NORMAN GRANZ:
The White Moses Of Black Jazz
By Dempsey J. Travis

Urban Research Press, Inc.

www.urbanresearchpress.com

Copyright© 2003 Urban Research Press, Inc.
840 East 87th Street, Chicago, Illinois 60619 USA
Printed in the United States of America
First Edition
ISBN 0-941484-34-3

Library of Congress Cataloging-in-Publication Data.

Dedicated To:

To those creative ones who prevailed in making American Jazz a world class music.

Acknowledgements

A good coach never changes the front line of a winning team. Therefore, with great pride, I salute the following players: Moselynne Travis, *my wife and motivator*, Ruby Davis, *senior researcher*, Pat Scott, *layout designer*, Lois Walker, Librarian at The Chicago Daily Defender, Jewell Diemer, Jasmine Dunning, a student trainee from the University of Illinois at Chicago and the Vivian G. Harsh Research Department of the Carter G. Woodson Regional Public Library.

Table of Contents

III

Studs Terkel and the Author

Introduction:

By Studs Terkel,
Pulitzer Prize Author

Travis' Black Jazz is like no other jazz memoir I have read. The author is not a jazz critic nor a professional jazz artist. He is simply a friend of the heroes and heroines, whose dreams, dark and sweet, he recounts. And whose hard truths he captures. Because he is simply a friend, there are things revealed that might otherwise be forever hidden or blown up into myths. Dempsey Travis offers us an informal, mostly oral, history of the way it was in the first six decades of the 20th century. That is all one can ask.

As I play, for the millionth time, Earl 'Fatha'

Extreme left Billy Eckstine, Franz Jackson, blowing tenor sax, Scoops Carry, George Dixon, clapping his hands. Facing camera at the rear is Earl Hines at the piano.

Earl "Fatha" Hines, born in Duquesne, Pennsylvania, December 28,1903; died in Oakland, California, April 22,1983. Became musical director of Carroll Dickerson Orchestra when Louis Armstrong assumed leadership in 1927. He opened with his own orchestra at the Grand Terrace in Chicago in December, 1928.

In the 1940's his band included many Be Bop musicians, such as Charlie Parker, Dizzy Gillespie, Bennie Green, Wardell Gray, Shadow Wilson, Billy Eckstine and Sarah Vaughan.

In 1947 he disbanded and joined Louis Armstrong and his All Stars.

Hines' "Boogie Woogie on the St. Louis Blues," I can still hear that distant voice, ebulliently calling out, "Play it until 1951." I always got a wallop out of Fatha's playing and George Dixon's impulsive shout. Now, thanks to Travis, I know more about these artists and the plantations on which they labored.

Oh, yes, I loved all those memories of the Grand Terrace, where Earl Hines and his gifted colleagues held forth. Though I was vaguely aware of the Syndicate connections, I had no idea of the power they held over the jazzmen, and of their meager salaries. The Mobsters, though at times grandly handed out C notes, to the artists they held bondage. In reading this work, you come to love

Ralph Capone,
The Cicero, Illinois Mob Boss

the artists even more - for their survival as much as for their gifts. I can envision the scene that Travis describes when Capone said:

"Hey, boy, come here!" Ralph Capone called out as he beckoned toward Lucius "Lucky" Millinder, the bandleader for the syndicate controlled Cotton Club   in Cicero, Illinois, a suburb on the West boundary of Chicago. Millinder, who was dressed formally in white tie and tails with a wing-tip shirt, hastily moved

VII

in his snow-white slippers from the bandstand to the boss's front row table.

> "Boy, I like the way you colored people play music and I get a big kick watching your jazzy steps and pearly smiles as you direct that band," said Capone. "My brother, Al, and I decided we're going to keep you boys working regularly, but you can't work for nobody but us."

There are certain things a man shares with a friend from his high school days that he might neglect to tell the most sophisticated of critics or dedicated historians. Those long-remembered hurts and humiliations. The little things that he shared with Dempsey Travis about some experience... hence, another revelation. Listen to this portrait of the most celebrated of all jazz clubs:

> The bandstand at the Harlem Cotton Club was a replica of a Southern mansion, with large white columns and a backdrop painted with weeping willow trees and slave quarters. The orchestra performed in front of the large double doors to the mansion. Down four steps was the dance floor, which was also used for floor shows. The waiters were dressed in red tuxedos, like butlers in a Southern mansion... The entire scene created a Gone With the Wind atmosphere that made every white male feel like Rhett Butler and every white woman like Scarlet O'Hara. Since the waiters were paid only one dollar a night, they had to hustle like Rochester and hope that Rhett Butler would leave a big tip.

Aside from his boyhood closeness to the jazzmen from Chicago, Dempsey's appreciation of his father's art molded him. Louis Travis was a "piano man." That meant

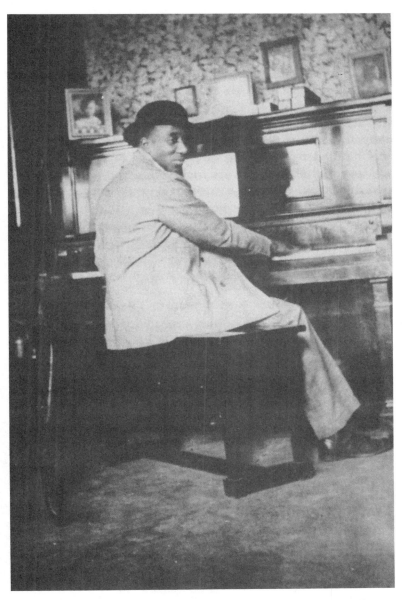

Louis Travis, the author's father and Blues piano man.

only one thing, during all those hard times, before and after the Depression. It meant the landlord house rent parties. It was the blues, of course: *"How Long Blues"*, *"The Five"* and *"The Boogie Woogie."* The room's atmosphere was filled with exhilaration and delight, as the little girl with the red dress on performed the "Black Bottom", the "Charleston" and the "Shimmy." Shot glasses of moonshine were lined up on the ledge of the piano as tribute to the man making all the music. The landlady served all the fried chicken, cole slaw and spaghetti you could eat. The money went a long way toward helping pay the rent for the host/hostess at Mecca Flats or the Baby Doll Building. Those multi-apartment buildings were cities, worlds in themselves. And the piano man was emperor.

Dempsey recalls his mother's pride in her husband's artistry and manner, who was a common laborer six days a week. "Your daddy would assume an air of extraordinary importance as he sat down at the upright piano with his black derby hat tilted forward and to the right with a ten-cent cigar hanging out of the left side of his mouth... the rent party dancers would shout: 'Louie! Louie! Play that thing because its tight like that!'"

Why, he was a mirror image of Willie "The Lion" Smith. Or was he simply a man named Louis Travis living out his dream, smack in the middle of a hard life? He was Meade Lux Lewis, the car washer; Jimmy Yancey, the ballpark groundskeeper; Albert Ammons, doing what he had to do. He was all these and himself. And a son remembers.

Here are the memories, too, of Milt Hinton, "the Judge", and Franz Jackson and an under-rated old piano friend, John Young. And the fabled band teacher at DuSable High, Captain Walter Dyett, who taught, and I do mean taught, some of our very best such as Nat "King" Cole; a Earl Hines protégé, Dorothy Donegan; Art Tatum an Earl Hines protégé, Gene Ammons; a Ben Webster disciple, Martha Davis; a Fats Waller follower, Johnny Hartman; a vocalist, and Johnny Griffin; a Coleman Hawkins man. As I read these pages, I remember a small white boy standing out in front of the Dreamland Ballroom on Chicago's West Side, listening hard to the strains coming from inside, where my older brother was dancing. I was hearing for the first time - this was in the Twenties - a kind of music that caught me and held my attention for the rest of my life. I was hearing jazz. Oh yeah, memories of Charlie Cook's Band and Lottie Hightower's are rekindling the dreams, as I read this book.

Studs Terkel
Pulitzer Author

The USS Arizona was one of the more seriously damaged United States ships at Pearl Harbor on December 7, 1941. Many of the more than 2,000 officers and enlisted men killed at Pearl Harbor were buried alive in ships like the Arizona.

Prologue:

Welcome To Granz's World of Jazz People

Norman "The White Moses" Granz was the impresario of a traveling musical jam session that was labeled Jazz at the Philharmonic. "White Moses" was born on August 6, 1918 in Los Angeles, California. He graduated from Roosevelt High School and he attended the University of California in Los Angeles where he briefly studied finance. Although both of his parents were foreign-born, he was a one hundred percent United States of America citizen.

His father Morris Granz was a Ukrainian Jew born in Russia in 1885 shortly after the reign of Nicholas Alexander. When the elder Granz was a young man he migrated in the bowels of a ship to the United States in January 1905 and subsequently became a naturalized citizen in front of a setting Federal court judge in the United States District Court in Los Angeles, California on Monday January 17, 1910.

His mother, Ida Clara like his father was Jewish and was born in Russia in 1895. She migrated with her parents to America in January 1906 eight years before the outbreak of World War I in Europe. She acquired her citizenship via marriage to Morris Granz.

Norman Granz a young patriot volunteered and enlisted in the United States Army Air Force cadet training school with dreams of becoming a fighter pilot against the Axis powers in February 1942. President Franklin Delano Roosevelt had declared war against Japan, Germany and Italy on December 7, 1941. The president's actions inspired thousands of volunteers to sign up for service as their fathers had for World War I in 1917.

A young Granz was downhearted and dispirited when he "washed out" of the air cadet training school at Tulare, California in May 1942.

A few weeks after being discharged from the Air Corps he was drafted into the United States Army where he served in the Special Service unit which was charged with keeping up the morale of the troops via USO Clubs, movies and live entertainment. He got an early honorable discharge from the armed forces in late fall of 1943 because of a medical problem.

Prior to and subsequent to his military service, he promoted Sunday night jam sessions at Herb Rose's 331 Club on Eighth Street in West Los Angeles. Granz was an addicted lover of jazz music. He was particularly fascinated by recordings of such Black artists as pianist Art Tatum, Thomas "Fats" Waller, Count Basie, Louis Armstrong, Duke Ellington, Andy Kirk and Jimmy Lunceford.

The politically astute Norman Granz observed the

ill treatment that Black musicians encountered when they were fortunate enough to get "Big Buck" gigs in white nightclubs, ballrooms and white owned hotels. They were always isolated after they came offstage because everything beyond the footlights was segregated.

Following his discharge from the United States Army in 1943, he jumped into promoting jazz concerts big time in the Los Angeles area. At the same time, he kept bread on his table by working on a daytime gig first as a laborer and later as a film editor for Metro-Goldwyn-Mayer in Burbank, California.

His early interest in jazz actually began in the early 1930s as a hobby collecting three-minute Blue Bird jazz records that sold for twenty-five cents. Fortunately for him his hobby ultimately developed into a very lucrative full time job.

Granz recognized that music was not all fun and games, therefore he found it necessary to grapple with the socio-economic and racial issues of the business. The Lincoln Bookshop on Highland Avenue, in Hollywood, California became his academic laboratory. The bookshop was best known as left wing because many of the books that it stocked were written by liberal Jewish authors. One afternoon the owner of the bookstore told Norman that many of the racial problems that he was concerned about could best be solved by joining a socially integrated organization that was geared to improving the economic and social conditions that plagued various minority groups.

In the late fall of 1944 Granz joined the Los Angeles County Communist Party (LACCP). His membership card number according to the files of the Federal Bureau of Investigation was 45039. Norman was assigned to work with the Hollywood cultural branch of the organization. He initially questioned the assignment because he was not a writer, actor or musician. (see FBI files at end of Chapter XIII Epilogue.)

Some years later during a Q and A interview with an FBI agent Granz stated that he could only recall attending between 8 and 10 CP meetings during the course of his membership. His cell usually met in private homes. He said attendance varied from eight to as many as sixty people. Granz identified John Howard Lawson, a screenwriter, and Mischa Altman, a musician as members who were introduced to him as hard core CP members.

The CP meetings were attended by both Blacks and whites. As a matter of fact, the Black members were treated as they should have been and that is, as equals. This open arm policy toward minorities was eye-opening for Granz when contrasted with the fact that the United States Armed Services during World War II and beyond was one hundred percent Jim Crow.

Billie "Strange Fruit" Holiday a friend of Granz's pulled his coat when she complained to him that Billy Berg, the owner of the Trouville Club in the Beverly Fairfax area of Hollywood where she was working would not admit Black patrons.

Granz followed Holiday's conversation with a nose to nose discussion with Billy Berg. He offered him a proposition that he could not turndown. He told Berg that he could make big bucks for both of them if he would agree to let him promote jam sessions in his club on Sunday nights when the regular musicians were not permitted to work because of a local union rule. To make Granz's suggestion a reality Berg would have to eliminate the color barrier which he finally did after a lot of deliberation.

Within a short period, Granz's Sunday-night jam sessions at Billy Berg's became the hottest entertainment ticket in the City of Angels. The jam sessions were packed wall to wall in concert style because dancing was not permitted. The crowds were so large Granz had to move his jam sessions from Billy Berg's place to a larger hall known as Music Town in South Los Angeles. He outgrew Music

A young Billie Holiday was Granz's friend.

The Place to be seen in the City of Angels on Sunday night.

Town within a couple of months. Thus he rented the Philharmonic Auditorium and ordered posters that were suppose to read "Jazz Concert at the Philharmonic Auditorium." Lacking sufficient space the printer designed a poster that read Jazz at the Philharmonic. This mistake caught Granz's fancy and he latched onto it.

On Sunday afternoon July 2, 1944 Norman Granz leaped into the big time at the Philharmonic Auditorium, which for decades had been the home of the staid tuxedo, black tie members of the L.A. Philharmonic Symphony Orchestra. He rescued post World War II jump music from the smoke filled nightclubs into a suitable concert music venue fit for the most delicate musicians' taste buds. The idea of a jazz concert was not original, he simply turned a musical scrimmage into a war between instrumentalists.

Marie Bryant, singer, Nat Cole and Illinois Jacquet, the little Texas tenor.

The swing warriors who participated on July 2, 1944 in Jazz At The Philharmonic were Nat "King" Cole, pianist/singer. Les Paul, then known as a jazz guitarist, was on the bill along with Benny Carter the talented saxophonist, trumpet player and arranger, Lee Young, drums; Barney Kessel, guitar; Corky Corcoran, trumpet; Al Killion, bass; Kenny Kersey, piano; Buck Clayton, trumpet; Helen Humes, vocalist; plus Illinois Jacquet, the Texas tenor saxophone player who made the song "Flying Home" a popular upbeat standard with the Lionel Hampton Orchestra.

In the early 50s the board of directors of the Philharmonic organization evicted Granz and his music

Norman Granz presents . . .

Jazz at the Philharmonic

Inasmuch as the heart of jazz, and, in fact, what sets it off from other types of music, is its improvisational quality, it's rather difficult to program the tunes which would be played. However, as a kind of compromise, here is a list of tunes which might be played. On the other hand, they might not.

Honeysuckle Rose	*Night and Day*	*Lady Be Good*
Body and Soul	*Tea for Two*	*I Surrender Dear*
Stardust	*Found a New Baby*	*Blues*

FIRST SET

BUDDY COLE — piano
OSCAR MOORE — guitar
RED CALLENDAR — bass
JOE MARSHALL — drums

JOE THOMAS — tenor sax
SHORTY CHEROCK — trumpet
BUMPS MYERS — tenor sax

SECOND SET

NAT KING COLE — piano
JOHNNY MILLER — bass
LEE YOUNG — drums
LES PAUL — guitar

ILLINOIS JACQUET — tenor sax
BENNY CARTER — alto sax and trumpet
JAMES JOHNSON — trombone

MARIE BRYANT — vocals

THIRD SET

MEADE LUX LEWIS — piano

FOURTH SET
Chicago Jazz

JOE SULLIVAN — piano
BUD HATCH — bass
SOMEBODY — drums

RANDALL MILLER — trombone
BARNEY BIGARD — clarinet
CHARLES PEPPIE — trumpet

FIFTH SET

NAT KING COLE — piano
RED CALLENDAR — bass
OSCAR MOORE — guitar
LEE YOUNG } — drums
BUDDY RICH }

ILLINOIS JACQUET — tenor sax
SHORTY CHEROCK — trumpet
JACK McVEA — tenor sax

CAROLYN RICHARDS — vocals

•

Benefit Sleepy Lagoon Defense Committee

XIX

makers and lovers out of their hall. They used the noise factor as an excuse for terminating their tenancy. Granz hit the road with his JATP entourage with the highest paid musicians in the world. The entire planet became their concert stage.

"The whole reason for Jazz at the Philharmonic was to take it places where it could break down color barriers," Granz stated: In Dizzy Gillespie's book "To Be or Not to Bop" he said: Well, the whole basis for forming Jazz at the Philharmonic was initially to fight discrimination. It wasn't formed just to do jazz concerts. I mean the whole reason for JATP, basically, was to take it to places where I could break down segregation and discrimination, present good jazz and make bread for myself and for the musicians as well. I felt that it made no kind of sense to treat a musician with any kind of respect and dignity onstage and then make him go around to the backdoor when he's offstage. I did not understand that kind of mistreatment. So wherever we went, we stayed in the best hotels. We traveled first class because I think that's all a part of the game. It didn't make sense for me to get a cat to work for me at Carnegie Hall, and then after work, he had to sleep in the bedbug ridden Woodside uptown on 7th Avenue or the Braddock and Alvin Hotels. That did not make sense. A musician is supposed to be treated as a great artist on and off the stage. It wasn't only antiblack discrimination, it was discrimination against top-flight musicians.... My musicians had to be treated with the same respect as Leonard Bernstein or Heifitz because they were just as good, both as men and musicians. It took a long time to convince the concert halls, even though I was paying the rent for the hall. It was hard to get those operators to bury their prejudices. We had to use out of tune pianos; bad mikes; we had the worse dressing rooms. I mean there was no reason in the world, when we'd go to those down in the mouth Middle Western cities that were prejudiced, they would not permit Dizzy to stay in a white hotel with me. That didn't make sense. So we always tried to stay in the very best hotels. I mean that's part of doing a show first-class; everybody had to go first-class.

Well, Houston is a very southern city in more ways than one.... In those days, it was a very tough city and very, very prejudiced, in many ways more so than Dallas, which wasn't too far behind. Because Houston was a much tougher city and a much more prejudiced city and a racist city, it was a difficult city to break open.

In any case I decided to take Jazz at the Philharmonic down there. And of course the first thing I'd do was rent the auditorium myself. Then I'd hire the ticket seller to sell tickets to my concert and tell him that there was to be no segregation whatsoever. Well, that was new for Houston. I removed the signs that said 'White toilets' and 'Negro toilets.' That was new. The whole idea was to break all that Jim Crow shit. And even the ticket seller who worked for me was a Texan, and I knew he didn't have eyes to do what I'd asked him to do, but he was getting paid, so he had to. Of course I'd bring in a 'mixed' show. In those days, all my shows were mixed, on purpose, because if a cat played, I don't care if he's green, Black, or whatever. It so happened, most of my cats were Black, but there were some white - Gene Krupa and people like that.

Anyway, we got down there early because I wanted to be sure we wouldn't have any problems at all, so I even hired local police, white, of course, to be sure there would be no kinda problems. And some whites came out and said, "This is mixed with Blacks, and I don't wanna sit here." They'd would ask, "Could they change their seat?"

I'd say, "No. Here's your money back. You sit where I seat you. If you say I don't like this seat because I can't hear, fine. But don't tell me there's a cat sitting next to you, and because he's Black, you don't wanna sit there. Here's your money back." We did everything we could, and of course I had a strong show.... When people wanna see your show, you can lay some conditions down.

Well, the show began. We had a double-header. There were some cats standing backstage, and one of my rules was never to let anybody backstage when my show was on. These were two or three white cats, and I asked them who they were. And they showed me their badges. They  were like plainclothes men, and they said, "We like jazz. We just wanna watch the jazz concert."

So I said, "O.K., if you stand back, that'll be all right." And I think Krupa was performing on stage at that time. Well, Prez and Illinois Jacquet and Birks started to play dice in Ella's dressing room. I mean the way musicians would do when they were wasting time because they didn't go on for another hour. And it was like for a dollar or something, just to pass the time. Ella was eating, and the woman

Gene Krupa

who dressed her was there eating with her, because we had sent out for food for these people. We didn't have time to go out and eat. And all of a sudden, these cats break the door down. These dudes did not have to do that because all they had to do was go turn the knob. They came in with flashlights and guns drawn and all that bullshit. The same guys that said to me, "Well, we're jazz fans." They were police, of course, and they said, "You're all under arrest for gambling!"

Well, Ella, first of all, was eating, and her secretary was eating, and just these three cats were playing, and it was really jive. And I ran in when I heard the commotion; and I saw one of the cats go in the bathroom, the police.

And I knew what it was then. I knew he was going to try and plant some shit. That's the first thing. That's for openers. Then it's easy, you see. 'Black musicians caught...' good headlines. So this cat said, "What're you doing?"

I said, "I'm watching you."

"I oughta kill you," he said, and he took his gun out and put it in my stomach. And this is in front of everybody, in front of Ella, in front of everyone.

I said, "Well, man, you've got the gun. If you wanna shoot me, there's nothing I can do about it." But he was serious. So I said, "What are you arresting me for?"

"Well, you're the manager of the show," he said, "so you're running a gambling house." The whole thing was just jive. The thing was that in the South they didn't like the idea that we'd 'mix' everything. Because that sets a precedent. That's the thing they were bugged about 'cause if you could prove that Black and white could sit next to each other, you could break up a lotta that shit down there. All they wanted to do was create an incident. I mean, if they could've gotten us on drinking backstage, anything.

"O.K., you're all under arrest," the cat said, "and we're taking you all down to the station."
And the manager, who's one of them, a Texan, came back down,so I said, "Look, you have a packed house out there, and you have a packed house waiting to come in,' 'cause we sold that thing out, we locked it up." I said, "You go out there and tell the people that the concert's finished, right now, and that the people can go on home, and there's no more concert, the second show, because we've been arrested by these police. And you can settle the riot that you're gonna have on your hands." I said, "Now you take it from here; I'm calling the show off, right now. You do what you want." Now, since I owned the show and rented the house, it was my bread, so he couldn't very well sue me or anything. By the same token it wouldn't look very good on his track record if the manager should suddenly have a riot.

XXIII

So he said, "Just a minute." And he talked to the cat in the corner, and they finally got it together. He said, "They'll take you down, now, between concerts. Finish this one, 'cause they're gonna have to book you, but they'll get you back in time for the second concert, see."

Well, they took us down there, and it was a very funny thing. All the newspaper photographers were down there. And you say, "Well, how these cats know about this?" See, all that shit had been laid out, the newspaper photographers and everything else. And they did what they do like

Nab Ella Fitzgerald, Gillespie in Dice Game

Houston Dice Cops Give Ella & Boys a Bad Shake

'Guys & Dolls' Dice Bit Cops, Aud Unsegregated

$10 Awaiting Singer At Police Station

Ella Fitzgerald But the show goes on.

if you're caught parking. You post a bond and then you forfeit the bond, which is in other words, a fine.

They said, "We're setting bail for you, each one ten dollars. And your case will be heard, like, October something." So I put up fifty dollars bail for the five of us. Well, now they know we were leaving the next day; we're doing one-nighters. We were like in Detroit the next day. So it was just a jive way of saying, "Now, you've got a record down here for gambling. You don't show up, you'll forfeit the bond, which means you'll be guilty and you'll lose the ten dollars." O.K., so we went back and we did the show, and the next day I had a press conference there. And one of the newspapers - it was strange, one of the big white papers said - '"After what happened last night, they oughta give the police a medal. It should be chicken on a field of yellow. "Because he said it was bullshit, you know, what the cops did to us. Well, anyway, we left the next day. Of course the story was in all the papers across the country. But I tricked them. I hired the best lawyer I could and we fought the case. We beat them. We won, got the bread back, and of course then I thought we'd never go down to Houston again, but we did - we went down the next year again, and nobody touched us. It cost me a lotta bread, but I got the best lawyer in Texas. Of course we beat those cats, 'cause it was jive.

A Historical Overview Of The Jazz Culture

Norman Granz came on the scene of black jazz in the early 1940's. The flavor of Black Music was best described in a November 1983 Chicago Tribune bestselling book entitled An Autobiography of Black Jazz.

Lucky Millinder

My old friend, the late Lucky Millinder, a Chicago South Sider and Wendell Phillips High School alumnus, once told the author that he did not realize before the late Nineteen Twenties the full implications of Ralph Capone's conversation about controlling Black jazz until he saw it in living color at the Cotton Club in the "Big Apple."

Harlem's Cotton Club

Capone's statement about Colored people's music became crystal clear during Lucky's first trip to New York City in the late 1920s shortly before the big Depression. There he saw the syndicate network unfold into the outstretched arms of Owney

Owney Madden, Owner of New York's Cotton Club.

Al Capone, Chicago's South Side Mob Boss

Madden, one of the most notorious of the prohibition bootleggers. Madden was a principal owner of Harlem's
famous Cotton Club. The mob network was tied together
like a four leaf clover. Madden controlled the East
Coast's booze and beer distribution; Al Capone reigned over
Chicago and its environs; Johnny Lazia controlled the
police, liquor and gambling in Kansas City, Missouri and
the Purple Gang dominated Detroit's subculture. Chicago,
New York and Kansas City housed a disproportionate percentage of all the great jazz talent in America during the
1920s and 30s. These cities were controlled by the " Jazz
Slave Masters" and some of the very best Black musicians
were their serfs.

   Talented jazz musicians were chained to bands and
specific nightclubs and saloons in the same manner as the

Chicago's Club DeLisa marquee

ante-bellum Negroes were shackled to plantations. Louis
Armstrong, Duke Ellington, Jimmie Lunceford, Cab
Calloway, and Earl Hines are a few of the many top artists
who were inmates behind the "Cotton Curtain" at various
points in their careers. All of the aforementioned stars
except Earl Hines had picked cotton on the Cotton Club
Plantation in New York City, which was the best known
entertainment plantation in the United States between 1924
and 1936. All Blacks other than entertainers, waiters,
cooks and the cleaning crew were excluded as guests from
the interior of the Jazz Slave Master's New York mansion.

**George Dixon,
Key member of the Earl Hines Orchestra**

**Ralph Cooper,
Producer of Chicago's Grand Terrace Show
productions**

Money was what the plantation system was all about. The Grand Terrace in Chicago was the most grandiose plantation in the country. Its appointments were more elaborate than New York's Cotton Club or Chicago's Club DeLisa. Everything and everybody in the club smelled like new money except the Black entertainers. They all sweated for a pittance, including Earl Hines, the internationally renowned piano player and bandleader. The band's star trumpet and saxophone player, George

Ed Fox, the manager of the Grand Terrace for Al Capone.

Frank Nitti, "The Enforcer"

Dixon, did not realize how the mob's plantation system worked until he decided to better his lot in life and gave notice of leaving Hines at the Grand Terrace to join Don Redman's band in Detroit at the Graystone Ballroom. Don Redman had been the brilliant former musical director of McKinney's Cotton Pickers. Omer Simeon, Hines' alto sax man, and Billy Franklin, the trombonist, decided to join Dixon in his move to Detroit.

Dixon told the author, "The day we left Chicago, Ralph Cooper, the producer of the show at the original Grand Terrace at 3955 South Parkway (Dr. Martin Luther King Drive), came out of the club and shook our hands while we were loading the trunk of my car. When I stepped into my little 1929 Ford and said "Goodbye," Cooper replied, "I am not going to say goodbye because you'll be back."

I said, "Not a chance."

Shortly after we arrived in Detroit,

Don called his first rehearsal at the Graystone Ballroom. Before we could assemble our instruments, Don's manager came up and said, "Where's the three fellows from Earl Hines' band?"

We all identified ourselves. Don's manager said, "Well, I just got a call from New York and I won't be able to use you guys."

The three of us yelled in unison, "Does that mean we have to go back to Earl?"

The manager replied, "Yeah, that's what it means."

After hearing that bad news, the three of us jumped into my little Ford and came back to Chicago. The mob, through intimidation and organization, had things so well-regulated we couldn't even change jobs.

Author interviewing Cab Calloway

Later Dixon accidentally overheard a conversation between Ed Fox, manager of the Grand Terrace, and Frank "The Enforcer" Nitti, the Capone treasurer, which shed some light on what had happened. It seemed that Joe Fusco, Al Capone's superintendent of breweries was also plantation overseer at the Grand Terrace.

Cab Calloway was once threatened with violence by the Owney Madden mob if he didn't do right. Cab was working and broadcasting from Madden's New York Cotton Club. His popularity was soaring and the mob had arranged to book him into the Paramount Theater in midtown Manhattan for a three-week engagement at a salary of $200 per week. Cab became obstinate about doubling on both gigs for that short bread.

Cab was given the word: "You'd better go into the Paramount on those terms or we'll see to it that you'll never be able to dance again."

With that message ringing in his ears, Cab hide-ho'd it to both his midtown gig at the Paramount Theater and his uptown gig at Harlem's Cotton Club for three consecutive weeks and was not late for a single performance.

The New York "Jazz Slave Masters" had long arms that frequently reached into Chicago to protect their chattel. Duke Ellington recalls an experience when he was scheduled for an engagement at the Paradise Theater on Chicago's Northwest Side. When he arrived at the theater the manager, Sam Fletcher, told Duke that some members of a West Side mob had been there that morning and said that Duke had to pay them $500 or he wouldn't leave the theater alive that night.

Duke Ellington

Duke called Owney Madden at the Cotton Club in New York and told him what had happened. Madden said: "Duke, don't worry about it. I can assure you that you won't have that kind of trouble anymore."

After reassuring Duke, Owney Madden carefully hung up the phone only to grab it again within minutes to call Ralph Capone in Chicago and told him about Duke's troubles with the West Side hoodlums. Capone immediately issued the following order: "Duke Ellington is not to be bothered on the West Side or in the Loop." Duke later said, "Those words closed the chapter on the gangster problem for me and the band in Chicago from that day forward."

Capone saved Duke Ellington from threats of violence, but chained Earl Hines to a $150 a week contract that was constructed to last forever. Capone, through his Grand Terrace manager, Ed Fox had a contract with Hines that literally would not permit Hines to use his own name if he attempted to leave the Grand Terrace plantation. His

contract was perpetual: In that if Ed Fox died, Hines would become the personal property of Fox's widow, and in the event of her death, Fox's eldest son would be the heir to the contract for a lifetime. If the oldest son died before Hines, the contract would pass to Fox's youngest son. The chattel contract on Earl Hines was in effect

James C. Petrillo, President of the National Federation of Musicians Union.

The facade of the old Grand Terrace at 3955 South Parkway (Dr. Martin Luther King Drive)

from December 1928 until a Thursday, April 10, 1941 engagement at the Regal Theater in Chicago where Hines collected his music after the last show and told the boys in the band:

"I am not working for Ed Fox anymore."

Hines had made this threat before, but this time he apparently intended to keep his word.

Early the following Monday, Hines and George Dixon, who was both a saxophone and trumpet player in Hine's orchestra, went to Harry Gray, the president of Local 208, at 3934 South State Street, which was the head-quarters of the Colored Musicians' Union. Earl told Gray the story and Gray called James (Jimmy) C. Petrillo, President of the National Federation of Musicians in New

The New Grand Terrace on the site of the old Sunset Garden which was located on the south-west corner of 35th and Calumet Avenue

York. Petrillo was also the President of Local 10, which was the Chicago downtown union for white musicians. Petrillo came into town that Wednesday and met Harry Gray, Earl Hines, Charlie Carpenter and George Dixon at the Palmer House Hotel.

According to Dixon, Petrillo read the contract and said, "This contract is not worth the paper it is written on. It's too much Ed Fox and not enough Earl Hines, so you go and work anywhere you want for anyone you want and I will protect you."

Dixon remembered that Fox did not give up on Hines even after the powerful Jimmy Petrillo had told Hines he was free. Shortly after his emancipation, Hines took a band into New York's Apollo Theater. Fox immediately procured an injunction through his New York lawyers and tied up the band's weekly salary. When Petrillo got the news he called Jack Schiffman, the manager of the Apollo and told him, "If you don't release the band's payroll, your show will not go on tonight!" Jack Schiffman immediately responded by releasing the payroll.

Fox subsequently enticed Earl Hines to return to Chicago and open at his New Grand Terrace, which was located in the Old Sunset Garden Building on the southwest corner of 35th and Calumet. [The original Grand Terrace which was located at 3955 South Parkway (now King Drive) had been reconverted to a theater and named The Park. It had been known as the Peerless Theater from October 1917 to December 1928.] Earl, the freedman, was now brighter in the ways of business and insisted that Fox put the band's four week's salary up in advance and place it in escrow with a third party. Fox agreed and the band opened. Fox then got an injunction to tie up the money he had placed in escrow. Since Fox owned this plantation, a call from Petrillo did not release the money. This time it was necessary for Petrillo to take Fox to court. The judge rendered a decision in Hines' favor. Hines was "free at

Duke, The Jungle Music King

Cab, the King of "Hi De Ho"

last!"

Ralph Fusco, a West Side hoodlum who also oper-
ated a Chicago version of the New York Cotton Club at 12th
Street and Blue Island Avenue on the near west side of
Chicago. Capone gave Erskine Tate and his entire fifteen-
man orchestra their freedom
one night. However, he
refused to pay the $1,500
weekly salary he owed them
and threatened to use his
weapon if they attempted to
remove their instruments
from the premises.

Harry "Fearless" Gray, who
was the musicians' business
agent, before he became
President of the Local 208

Harry "Fearless" Gray came to their rescue. He
described the events that took place:
"When I heard what had happened the next day, I jumped
in my car and went directly to the Cotton Club to talk to
Ralph Fusco. When I walked through the double doors
leading to the cabaret, there was a tough-looking guy sitting
at the end of the bar shuffling bullets in and out of a large
automatic pistol.

He said to me, "What do you want?"

I said I wanted to see Ralph Fusco. About this time
Ralph walked out of a back office. His henchman said,
"Here's a crazy guy who wants to take over the joint."

Fusco said, "What do you want?"

I replied, "I want the $1,500 due Tate's band and the
instruments."

Fusco turned around and went back into his office
without any further conversation and came back with fifteen $100 bills and put the bundle in my hand. His final
message was, "Tell the boys to come back to work tonight

and I assure you they won't have any more problems."

Harry Gray could deal effectively with hoodlums because he was not afraid to die in his quest to free Black musicians from the slave masters.

Although jazz is a music known for its free form, the Black people who played it were never free agents. Owney Madden once told Duke Ellington that he would never be free to leave the New York Cotton Club plantation unless he agreed to pay the orchestra that replaced him out of the money he made on the road tours during the entire period his band was absent from the mansion. Duke's leave would vary from two weeks to three months, depending upon the nature of the engagements. Sometimes the gigs were extended theater tours or maybe a fourteen-day movie assignment in Hollywood. Ellington's first replacement was the Missourians, with Cab Calloway fronting the band. Duke paid Cab $200 a week to conduct and act as the master of ceremonies. The actual choice of Cab and the Missourians was made by the Cotton Club mob. The gangsters simply took control of Cab and his band from a white booking agent named Moe Gale with pure muscle and threats to the agent's health. The mob closed the deal by kissing Gale on the left cheek and offering him ten percent of Cab Calloway's annual earnings.

The Ellington and Calloway Cotton Club venture was ultimately structured with Duke and Irving Mills, song publisher and booking agent, owning fifty percent of Cab Calloway Enterprises. In addition, Mills owned fifty percent of Duke Ellington Inc. In the post-bellum period, the Jazz Slave Masters permitted some serfs to own at least fifty percent of themselves.

Remember, the Jazz Slave Masters always controlled the cash register, paid the piper and called the tune. The keepers of the cash box were usually Jewish or Italian and, occasionally, they were mob-connected Blacks. The creators of jazz music were Black. All this had a positive side.

Wherever there was a generous segment of Jews, Italians and Blacks coexisting within an urban area, the results favored jazz music. A population survey taken between 1927-1930 supports these observations. The important jazz centers which had the aforementioned population mix were New Orleans, Kansas City, Chicago and New York. Philadelphia was the only major exception: it had the ethnic mix, but never became an important jazz center.

Dempsey J. Travis

LUCKY MILLINDER

Lucky Millinder, leader of the Mills Blue Rhythm Band. Lucky was born in Anniston, Alabama, August 8,1900; reared and educated in Chicago. He died in New York City on September 28,1966.

In 1934 he took over leadership of the Mills Blue Rhythm Band. His sidemen included Red Allen, Charlie Shavers, Harry Edison, J.C. Higginbottom, Wilbur DeParis, Joe Garland, Tab Smith, Buster Bailey, Edgar Hayes, Billy Kyle and John Kirby. In the 1940's band members included Joe Guy, Freddy Webster, Dizzy Gillespie, Lucky Thompson, Eddie "Lockjaw" Davis, Bull Moose Jackson, Ellis Larkin, Bill Doggett and George Duvivier.

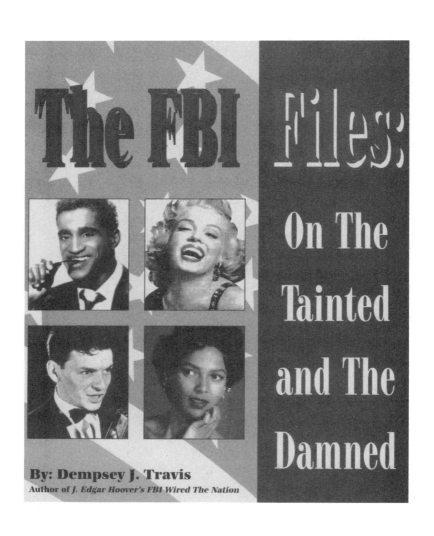

The FBI Files:

On The Tainted and The Damned

By: Dempsey J. Travis
Author of *J. Edgar Hoover's FBI Wired The Nation*

Ella at age seventeen.

Cut I
Ella Fitzgerald:
How The Ragamuffin From Yonkers, New York Became America's First Lady of Song

Ella Fitzgerald began her public school education in Yonkers, New York in September, 1923 at Public School #10. It was the same year her mother Tempie gave birth to a second daughter whose given name was Frances and surname was Du Silva. Until Frances' death in 1960, Ella had remained very close to her half-sister, which undoubtedly was one of the few enduring relationships that she formed during her entire lifetime.

Ella is remembered by some of the Yonkers old timers as a shy, tall double jointed loner who displayed flashes of show business ambitions early in her life. When she was in the third grade she started street dancing for pennies in her neighborhood along with other kids. She danced with a lot more enthusiasm than other juvenile

3

street dancers. The ragamuffin pre-teenager could do some mean rug cutting (dance) with the best of them when she did the Charleston, which was the dance craze of the Roaring Nineteen Twenties. On the other hand, when she was not feeling shy she could belt out songs with the volume of such stars as Ethel Waters, Sophie Tucker, Kate Smith and Bessie

"Fats" Waller

**Bing Crosby
and
Louis Armstrong**

*Smith without the benefit of a microphone. Her favorite melodies were **Some of These Days** by Shelton Brooks, **My Blue Heaven** by George Whiting and Walter Donaldson, and **Black & Blue** by Thomas "Fats" Waller and Harry Brooks. She could sing those songs with a sensitivity that was very reminiscent of Louis Armstrong whom she admired. The girl actually considered herself a better hoofer than a singer. Her loose dancing style was influenced greatly by Snake Hips Tucker the Cotton Club dancing star with the swiveling rubber hips and Bill "Bojangles" Robinson, the world's greatest tap dancer.*

Although Armstrong was the first singer to leave a permanent footprint on Ella's style, she was also attracted to Bing Crosby, the Crooner and the three Boswell Sisters who had

4

"Snake Hips" Tucker of Cotton Club fame.

grown up in New Orleans. She specifically wanted to copy the vocal style of Connee Boswell, the Boswells' lead singer. Tempie, in an effort to help her daughter learn how to sing like Connee bought a Boswell record for little Ella to listen to.

Connee Boswell's talents were not limited to singing in that she was also a composer and arranger a la Mary Lou Williams the Pittsburgh genius who played the piano, composed and arranged for Andy Kirk and his Twelve Clouds of Joy Orchestra in Kansas City, Missouri. Mary Lou also wrote musical arrangements for Benny Goodman, Tommy Dorsey, Earl Hines, Louis Armstrong, Jimmy Lunceford, and many other orchestra leaders.

To keep abreast of the dancing trends the fourteen year old Ella occasionally would sneak out of the house with Charles Gulliver, who was a next door neighbor. They would go down to New York City's Savoy Ballroom at 140th and Lenox Avenue to pick up on the latest dance steps. Going to the Savoy was no short trip because they had to take a half hour trolley ride down to the subway station and then catch a subway train to uptown Harlem, where they got off at the 125th Street Station, and then walked an additional 15 short city blocks north to the Savoy Ballroom at 140th Street. The Savoy ballroom was also known by the jitterbugs of that period as the Home of Happy Feet. It was there that Ella learned how to do The Shuffle Off to Buffalo, Trucking, The Susie Q and the fast moving finger popping over your head Lindy Hop dance steps which were precursors to the jitterbug dance.

A heavy burden fell on young Ella's shoulders when her mother Tempie dropped dead from a fatal heart attack at the age of 38. Ella's school records indicated that she stopped going to Benjamin Franklin Junior High on April 21, 1931. Ella had to move out of the Yonkers apartment building shortly after her mother's death because her stepfather began making wifely demands on her. Hence, it

6

became necessary for her to move into her Aunt Virginia's Harlem four story walk-up apartment on West 145th Street in New York City.

The next two years for Ella were hell on earth. She skipped school and ran policy numbers door to door for the number kings in Harlem just as a means to keep her skin and bone together. In addition, to being a policy runner she also worked as a lookout girl for a house of prostitution. The warning signal was four hard knocks on the front door to alert the ladies of evening that the precinct flat feet were in close proximity.

Playing hookey from school to perform her various tasks brought Ella to the attention of the New York School truant authorities. She was apprehended on the street one day by a truant officer and sent to Public School #49, which had formerly been the Colored Orphan Asylum until the Board of Education took over the facility in 1911. Since she was determined to get into show business she ran away from that institution early in the fall of 1934 with no intention of ever returning. The poor girl was afflicted with a mild case of claustrophobia, a malady which caused her to panic whenever she was locked into some of the cubicals at Public School #49.

Ella could never return to her Aunt Virginia's apartment because the truant authorities would be able to track her down easily and incarcerate her in a lock down juvenile home. The tall skinny girl's only option was to hangout on Seventh Avenue, the main drag in a section of New York's Harlem known as the "Black Broadway" between 125th and 140th Streets. This fifteen block stretch along Seventh Avenue was a candy store for every kind of vice known to man in addition to having more than its quota of down on their luck entertainers such as musicians, dancers and singers.

During the depression years of the 1930s it was possible for a musically gifted person to enter a talent contest

7

with dreams of winning mini lottery every night at some major theater or nightclub amateur hour. Talent shows were a cheap means of entertainment for show business entrepreneurs who were beating on the walls of hard times themselves. The amateur shows rewarded the winner of the contest with a crisp ten dollar bill. Ten dollars during the 1930s represented seventy-five percent of a Negro common laborer's weekly wages. However, the average Colored postal worker at that time was only earning twelve hundred dollars a year. On the other hand postal workers were counted among the cream of the Black society ranking alongside of medical doctors, lawyers, dentists, public schoolteachers and Pullman porters. The typical postal worker was better educated than most day laborers.

Ella decided she would try her luck for the big bucks at the newly opened Apollo Theater for Colored, which was located at 253 West 125th Street in Harlem. Up until 1934, the theater had been a burlesque house for "Whites Only". One of the Apollo Theater attractions with the change of management was the Wednesday night amateur show which

The Edward Sisters

was presided over by the popular Colored movie star Ralph Cooper who also acted as the master of ceremonies.

Miss Fitzgerald actually made her stage debut at the Apollo on Wednesday night, November 21, 1934. Ella's initial intention was to perform a dance number in the amateur contest, that is until she learned that the smooth dancing Edward Sisters would be her competition. The Edwards girls had been trained by their father who was also a professional dancer and they had no

8

*juvenile peers on the national scene other than the popular Nicholas Brothers during that period. Ella was not stupid, therefore she quickly switched from dancing and entered the contest as a singer. Although her appearance was that of a ragamuffin her voice and singing style overrode all the negatives and she won the first prize hands down and one week's work in a regular stage show. Her winning songs were **The Object Of My Affection** and her encore was **Judy**.*

The leader of the backup band for Ella that night at the Apollo was Benny Carter. In the year 2002, Benny at age 95, is still rated among the top musicians. He was impressed by Ella's style to the point that he later took her to meet Fletcher Henderson his former band leading boss in his home on Strivers Row at 110 West 138th Street for a second opinion. Henderson was instantly turned off by Ella's appearance. His opinion was influenced by the fact that she was sloppily dressed and not Mulatto, he was definitely partial to high yellow complexioned women.

Incidentally, Ella did not get the one week's work she was promised after winning the first prize at the Apollo. Therefore, she was thrown back into the midst of the Seventh Avenue wolves, broke and disgusted but not downhearted. In January 1935 she started hanging out at the stage door of the Harlem Opera House which was just a short distance from the Apollo, and where she finally got a second opportunity to enter another "Amateur Hour". Again, she won first prize hands down. However, this time the seventeen year old girl got the promised one week gig. She opened at the Harlem Opera House on Friday, February 15, 1935.

Others in the show with Ella were Tiny Bradshaw and his band, Mae Alex, the blues singer and several lesser known acts. This engagement marked the first time Ella's name appeared in very small print on a Harlem Opera House poster. A little publicity was the only thing that she got out of that date. The manager refused to pay her after

9

she finished the week. There are several versions of why she was denied a paycheck. The one that appears to hold the most water is told with authority by Frank Schiffman the manager of the Apollo who said the money was used to buy Ella some suitable clothing to wear for her stage appearance. Ella's press people said some years later that Schiffman had lied because the chorus girls had chipped in to buy her a dress, shoes, undergarments and a hair treatment.

1935 was Ella's good luck year. Chick Webb was looking for a girl singer to join his band which was opening at the Harlem Opera House. He assigned Charles Linton his male singer the task of finding one. An Italian chorus girl who was a friend of Linton's, recommended Ella Fitzgerald because she had heard her sing at the Apollo Theater the night that she won her first amateur contest.

The problem of getting in touch with Ella was a tough one because she was a street person who could not be reached by telephone and she did not have a permanent street address. The only hope of locating Ella was to scour both 125th Street and also the fifteen block area on Seventh Avenue known as the "Black Broadway."

Linton and the Italian girl finally found Ella forty-eight hours later hanging out in front of Smalls Paradise Night Club at 135th and Seventh Avenue. Linton rushed Ella over to Chick's dressing room at the Harlem Opera House where he was working with Burdu Ali, a part time musical director of the Chick Webb Orchestra. The first thing Chick said to Linton when he saw Ella was "You are robbing the cradle my man." Chick then asked Ella to step outside of the door. Before the door could hit Ella in the back Chick grabbed Linton by the collar and whispered: "Man, you are not putting that broad in my band."

Several minutes after Chick regained his cool Charlie Buchanan, the manager of the Savoy Ballroom walked into the dressing room and Chick asked if he had

10

seen that girl standing outside the door. Buchanan nodded in the positive. Chick then said: "That is what Linton wants to put in my band." Buchanan opened the door and took a second look at Ella and said, "No, no, out!" He didn't want her either.

Ella was not aware of all the low tone bickering that was going on about her. Linton said to Buchanan when he was about to leave the room, "If you don't listen to her sing I am going to quit Chick's band!" Buchanan stopped cold in his footsteps and said, "Oh, no. Okay! When you finish the theater gig, you have got a two-week gig at the Savoy Ballroom. Bring her up, let her sing along with the band, and if the public likes her we will keep her and if they don't, she is out with no pay!"

Chick Webb did not realize that Linton had found a gold mine for him in Ella Fitzgerald. However, Webb did not pay Ella a regular salary he simply gave her a couple of bucks from time to time. She always wore one of two street dresses because they represented the only dress up clothes she had in this world. She never worked before a formal dance audience because she did not own or could afford an evening gown.

It wasn't until May 1935 that Ella began to get some

Ella Fitzgerald

bonifide recognition. A young white music critic named George T. Simon from the Metronome Magazine came uptown to the Savoy Ballroom and was figuratively knocked out by her, not only by the way she sang but also by the spirit that she put into a song. Instead of sitting with the band like a canary in a bird- cage as was the custom in

11

those days she exhibited her dance talents alongside of the orchestra. The energetic Ella was finger popping making rhythmic arm movements when certain trumpet and sax riffs were being played. She really put additional life in a band that could use a few swift kicks from time to time. Simon gave the Webb Orchestra a B-plus rating in the June edition of Metronome Magazine, and concluded his review by saying that Ella Fitzgerald was going places. This was Ella Fitzgerald's first press mention and one that she would remember for the rest of her life.

George T. Simon made the following comments in predicting Ella's meteoric rise to the top of her profession. As a matter of fact he made the following forecast in Metronome Magazine: The seventeen-year old girl singing up at Harlem's Savoy Ballroom with Chick Webb's fine band...she is unheralded and practically unknown right now, but what a future... a great natural flair for singing... extraordinary intonation and figure... As she is right now, she's one of the best femme hot warblers... and there is no reason why she shouldn't be just about the best in time to come.

*On November 14, 1936 Ella appeared on Benny Goodman's coast to coast radio show, sponsored by the Camel Cigarette Company. The show was called the "Camel Caravan", it was one of the most popular music shows in America. She sang a bouncy song entitled: **You Turned The Tables On Me.** Later Benny offered Webb $5,000.00 to buy out her contract. Ella had truly made the first step on the stairway to stardom. Even the calcified sidemen in Chick Webb's orchestra began to sit back and take notice of this little girl who was now positioned to get into show business big time. Rival orchestra leader, Jimmy Lunceford made her a very attractive offer which included a $2,000.00 advanced bonus. It was for naught, because she was hogtied to a binding contract with the Moe Gale Agency.*

*In November 1937 Ella was voted the number one female vocalist in both the Downbeat and The Melody Maker Magazine readers' polls, she topped her main rivals Billie Holiday and Red Norvo's vocalist Mildred Bailey. On May 2, 1938 Chick and Ella went into the Decca recording studio and recorded, **A-Tisket, A-Tasket!** It was Ella's idea to take a nursery rhyme and make it a popular song. Actually, the origin of the nursery rhyme dated back to 1879. However, the rhyme had not been copyrighted as a song until 1938. Thus, the credit for the words and music were attributed to Ella Fitzgerald and Al Feldman.*

The song went on the music scoreboard as number 10 in June 1938, and zoomed to number 1 a week later; it stayed on the Musical Hit Parade list for a total of 19 weeks. It eventually reached the million sales mark in 1950.

Dempsey J. Travis the author of this work said: I will always remember the night of nights at Chicago's Savoy Ballroom on July 31, 1938. It was billed as the

Ella is seated fourth from the right next to Lonnie Simmons on her left.

"Swing Band Battle of the Century". Oh! But this was a night that this writer will never forget. The marquee in front of the Savoy read: Harlem's Chick Webb, America's

Outstanding Swing band versus Bronzeville's Horace Henderson, the creator of the Jump Rhythm.. Fletcher Henderson, Horace's elder brother had become Benny Goodman's full time arranger.

*Ella Fitzgerald was the featured vocalist with the Chick Webb Orchestra and Viola Jefferson was the songbird with the Horace Henderson Band.. Horace had made an arrangement of **"A-Tisket-A Tasket"** for Viola that was almost identical to the one Chick Webb had made for Ella Fitzgerald. The Savoy's Bronzeville audience kept yelling for Viola Jefferson to sing **"A-Tisket-A-Tasket!"** Ella had just finished singing the song during the Chick Webb set. Viola Jefferson appeared to be both scared and reluctant to follow the great Ella Fitzgerald.*

*However, when Horace Henderson opened his set with **"A-Tisket-A-Tasket"**, Viola had no alternative except to go out there and do her stuff. When she finished singing the nursery rhyme, the crowd just roared, screamed, and stomped. This writer was standing in front of the bandstand*

no more than one foot from the stage listening intently when I noticed my white linen suit was damp with sweat from my own body heat and the heat of the music lovers who were elbowing to get closer to the bandstand. It was hot as the devil's oven in the Savoy Ballroom that evening. In fact, it was so hot that the management stopped the music and moved a portable bandstand to the outdoor pavilion which was south and adjacent to the main ballroom. That was probably one of the largest crowds in the Savoy Ballroom's history. I say probably because I had witnessed capacity crowds in that ballroom when Duke Ellington, Cab Calloway, Louis Armstrong and Jimmy Lunceford played gigs there.

On the ninth of June, 1939, Chick Webb was admitted to the Johns Hopkins Hospital in Baltimore, Maryland with kidney problems that were compounded by the lifelong difficulties he was having with spinal tuberculosis. On June 16th the little drummer man gave up the struggle for life on this planet and died quietly in his mother's arms.

After Webb's death the Moe Gale Agency made Ella Fitzgerald the leader of Webb's all male orchestra. The jazz band was billed as Ella Fitzgerald and the Famous Chick Webb Orchestra. In September of 1939, the Fitzgerald band was booked into Ed Fox's Grand Terrace nightclub which was located at 35th and Calumet Avenue in Chicago, Illinois. They were the replacement band for the Earl "Fatha" Hines Orchestra which had been booked by Fox to make a four week road trip through the southern part of the country. It was during the Grand Terrace engagement that Chick Webb's name was dropped from his old band. The new orchestra with the Chick Webb personnel was billed as Ella Fitzgerald and her Famous Orchestra. Members of the band such as Lonnie Simmons, Louis Jordan and other old timers, began leaving the band because of personality conflicts with Ella and more importantly because of the extremely low salaries.

*In August of 1942, the old Chick Webb band was totally dissolved because many of the musicians were being drafted into the military service. Ella began working with a smaller group in Philadelphia known as the "Three Keys". By late summer of 1943 the Furness Brothers were claimed by the draft board, forcing the "Keys" to disband. In 1944 Ella Fitzgerald entered a joint venture with the Ink Spots and recorded with **Into Each Life Some Rain Must Fall,** which sold more than a million records. In 1945 Ella and the Ink Spots struck gold a second time with another million disc best seller. It was a Duke Ellington creation entitled: **I'm Beginning To See The Light.***

In 1947, Ella married Ray Brown, a bass player from the hills of Pittsburgh (Smoky Town). Their marriage ended in 1953. Several years earlier on December 26, 1941 Ella married Benjamin Kornegay in St. Louis, Missouri. Moe Gale, her manager was both disappointed and shocked by her sudden rush into marriage. He decided to check out this mysterious man who had married this fine chick that was laying golden eggs for his agency. His finding revealed that Kornegay had a criminal record. He had been convicted of drug charges in the 1930s and had served jail time. Based on those facts Moe Gale's lawyers succeeded in getting the marriage annulled. There was overwhelming evidence that the marriage was motivated for criminal intent and not love. Prior to Kornegay, she was married to a shipyard worker in 1939. That marriage was annulled ten days after it took place.

*Among Ella's other brand name suitors were Louis Jordan who worked with her in the Chick Webb Orchestra and later gained fame as the leader of the Tympany Five. Jordan was also the composer of **Five Guys Name Moe, Is You Is Or Is You Ain't My Baby,** and **Choo Choo Boogie.** Joe Jones, the flashy and sharp dressing drummer with the Count Basie Orchestra was also on her known list of lovers. Everlasting love was something Ella never found in her life-*

Marriage #2

Although there has never been any doubt about Ella's marriage to Ray Brown, the actual date of the nuptials has always been shrouded in mystery. In fact, she was married on December 10, 1947, in Ohio, as this copy of her marriage certificate reveals. The designation "Colored," top right, is another reminder of the racial climate at the time.

Marriage #3

time outside of the lyrics of a song.

During the World War II years Ella's career took a nose dive, in that she slipped from fourth place to thirteenth on the musical popularity chart; however she went into orbit again when she joined forces with impresario Norman Granz and his Jazz at the Philharmonic (JATP) Concerts. With Granz, she toured worldwide with some of America's most prominent jazz instrumentalists such as Willie Smith, Clark Terry, Nat Cole, Oscar Peterson, Illinois Jacquet, Lionel Hampton, Coleman Hawkins and many others.

Norman Granz opened the door of racial equality for Afro-American musicians. He refused to let his group play to segregated audiences. He had clauses in his contracts that demanded equality in the selling of tickets and seating. If the clause was broken, Granz was legally entitled to collect the contracted fee and also refused to play. More often than not he prevailed.

The concert halls and nightclubs were not the only places the JATP-ers had problems and the south did not have an exclusive on Jim Crow. On a tour of the Midwest, a Ohio hotel manager refused to allow Black and white musicians to share the same room. Europe did not escape the shame of racism either. A German promoter refused to make arrangements for a private dressing room for Ella who was the only woman on this particular JATP tour - Granz refused to let his people play for an audience of 80,000 in an oversold concert facility. He paid his entourage their full fee and gave them the night off.

Clark Terry, the trumpet player was a member of the JATP touring group. He earlier had been a sideman with Count Basie, Duke Ellington and Quincy Jones. He was known for his photographic memory thus, he describes in detail a conversation that took place between Norman Granz and a German concert promoter as follows:
When we got off the bus the promoter met Norman and said, "Glad you are here."

19

Norman replied, "We are happy to be here."
"We got to hit (play) in an hour, where is Miss Fitzgerald's dressing room?"
The promoter recoiled and retorted, "We don't have a dressing room for anybody!"
A few moments lapsed, before Norman snapped "Where will Miss Fitzgerald dress?"
The promoter haughtily replied, "She can dress on the bus like the other band members."
Norman displaying a streak of anger in his voice said, "I am not talking about the band I am talking about Miss Fitzgerald. If you don't have a dressing room for Miss Fitzgerald you don't have a concert."
The promoter shouted, "What the hell do you mean?" "I have 80,000 people waiting in that hall to hear you people."
Norman recoiled, "Give them their money back."
The German promoter blasted, "I will sue you."
Norman rebutted, "That is exactly what I want you to do however, before you file suit look in the upper left-hand corner of your contract on the second page and you will see that Miss Fitzgerald is entitled to a dressing room."
Granz yelled, "Let's go back to the hotel gang, this fellow don't seem to understand English." Norman, Ella and the band got back on the bus, went to the largest and most expensive restaurant in town and had dinner that was followed by a night on the town as the guest of the President of the JATP Corporation.

Six years prior to the first European tour Norman Granz officially became Ella Fitzgerald's manager following the expiration of her contract with Moe Gale. Norman solidified the relationship by paying her delinquent Internal Revenue taxes out of his own personal funds.

Ella entered into a handshake agreement with Norman Granz and his Verve Recording Company in 1956. The "arrangement in wax" yielded more hit records than either one of them could have anticipated. She was one of a very few Black artists to become a millionaire and he in turn became a multimillionaire.

Granz had been acting as Fitzgerald's manager for several years prior to the handshake agreement. Inasmuch as he was the President of Verve Records her output of recordings could not be matched by any other recording artist including Frank Sinatra with Capitol Records. It was with Verve that she began her legendary songbook series commencing with Cole Porter compositions followed by the Rogers & Hart Songbook and then the Duke Ellington Songbook and others.

Getting Ella released from Decca Records was a judgmental blunder on the part of Universal Movie Studio which owned Decca Records.

UMS had enjoyed a big financial success with the release of The Glenn Miller Story in 1954. Thus, in 1955 they decided to dig deeper for more gold in a Benny Goodman Story. This movie production could not take place without a copyright release from Granz who had both the musicians and the soundtrack under his corporate umbrella. Universal pictures was so hungry for the material they agreed to release Ella Fitzgerald from her Decca recording contract in exchange for the use of Granz's men and material.

Ella had grown like topsy in that on the evening of July 20, 1957 the fortieth year of her birth was declared "Ella Fitzgerald Night" at the Hollywood Bowl. On that starlit night she performed before a sellout crowd of 17,000. She was accompanied by the Los Angeles Philharmonic with its 102 member orchestra, Frank Devol was the conductor. This represented the first of many sellouts for a period covering the next thirty-five years.

On another European Trip, Ella Fitzgerald and her entourage boarded an airline with the expectation that they would sit in their comfortable first-class, reserved seats. To their surprise they were told that they had been bumped in spite of their reservation. Granz filed suit against Pan American World Airways and won an out of court settlement from the airlines. It was Norman Granz's fight for civil rights activity that generated surveillance by J. Edgar Hoover's Federal Bureau of Investigation for both he and Ella Fitzgerald.

Ella Fitzgerald was at the apex of her career when she recorded the songbooks of Cole Porter, Duke Ellington, George and Ira Gershwin and others between 1956 and 1964. She was accompanied on different recording dates by Nelson Riddle, Billy May, Duke Ellington, Count Basie, Oscar Peterson, Joe Pass, Louis Armstrong, et al. Out of the songbooks she sang dozens of songs by Duke Ellington, Cole Porter, Richard Rodgers, Irving Berlin, Johnny Mercer, Jerome Kern, George and Ira Gershwin, and Harold Arlen. These composers and lyricists represented some of America's most elite talents.

In the early 1970s, Ella was plagued by Granz's desire to overbook the songbird that laid the golden eggs in spite of her poor health which started with eye problems related to her diabetes. As a result of her high blood pressure she developed a heart condition in the 1980s. As a matter of fact she had several heart bypasses. In 1989, she was advised to cut her schedule down to an occasional concert. In 1993 she had both legs amputated below the knee because of complication from her diabetes. Her spokesperson did not release news of the amputations until a year later in 1994 at which time she was confined to a wheelchair. On June 15, 1996, Ella an American Original died at her home in Beverly Hills, California at age 78. She was surrounded by Ray Brown, Jr. her son and other family members.

Jazz at the Philharmonic troupe photographed on arrival at the Honolulu airport, 1952. Standing left to right: Ray Brown, pianist Oscar Peterson, guitarist Barney Kessel, Norman Granz, unidentified Hawaiian promoter, Roy Eldridge, pianist Hank Jones, Lester Young. Seated, alto saxophonist Willie Smith, tenor saxophonist Flip Phillips sharing his garland with trumpeter Charley Shavers, Ella Fitzgerald, drummers Buddy Rich and Gene Krupa, and clarinetist Buddy De GFranco.

FEDERAL BUREAU OF INVESTIGATION

FREEDOM OF INFORMATION/PRIVACY ACTS SECTION

COVER SHEET

SUBJECT: <u>ELLA FITZGERALD</u>

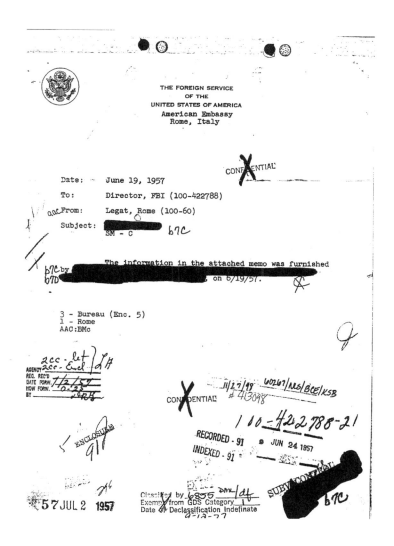

THE FOREIGN SERVICE
OF THE
UNITED STATES OF AMERICA
American Embassy
Rome, Italy

CONFIDENTIAL

Date: June 19, 1957

To: Director, FBI (100-422788)

From: Legat, Rome (100-60)

Subject: ▓▓▓▓▓▓▓▓
            SM - C   b7C

The information in the attached memo was furnished
▓▓▓▓▓▓▓▓▓▓▓▓▓▓▓▓▓▓▓▓▓▓▓, on 6/19/57.

3 - Bureau (Enc. 5)
1 - Rome
AAC:BMc

CONFIDENTIAL   # 413098

100-422788-21

RECORDED - 91   JUN 24 1957
INDEXED - 91

57 JUL 2 1957

Classified by 6855
Exempt from GDS Category I
Date of Declassification Indefinate

UNITED STATES DEPARTMENT OF JUSTICE
FEDERAL BUREAU OF INVESTIGATION

Reply, Please Refer to
No.

WASHINGTON 25, D. C.

June 19, 1957

CON̶F̶I̶D̶E̶NTIAL

b7C ▬▬▬▬▬

The following information was furnished by a confidential source abroad on June 19, 1957.

▬▬▬▬▬ and his musical orchestra, known as
"Jazz at the Philharmonic," performed in Rome, Italy from
May 25 to June 6, 1957. The orchestra was composed of nine
musicians, among whom was the singer, ELLA FITZGERALD.

b7C No information was received indicating that ▬▬
engaged in any political activities while in Italy.

APPROPRIATE A▬▬▬▬▬
▬▬ FIELD OFFICE
ADVISED BY ROUTING
SLIP(✗) OF CLASSIFICATION
DATE 9-14-77 DML REC

CONF̶IDENTIAL

Classified by 6855 DML/df
Exempt from GDS Category 1
Date of Declassification Indefinate
9-12-77

DESTROYED
OCT 24 1963

100-422788-21

ENCLOSURE

26

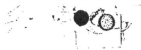

February 18, 1970

BY LIAISON

Honorable Alexander P. Butterfield
Deputy Assistant to the President
The White House
Washington, D. C.

Dear Mr. Butterfield:

Reference is made to your name check request concerning Ella Fitzgerald, █████████████████

The central files of the FBI reveal no pertinent information concerning ███████████

The fingerprint files of the Identification Division of the FBI contain no arrest data identifiable with ███████ based upon background information submitted in connection with this name check request.

Attached are separate memoranda concerning Ella Fitzgerald and ██████████

Sincerely yours,

ENCLOSURE

CC TO: White
REQ. REC'D 5-12
SEP 16 197,
ANS.
BY:

closures (2)

Mr. DeLoach (sent direct) REC-33   62-5-35583
Mr. Gale (sent direct)

mcb

17 FEB 20 1970

TELETYPE UNIT ☐

February 18, 1970

BY LIAISON

Honorable Alexander P. Butterfield
Deputy Assistant to the President
The White House
Washington, D. C.

Dear Mr. Butterfield:

      Reference is made to your name check request
concerning Ella Fitzgerald, ███████████████████████

      The central files of the FBI reveal no pertinent
information concerning ████████████

      The fingerprint files of the Identification Division
of the FBI contain no arrest data identifiable with ████████
based upon background information submitted in connection with
this name check request.

      Attached are separate memoranda concerning
Ella Fitzgerald and ██████████

Sincerely yours,

ENCLOSURE

Enclosures (2)

Mr. DeLoach (sent direct)
Mr. Gale (sent direct)

mcb

February 18, 1970

ELLA FITZGERALD

Summary

Ella Fitzgerald, who was born on April 25, 1918, at Newport News, Virginia, has not been the subject of an investigation conducted by the FBI. However, our files reveal the following information concerning her.

In June, 1957, it was reported that one ▓▓▓▓▓ and his musical orchestra performed in Rome, Italy, from May 25 to June 6, 1957. This orchestra was reportedly composed of nine musicians and Ella Fitzgerald, a singer. ▓▓▓▓▓ was allegedly a member of the Communist Party in the early 1940's. He was interviewed by representatives of the FBI in 1956 and displayed a cooperative attitude. (100-422788-21

A newspaper article in January, 1957, indicated that Fitzgerald and three other members of her staff had accepted out-of-court settlements on four damage suits they brought against a major air line charging racial discrimination. (62-101087-A-26)

The fingerprint files of the Identification Division of the FBI contain no arrest data identifiable with captioned individual based upon background information submitted in connection with this name check request.

NOTE: Per request of Alexander P. Butterfield, Deputy Assistant to the President.

ALA:mcb (7)

62-5-35583   ENCLOSURE

SEE REVERSE S
ADD. DISSEMIN.

MAIL ROOM ☐ TELETYPE UNIT ☐

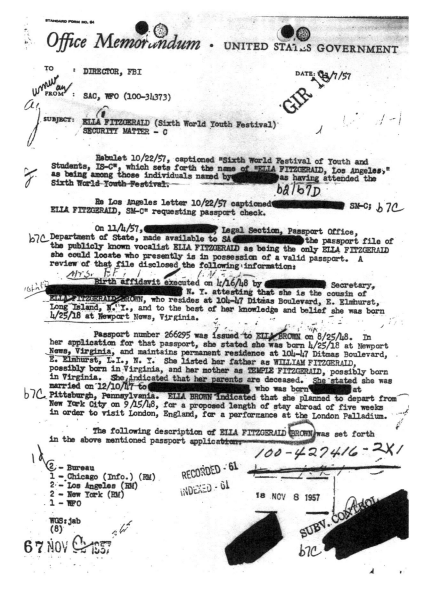

STANDARD FORM NO. 64

Office Memorandum • UNITED STATES GOVERNMENT

TO : DIRECTOR, FBI

DATE: 13/7/57

FROM : SAC, WFO (100-34373)

SUBJECT: ELLA FITZGERALD (Sixth World Youth Festival)
SECURITY MATTER - C

Rebulet 10/22/57, captioned "Sixth World Festival of Youth and Students, IS-C", which sets forth the name of "ELLA FITZGERALD, Los Angeles," as being among those individuals named by ▮▮▮▮ as having attended the Sixth World Youth Festival.

Re Los Angeles letter 10/22/57 captioned ▮▮▮▮ SM-C; ELLA FITZGERALD, SM-C" requesting passport check.

On 11/4/57, ▮▮▮▮, Legal Section, Passport Office, Department of State, made available to SA ▮▮▮▮ the passport file of the publicly known vocalist ELLA FITZGERALD as being the only ELLA FITZGERALD she could locate who presently is in possession of a valid passport. A review of that file disclosed the following information:

Birth affidavit executed on 4/16/48 by ▮▮▮▮ Secretary, ▮▮▮▮, N. Y. attesting that she is the cousin of ELLA FITZGERALD BROWN, who resides at 104-47 Ditmas Boulevard, E. Elmhurst, Long Island, N. Y., and to the best of her knowledge and belief she was born 4/25/18 at Newport News, Virginia.

Passport number 266295 was issued to ELLA BROWN on 8/25/48. In her application for that passport, she stated she was born 4/25/18 at Newport News, Virginia, and maintains permanent residence at 104-47 Ditmas Boulevard, E. Elmhurst, L.I., N. Y. She listed her father as WILLIAM FITZGERALD, possibly born in Virginia, and her mother as TEMPLE FITZGERALD, possibly born in Virginia. She indicated that her parents are deceased. She stated she was married on 12/10/47 to ▮▮▮▮ who was born ▮▮▮▮ at Pittsburgh, Pennsylvania. ELLA BROWN indicated that she planned to depart from New York City on 9/15/48, for a proposed length of stay abroad of five weeks in order to visit London, England, for a performance at the London Palladium.

The following description of ELLA FITZGERALD BROWN was set forth in the above mentioned passport application.

100-427416-2X1

2 - Bureau
1 - Chicago (Info.) (RM)
2 - Los Angeles (RM)
2 - New York (RM)
1 - WFO

WGS:jab
(8)

RECORDED - 61
INDEXED - 61

18 NOV 8 1957

67 NOV 8 1957

WFO 100-34373

Height:	5' 5½"
Hair:	Black
Eyes:	Brown
Occupation:	Vocalist

Passport number 266295 was renewed on 3/21/52, and in her renewal application, ELLA BROWN stated she intended to depart from New York City on 3/28/52 for a proposed length of stay abroad of two weeks in order to visit Scandanavian countries, France, Switzerland, Belgium, and Germany for the purpose of performing at jazz concerts.

New York Series passport number 1412 was issued on 2/5/53 to ELLA BROWN, known professionally as ELLA FITZGERALD. In her application for that passport, she indicated she resides at 179-07 Murdock Avenue, St. Albans, L.I., N. Y. She stated she was residing at ▓▓▓▓▓▓▓ N. Y. She stated her maiden name was ELLA FITZGERALD; that she was previously married to ▓▓▓▓▓▓ in 1941 at ▓▓▓▓▓ Missouri, and that this marriage was annulled in 1942. ELLA BROWN stated she would depart from the United States on 2/14/53, for a proposed length of stay abroad of from six to eight weeks in order to visit Sweden, Holland, Belgium, France, Italy, and Denmark for the purpose of performance at concerts.

On 1/20/55, passport number 521063 was issued to "ELLA BROWN, known professionally as ELLA FITZGERALD". In her application for that passport, she stated her marriage to ▓▓▓▓▓▓ was terminated by divorce on 8/13/53. She stated her permanent residence was at 179-07 Murdock Avenue, St. Albans, L.I., N. Y. She indicated she would depart from the United States on 2/5/55 for a proposed length of stay abroad of six weeks in order to visit Sweden, Denmark, Norway, Germany, France, and England for the purpose of concert tour with Jazz at the Philharmonic, Inc.

Her passport was renewed on 1/15/57, and in her renewal application she stated she intended to leave the United States on 2/9/57, for a proposed length of stay abroad until April, 1957, in order to visit Norway, Sweden, Denmark, Italy, Germany, and France for the purpose of entertaining.

There was no additional pertinent information set forth in her file.

WFO will forward copies of ELLA FITZGERALD BROWN's passport application photograph to New York. Copies will also be furnished to Chicago for display to ▓▓▓▓▓▓ to ascertain if informant can identify same. P.

- 2 -

Nat "King" Cole

Cut II
The Unforgettable:
Nat "King" Cole

ﾉ

Nathaniel Adam Coles was born under a constellation sign known as Pisces, the 12th sign of the Zodiac on March 17, 1917. His place of birth was a frame house at 1524 Saint Johns Street in Montgomery, Alabama. Nat's father James Edward Coles was a skilled butcher at a local grocery and meat market store. On Sunday he served as one of the church deacons and jackleg preacher at the Buelah Baptist Church. His mother Perlina Adam Coles played the piano for the choir at the 10:30 A.M. Sunday morning service.

In 1923 Deacon James Edward Coles was called from the mountain top by the thunderous voice of the Lord early one Sunday morning just before daybreak and told to go north and do his work. He specifically instructed him to

The Illinois Central Railroad Station

go to Abraham Lincoln's City on the western shores of Lake Michigan and preach.

Shortly after arriving at the Illinois Central Railroad Station located at 12th and Michigan Avenue in Chicago with his wife and four children, he was advised to walk west two blocks and catch a #7 streetcar commonly known as "Big

The Union Stockyards

34

Red" going south on State Street through the heart of the colored community. Without too much trouble he immediately found and rented a small two bedroom unfurnished apartment in the Black Belt in the 4200 block on South Prairie Avenue. His second act in the city labeled the "Hog Butchers for the World", by Carl Sandburg, was to find a job as a meat cutter in the union stockyards at either the Wilson or Swift meatpacking companies where several of his Alabama hometown boys worked.

Reverend James Coles was only in Chicago for approximately two months when he organized the Second Progressive Baptist Church in a 43rd and State Street storefront several blocks from his abode. His fame as a preacher of the Lord's work began to spread like a California wildfire. Thus, within months after his arrival in 1924 he was invited by the board of Deacons of the Truelight Baptist Church to fill the vacancy of their retiring minister. The Truelight edifice was located on the south-east corner of 45th and Dearborn, its main auditorium could accommodate approximately two hundred parishioners.

At age eleven, Nat Cole began sharing the piano chores with his mother at his father's church. Although he could not read music, he could play by ear any songs he had heard once.

The Evelyn Cole apartment was in the second building from the corner.

Some thirty years later Nat's sister Evelyn Cole was the writer's tenant and neighbor in an apartment building located at 8007 South Champlain Avenue in the Chatham community on the South East Side of Chicago. She told the writer: "The first song that Nat learned to play

35

was not a religious hymn but a popular song written in 1923 by Frank Silver and Irving Cohn entitled *"Yes! We Have No Bananas."*

This writer who was also a piano player first met the jet black, bumpy face, tall, slender Nat Cole on Easter Sunday in 1934. He was leading a Teenage Orchestra at a Matinee dance being held at the Warwick Dance Hall located at 543 East 47th Street in Chicago. By this time he had dropped the (s) from Coles. The dropping of the (s) from Coles was further noted in February 1935 by this writer in a 1st year Spanish class where they were both students at the New Wendell Phillips / DuSable High School located at 4934 South Wabash Ave. Cole dropped out of school shortly before the end of that semester.

DuSable High School

Henry E. Fort a string bass player and mutual friend of both Nat Cole and the writer, made the following observation during an interview for <u>An Autobiography of Black Jazz</u> written by this author in 1983. Fort said:

In January of 1934, I was a young bass player and childhood friend of Nat Cole. I received a telephone call from Cole asking me to join a teenaged band he was organizing. I went to the first rehearsal of the new twelve-piece band in the tiny apartment of Nat's parents, the Reverend James and Mrs. Perlina Cole in the 4200 block on South Prairie Avenue in Chicago. Cole had called together a group of young cats that included four saxophone players, three trumpet players, a trombone player and a full rhythm section which included a guitar, myself on bass, Russell Shores a physician's son on drums and Nat on piano.

Nat acted very mature for a seventeen year old boy. He was very serious and intense. The crack in his youthful and cool façade could be noted by the way he frequently bit his fingernails. Nat scratched his chin with the back of his fingers because he didn't have any fingernails. He was authoritative without being dictatorial, and he was able to whip a bunch of undisciplined teenagers into a music unit in less than sixty days. His objective was to make his orchestra sound like Earl 'Fatha' Hines' band; Earl was Nat's idol.

Nat lived within a few blocks of the old Grand Terrace nightclub which was located at 3955 South Parkway (Martin Luther King Drive) where Hines' orchestra played and broadcasted over the radio air waves nightly. Nat use to hang out regularly in the gangway under the Oakwood - Stockyard elevator tracks next to the Terrace and listen to the Hines Orchestra practice. Nat's musical memory was phenomenal. He could hear something once and repeat it note by note without skipping a single chord. His talents were a great asset to our young group. Nat lifted so much of the Hines material intact other musicians called our group the Rogues of Rhythm.

Nat's father objected to young Cole's intense interest in jazz piano. But his mother, Perlina, had a different opinion. Finally the family reached a compromise: Nat could play jazz on Sunday afternoons as long as he played organ for the morning service at his father's True Light Baptist Church. Nat's mother made our first uniforms, Cossack shirts, to give the band a professional look.

Malcolm Smith a dance promoter and manager made arrangements with Mr. Hall for us to play at the Warwick Hall 543 East 47th Street every Sunday afternoon. Consequently we began to get a lot of press and notoriety especially when we had a battle of the bands with Tony Fambro and his Jungle Rhythm Orchestra, another teenaged group. Tony played a lot of Ellington's material whereas Nat wanted his band to sound like the Hines Orchestra.

By early 1935, the band had become so popular among South Side youth that Malcolm Smith arranged a tour of Illinois for us. I recall our first trip, we went by bus down to Aurora, Joliet and then Kankakee, where we suffered our first casualty. A trumpet player named "Rail" became caught in the undertow while he was swimming in the Kankakee River, and was never seen again. That incident disturbed Nat's mother to the extent that she decided that Nat's oldest brother Eddie, should leave Noble Sissle's band, one of the top popular bands of the period, and come back to Chicago and give Nat the benefit of his experience. Nat had three brothers and one sister, Evelyn and Eddie were a good ten years or more older than Nat. Eddie was one of the best musicians Chicago had produced: a master bass player, as a matter of fact he could play any number of instruments, including the piano. All the Cole boys were musically inclined. On the other hand, none had the style of Nat "King" Cole. Nat played like Earl Hines and sat sidesaddle at the piano like Hines, his body carriage was that of a straight arrow and he walked in a strut like Duke Ellington. Nat was a proud young man. Even when he couldn't afford a new suit, he was always neat and he was always professional on the stage. It was just in him, and in his whole family.

"Nat could sit down at a piano, and point and tell the horn player to play a B-flat here or a C minor there and believe it or not it came out harmonically perfect. But I

never saw Nat read a piece of music the entire time I was with him. If he heard something once, he could play it as if he had been playing it all his life. If someone hummed a tune around Nat, before the last sixteen bars were finished, he would pick up the tune and play it to the finish as if it were his own. He could play anything he heard. At rehearsal when the band played a number Nat hadn't heard yet, he usually got up and directed. Then he could sit down at the piano and play that number a second time around as if he had written the arrangement, which was phenomenal. I'm certain that Nat couldn't read music during our early years, but I'm equally certain that he must have learned how to read and write later on after I left the band.

"In 1936 after Nat finished a six-month engagement with his brother Eddie at the Panama Café at 58th and Prairie Avenue in Chicago, he organized a big band to go on the road with a revival of Eubie Blake and Noble Sissle's 1923 Shuffle Along Revue starring Miller and Lyles. Our first stops were in Michigan, where we toured five cities, including Ann Arbor. We played the University of Michigan auditorium there, and Nat got married in 1937 to a chorus girl in the show named Nadine Robinson. I was his best man.

"After we completed the Michigan tour, we headed West, our goal was Los Angeles the City of Angels. The Angels did not welcome Shuffle Along with open arms. Miller and Lyles east coast fame were not household names on the west coast. The show flopped and the cast scattered like dry leaves in a windstorm.

We used an old Chicago trick to get a job while in L.A. Six or seven of us went separately into a nightclub. Of course Nat was the star attraction, and the local bandleader would ask him to come up and play a number on the piano. Nat did that, and after about ten or fifteen minutes, I went up and told the bass player that I would relieve him. A little later somebody else from our group relieved the sax

The Nat "King" Cole Trio

man, and before the set was over the entire Cole ensemble was on the bandstand. We outplayed the house band. Management approached us and offered us the job if we would work below scale. Scale at that time was thirty-five to forty dollars a week in California, but they offered us twenty-five dollars. We obviously couldn't accept that offer and remain in the union, so at that point I left Nat and returned to Chicago.

Nat decided that he would stay on the West Coast and work as a single. Bob Lewis of the Swanee Inn suggested that Nat add a bass, guitar and a drum. The first person Nat contacted was Oscar Miller, a guitarist, who jumped at the chance to get a steady job. Next he called bassist Wesley Prince and then a drummer who did not show up for the first night. The drummer was not needed on the second night because the Nat "King" Cole Trio had been born. His trio was accepted overwhelmingly by the clientele of the Swanee Inn on North LaBrea. The salary was $35.00 a week per man. In 1937 in the heart of President Herbert Hoover's lingering Depression a postal worker was making $1,200 per year.

Economic conditions began to improve with the outbreak of World War II in Europe in September 1939. Granz paid the Trio $11.00 per man to play at Billy Berg's place on Sunday night as the rhythm section for the jazz jam sessions. The extra money from the gig was cream in black coffee.

Carlos Gastel who months later became Nat's manager followed the King Cole Trio from the Fox Hills Café across the street from the 20th Century Fox movie lot to the 331 Club, Shep Kelley's in Hollywood and Club Circle in Beverly Hills. Many were the times when Carlos would weep softly as Nat played and sang **Sweet Lorraine.**

When Norman Granz staged his first Jazz at The Philharmonic on July 2, 1944 The Nat Cole Trio was on the top of his list to appear on the program along with Marie

In action on the stage at the Philharmonic left to right: Helen Humes, Trummie Young and Illinois Jacquets.

Bryant, singer; Illinois Jacquet, tenor sax; Benny Carter, alto sax and trumpet, Oscar Moore, guitar; Red Callendar, bass; Meade Lux Lewis, boogie woogie piano player; Barney Bigard, clarinet; Lee Young, Lester's brother on drum; et al.

Some 15 years later in 1959 Granz rescued Quincy Jones who was stranded with his band which featured Clark Terry in Europe when his Free and Easy show bellied up thousands of miles from home. Granz put Jones in touch with Nat "King" Cole, who hired his band to back his show in Sweden, Denmark, Germany, Switzerland, and Italy.

Quincy made the following observation: *One night Nat came offstage, ruffled, and Nat said "Quincy, call the cats in the band back onstage and let them play a few more numbers. Quincy said, "with all due respect, Nat - go back out there and play **Sweet Lorraine"** on the piano with just the rhythm section. He turned around, and walked back onstage, and played the shit out of **Sweet Lorraine,** he tore it up. He sang again and this time they loved it. He was the best who ever did it, a talented highly intelligent man, with perfect pitch on top of it all."*

To maintain a professional lifestyle in the states required four working hands. Nadine his first wife had to wait tables, dance, and sometimes act as a nightclub hostess and do a sundry of other things to keep a roof over their heads and food on the table in a small rented house at 2910 South St. Andrews Place. In addition, she was not critical of Nat's lifestyle. Many nights he did not come home from work until the following afternoon.

To make bad matters worse, she frequently found notes in his shirt pockets from other women when she took his clothes to the cleaners.

In 1939 Nat came up with a string of novelty songs that became hits during World War II such as **"Gone With The Draft"** and **"Straighten Up and Fly Right**." In the same year he recorded his friend Jimmy Noone's theme

43

Left to right: Nat, daughter Natalie and wife Maria dine at Morris Eat Shop, 410 East 47th Street, between stage shows at the Regal Theatre in Chicago.

song "**Sweet Lorraine**" and also Earl Hines' "**Rosetta**" often vocalized by Walter Fuller, the Hines trumpet player.

In 1941 Nat recorded songs that became jazz classics. Such tunes as "**I Like to Riff**", "**That Ain't Right**" and "**Hit That Jive, Jack**" they were all hip tunes that slid over the tongue and lips of jitterbugs from coast to coast. Traveling around the country alone did not help Nat and Nadine's marital relationship.

Nadine filed for a divorce in a L.A. court in January 1947. She claimed that Nat had inflicted extreme mental cruelty and all of the other boiler plate garbage that lawyers usually plead. Two weeks after she filed, Nat signed an agreement in New York City to pay Nadine $200 per week every week until the divorce was final. He further agreed to give her the L.A. home which had been appraised at $75,000, and also pay off a second mortgage lien of $8,357. At that time her lawyers Loeb and Loeb estimated Nat's

Left is Ralph Edwards' host of <u>This is Your Life Show</u> featuring Nat Cole and some family members and friends. Standing directly behind Cole is his father Rev. Cole and his sister Evelyn.

weekly income to be between $3,000 and $5,000 per week. The date for the divorce was set for March 22, 1948.

The Cole family did not like Maria Ellington his future wife who had been a former singer with the Duke Ellington Orchestra. She was not related to Duke Ellington. Nat's future bride was bubbling over with her own high middle class breeding which turned the Cole family off. In spite of the fact that her father was simply an ordinary postal employee she had this mirror, mirror on the wall attitude. She acted, talked and walked like a member of the English Aristocracy.

Henry Fort recalls: *"The years changed Nat. I recall after he divorced Nadine Robinson and married Maria Ellington some people blamed the change in him toward his old friends on his new marriage. I remember in 1958 I took my family to Hawaii and stopped off in Los Angeles. I called Nat and left a message with his answering service, but he never called me back. Shortly after I got back to Chicago from the Islands I received a call from Ralph Edwards, the television host of* **This Is Your Life.** *Nat had told him that I was one of the original members of his band, and Edwards wanted me to come back to California and appear on the show with Nat. My first inclination was to refuse, because Nat had not returned my call. My wife Catherine persuaded me to return to California and appear on the show in 1958."*

Nat hired Baldwin "Sparky" Tavares as his valet in 1949 while playing at the Blue Note in Chicago. Baldwin "Sparky" said:

I had met Nat earlier in New York through my brother-in-law Ervin Ashby, who played bass for Nat. "The valet work was actually too much for one man because Nat always carried big trunks filled with a dozen or more suits and at least fifty shirts, so he had to hire an ex-railroad man to help me. If Nat was going to do six shows a day, he would have nine or ten changes of clothing. That meant everyone in the trio had to have nine uniforms. They were all single or double-breasted suits, not one tuxedo. Nat was a perfectionist and a slavemaster. He worked the hell out of me. By the time I got to California several months later, I had dropped from one hundred twenty-seven to one hundred nine pounds. But I was stuck, I was his man. Around strangers he was very shy and quiet, but with his friends he acted like just another one of the cats. He liked to sit around and have a taste, argue sports and joke. He loved comedy and had a great sense of humor. He had the loudest laugh I ever heard.

He could laugh at himself. I remember one afternoon in Chicago we were coming out of the stage door of the Regal Theater and found ourselves facing a big group of kids in the alley. I asked them if they wanted an autograph? One kid said, "No, he wanted a hat." Another kid said, 'I want to see the show and you better let me in that door. I am Nat Cole's brother.'

I said, 'What's your name?'

He said, 'My name is Charcoal.'

Nat laughed louder than anyone in that alley. The boy apologized to Nat when he recognized him. And Nat said, 'Come on over here son, and tell me your name.' When the kid told him his name, Nat told him not to tell lies like that again. Then he said to me, 'Take those kids out front and tell Ken Blewett, the theater manager to give them good seats.'

A good way to wipe the smile off Nat's face was to mention the NAACP. The only time I've seen Nat really upset was after he sent a telegram to Roy Wilkins of the NAACP which read:

I will not join the NAACP in speech making, but I am willing to do everything within my power to further our cause.

Wilkins immediately issued a press release paraphrasing the telegram and implying that Nat had refused to join the NAACP. A legal official by the name of Walter White of that organization phoned and had the nerve to call Nat a handkerchief-head. The son-of-a-bitch that called him that was married to a white woman. One ironic thing about the whole National Association for the Advancement of Colored People episode was that Nat had been doing benefits for the NAACP since Day One, probably as many if not more than most entertainers-and yet he was being publicly insulted just because he didn't want to make speeches or be a card-carrying member. The thing came to a head in Detroit when civic leaders there asked Nat why he wouldn't join the NAACP.

Nat said, 'I have done more benefits for you people than anyone else you have mentioned.'

The Detroit officials said, 'Well, join anyway.'

Nat finally joined on his wife's advice and the advice

Lena Horne

of his manager Collis Gastell and others he respected. But that incident really hurt him and he carried the bruise to his grave.

He was hurt again in 1950 when we played the Thunderbird Hotel in Las Vegas. We had a congo player at the time named Jack Coustanza, an Italian boy from Chicago. He was working for Nat but since he was white he could get a room in the Thunderbird and Nat and the rest of us couldn't. To make bad matters worse, the Nat "King" Cole name was on the top of the marquee. However, we had to stay at Mrs. Shaw's on the west side of town, known as Darkie City. On top of that, although we were the stars of the show we had to enter the hotel through a side door and stay in our dressing rooms until we went onstage and our food was brought up and served buffet style every night. We refused to eat it. We did the show, returned to the dressing rooms to change our clothes and then left, because there was nothing they could do for us. When Nat finished that engagement, he told Collis, 'I don't want to play this town anymore until I can walk through the front door.' Collis agreed.

We did not go back to Vegas again until 1953, when we played at a place called El Rancho Vegas. It was managed by Jack Entrotter, former head man of the Copacabana in New York. He had an unwritten rule that all facilities must be open to all entertainers who worked in the hotel. Nat was given a large cabin and I also had a cabin. They told Nat he could use all facilities and they meant it. Nat was the first to break the color barrier for Black entertainers in Las Vegas and for Black people in general there. Shortly afterward, the Sands Hotel brought in Lena Horne and opened the entire place to her. She could have guests and do whatever she pleased.

We had a strange experience at the Sahara Hotel. Bill Miller, the manager from New York, called Nat and invited our group over to see the show, and we were treat-

ed royally. We had good food and drinks, and everything was beautiful. The next night we decided to go back on our own and see the show. But when we got to the Sahara, the security man stopped us at the door. Nat got on the telephone and called Miller who said he was sorry but his hands were tied and he couldn't do a thing about it. We were their guests one night and turned away from the door the next. Strange things happen in America.

*Life is full of peaks and valleys and one of the peaks for Nat occurred at the Brown Derby in Hollywood. We were sitting around having drinks and talking, when Hoagy Carmichael the composer of **Stardust** and many other hits came over and joined us. After a few minutes of general conversation Hoagy said to Nat, 'You know, the prettiest vocal version I ever heard of my song **Stardust** was by you. I have felt more honored by your version than any other I know.' Nat bubbled for the rest of the evening; **Stardust** was one of his favorite songs, but he had no idea that Hoagy felt that way about his version.*

Nat's mother was the leader of that family. She had an incredibly strong influence over her daughter and her sons. They all respected her. Although she was not educated, she was articulate and she spoke as crisply and distinctly as Nat sang. She treated all her children equally, and made no bigger fuss over one that was a star than over the others. When she died, it hit Nat hard. He fainted at the funeral services, which were held at a church pastored by the Reverend Rawls, Lou Rawls' uncle, at 42nd and Indiana.

In October, 1964, we were working a club in Lake Tahoe, doing two shows a night and flying to Hollywood every day to do a picture called Cat Ballou with Lee Marvin. One evening after we returned from Hollywood, we napped for an hour and went over to the club for dinner. While we were sitting around, I noticed that one of Nat's valets was making extra holes in Nat's belt. I asked him what the hell he was doing. He told me that the belt had gotten too large for Nat.

I turned to Nat and said, 'What's wrong?'

'I'm losing weight,' Nat said. He never weighed more than one hundred seventy-four pounds.

I looked at him and said, 'Yeah, I guess you are losing a little weight, Dick.' I always called him Dick. When I handed him his clothes that night I asked him when he had started losing weight.

'I don't know,' he said. 'Maybe I've been working too hard. I should probably take a few days off. I seem to stay tired.'

After we left Lake Tahoe, we went to Vegas to play an engagement at The Sands and one night Nat got dizzy while performing, and that's when he knew he was really sick and it was more than just fatigue. We called a doctor and they sent us a 'Feel Good' doctor who gave him a shot and said he would be all right. The doctors down there will do anything to stay in good with the hotels. They come in and treat entertainers, but the treatment mostly consists of making the entertainers feel good.

In November of 1963, Nat saw a doctor in Chicago and that's when he found out he had lung cancer. He had no idea before that that there was anything seriously wrong with him. We finished an engagement at the Fairmont Hotel in San Francisco on December tenth and on the twelfth Nat went back to Los Angeles and checked into a hospital. While we were driving to the hospital, Nat leaned over to me in the car and asked me for a cigarette.

On the morning of February 15, 1965, when I was in Miami Beach working with Nancy Wilson at the Diplomat Hotel, the clerk called and asked me if I had heard the news that morning. I hadn't. 'Nat Cole is dead,' he said. I called Nancy and told her I had to go home. I took a flight back to Los Angeles and went directly to the funeral parlor. When I saw Nat's body lying there on a table

I walked up and lifted him and held him in my arms. He was as cold as an ice cube, but I just had to hold the boss for the last time.

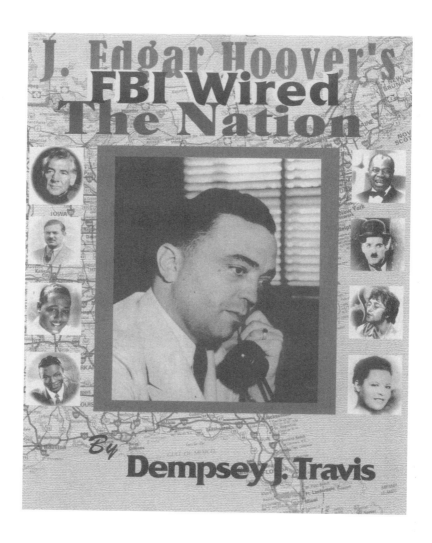

Federal Bureau of Investigation

Freedom of Information/Privacy Acts Section

Subject: <u>Nat "King" Cole</u>

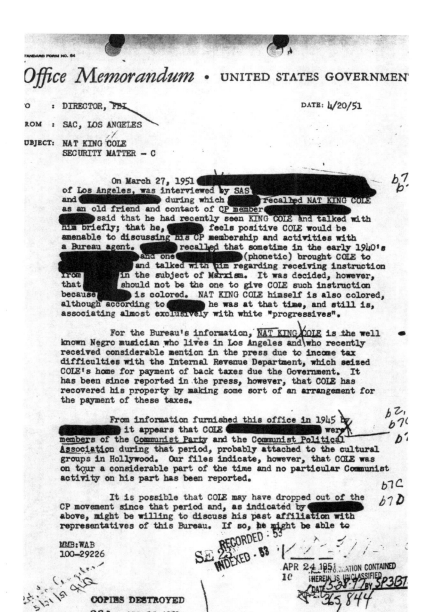

STANDARD FORM NO. 64

Office Memorandum • UNITED STATES GOVERNMENT

O : DIRECTOR, FBI   DATE: 4/20/51

ROM : SAC, LOS ANGELES

UBJECT: NAT KING COLE
SECURITY MATTER — C

On March 27, 1951 ████████ of Los Angeles, was interviewed by SAS ████████ and ████████ during which ████████ recalled NAT KING COLE as an old friend and contact of CP member ████████ said that he had recently seen KING COLE and talked with him briefly; that he, ████████ feels positive COLE would be amenable to discussing his CP membership and activities with a Bureau agent. ████████ recalled that sometime in the early 1940's ████████ and one ████████ (phonetic) brought COLE to ████████ and talked with him regarding receiving instruction from ████████ in the subject of Marxism. It was decided, however, that ████████ should not be the one to give COLE such instruction because ████████ is colored. NAT KING COLE himself is also colored, although according to ████████ he was at that time, and still is, associating almost exclusively with white "progressives".

For the Bureau's information, NAT KING COLE is the well known Negro musician who lives in Los Angeles and who recently received considerable mention in the press due to income tax difficulties with the Internal Revenue Department, which seized COLE's home for payment of back taxes due the Government. It has been since reported in the press, however, that COLE has recovered his property by making some sort of an arrangement for the payment of these taxes.

From information furnished this office in 1945 by ████████ it appears that COLE ████████ were members of the Communist Party and the Communist Political Association during that period, probably attached to the cultural groups in Hollywood. Our files indicate, however, that COLE was on tour a considerable part of the time and no particular Communist activity on his part has been reported.

It is possible that COLE may have dropped out of the CP movement since that period and, as indicated by ████████ above, might be willing to discuss his past affiliation with representatives of this Bureau. If so, he might be able to

MMB:WAB
100-29226

RECORDED : 53
INDEXED - 53

SE 23

APR 24 1951
ATION CONTAINED
HEREIN IS UNCLASSIFIED
DATE ████ BY SP3B7

COPIES DESTROYED

LA 100-29226

furnish pertinent information, depending upon the length of the period of his affiliation and the degree of activity on his part.

It is suggested that the Bureau might deem it desirable to arrange such an interview with COLE. However, no such step is being taken unless the Bureau authorizes it.

- 2 -

SAC, Los Angeles   May 21, 1951

Director, FBI

NAT KING COLE
SECURITY MATTER - C
Your file 100-29226
RECORDED - 57   Bureau file 100-379380 — |

01 — 10/1
3

Reurlet dated April 20, 1951.

      Before further consideration will be given to allow- 67
ing your Office to contact Cole, the Bureau would like to have
the benefit of your reasons why   believed that Cole 67.
would be receptive to an interview by this Bureau. If you do
not have this information available, you should recontact
for such and thereafter advise the Bureau.

      For your information, Bureau files reflect several
references to Cole's activities in the Communist Party;
however, all of these references have been furnished to the
Bureau by your Office.

JLQ:ban

Justice In The Cole Case

Conviction of four men in Recorder's Court on charges growing out of the attack last week on singer Nat (King) Cole in Municipal Auditorium should give the world notice that Birmingham does not tolerate that kind of despicable business.

Each of the four men was sentenced to 180 days in jail and fines also were assessed.

Evidence developed by police indicates that a large scale attack on the Negro singer was planned but that the majority of those involved apparently backed out, leaving only a small group to make the attempt.

Members of the Police Department especially are to be praised for their work in breaking up this attack and in helping to bring the men accused to justice.

BIRMINGHAM PO
Birmingham, A
April 19, 195
Final Edition
Editorial
JAMES E. MILL

RACON.

ALL INFORMATION CONTAINED
HEREIN IS UNCLASSIFIED
DATE 5-28-9 BY SP3BTJPW

RDED
1 1956

58 MAY 2 1956

Resumes Monday

Four go on trial, attack details told

The slow-moving trial of four men accused in an assault on Negro Singer Nat (King) Cole resumes in Recorder's Court Monday morning.

Only one witness testified after the proceeding got under way Friday in Judge Ralph Parker's court. Fifteen were sworn in.

POLICE OFFICER H. E. Schatz, first to reach the Negro entertainer when he was felled on the stage of Municipal Auditorium last Tuesday night, told the court how police dragged two men forcibly out of the building after the assault.

Schatz testified he and Officer A. A. Norman knocked the two men into the orchestra pit when one tried to drag Cole off the stage.

Schatz's testimony mainly concerned two men not yet on trial. The four being tried are accused of a variety of misdemeanors in connection with the assault.

JUDGE PARKER ordered the trial to begin over vigorous defense objections. He overruled motions by Defense Atty. Roderick Beddow for a two-week continuance and separate trials for the four defendants.

Beddow contended the four were "dissociated from each other."

Police investigators have charged that the assault was a conspiracy in which 150 men were to take part.

Another delay of more than an hour came when Judge Parker ordered the prosecution to prepare separate warrants in each case. He pointed out that the defendants could be found guilty of only one charge contained in a warrant.

OFFICER H. E. SCHATZ
First witness

63 APR 27 1956

THE BIRMINGHAM NEWS
Birmingham, Alabama
April 14, 1956
(Front Page)

RACON;
IS-X.

191 APR 26 956

One charge against each of three of the defendants was dropped in the proceedings.

ALL SIX MEN, the four now on trial and the two facing preliminary hearing on felony counts, are members of the North Alabama Citizens Council, a strongly pro-segregation organization.

The defendants and the charges against them now are:

Mike Fox, 36, conspiracy to commit a breach of the peace and conspiracy to commit assault and battery (one warrant).

Edgar Leo Vinson, 25, disorderly conduct and conspiracy to commit assault and battery.

Orliss Wade Clevenger, 18, disorderly conduct, carrying a concealed weapon and conspiracy to commit assault and battery.

Jesse W. Mabry, 43, disorderly conduct, refusal to obey the lawful command of an officer and conspiracy to commit a breach of the peace.

All but Mabry are from Anniston. Mabry, who lives at 960 West-blvd, Roebuck, is associate editor of The Southerner, a publication of the North Alabama Citizens Council.

OFFICER SCHATZ said he was at the east end of the Auditorium stage about 8:50 p.m. Tuesday night when he saw Willie Robert Vinson, 23, and Kenneth Adams, 35, running down the east aisle.

W. R. Vinson and Adams, also of Anniston, face preliminary hearing April 20 on charges of assault with intent to murder. Adams is an official of the Anniston White Citizens Council.

Schatz testified W. R. Vinson leaped on stage and grabbed Cole by his legs, dragging him down. Adams dived over Vinson's shoulders, the witness said.

"I went over and knocked Vinson from his hold. About that time Officer A. A. Norman grabbed Adams. Adams jerked like he was going to run and I knocked him off the stage. Norman went with him. We arrested Vinson and Adams," Schatz said.

SCHATZ SAID he saw Mabry, who followed the officers out, asking, "why we had the white boys under arrest when we ought to be in the Auditorium beating the _____ Negro."

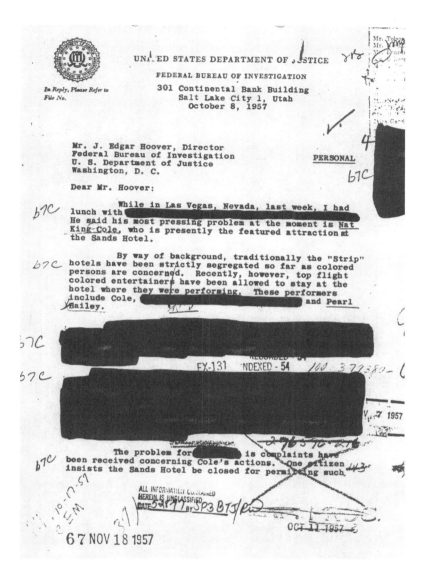

activity. This individual personally called at all "Strip"
hotels to inquire whether they would accept colored guests.
The Sands, Flamingo and Riviera Hotels all stated they would
register any presentable person, regardless of color. All
other hotels said they would refuse to register colored
persons. ███████ said he would keep me advised of develop-
ments in this matter.

In Reno the newest hotel is the Holiday. It is an
extremely modern building and was built by the Dollar Steamship family. The Hotel had slot machines but was losing money
until recently purchased by a syndicate headed by ███████

is a close personal friend of Bing Crosby.

Under ███████ a casino with all types of gambling
was placed in the Hotel. To stimulate business they have
instituted a contest called "In 80 Days, Around the World."
Each jackpot winner receives a chance on a nightly drawing,
and the winner of each nightly drawing is entitled to a chance
during the final drawing. Needless to say, the grand prize
is a first class trip for two around the world. To feature
this contest, a large replica of the balloon used in the
motion picture of a similar name has been placed in front of
the Hotel.

I have insisted to the Agents at both Las Vegas and
Reno that materially increased informant coverage is necessary,
and you can be sure I will personally follow this important
matter.

Respectfully,

W. MARK FELT
Special Agent in Charge

-2-

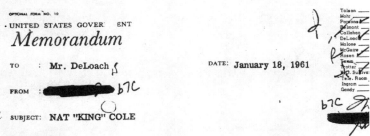

OPTIONAL FORM NO. 10

· UNITED STATES GOVER: ENT

Memorandum

TO : Mr. DeLoach

DATE: January 18, 1961

FROM :

SUBJECT: NAT "KING" COLE

PURPOSE:

Mr. Tolson requested a file check on Nat "King" Cole the singer. It is pointed out that we have a main file on Cole as well as approximately 100 See references. In the interest of expediency review has been limited to a review of Cole's main file and recent See references.

BACKGROUND DATA:

Nat "King" Cole was born Nathaniel Adams Coles on March 17, 1919 in Montgomery, Alabama. He began his career as a pianist and in 1939 formed a trio and while playing the piano in a California club started to sing and is now better known as a singer of popular jazz music. He has capitalized on his voice and now earns approximately $400,000 a year from records. Cole was the first Negro to host his own TV show starting in 1957. In 1937 Cole married but this marriage ended in divorce. In 1948 he wed singer He has two daughters and is active in the fight for equal rights for Negroes. Cole is a member of the National Association for the Advancement of Colored People (NAACP). He resides in Hollywood, California. (Celebrity Register)

INFORMATION IN BUREAU FILES:

No investigation has been conducted by the Bureau concerning Cole, however, files reflect the following salient information.

A confidential informant who has furnished reliable information in the past advised in 1945 that Nat "King" Cole were then members of the Communist Political Association in Hollywood.

A confidential informant who has furnished reliable information in the past advised in August, 1949, that "King" Cole was a member of the music division of the Southern California Chapter of the Arts, Sciences, and Professio Council (Hollywood Arts, Sciences, and Professions Council)

ALL INFORMATION CONTAINED
HEREIN IS UNCLASSIFIED
DATE 5-21-97 BY SP3BTJ/RW

JAN 26 1961

621 Mr. DeLoach
DGH:dau (7)

(Continued, next page) CORRESPONDENC

████ to DeLoach
Re: NAT "KING" COLE

The National Council of Arts, Sciences, and Professions has been cited as a communist front by the Congressional Committee on Un-American Activities.

A Salt Lake City criminal informant advised Bureau Agents on February 21, 1955, that ████████████████████ Las Vegas, Nevada, informed him, the informant, that ████████████████

████████████ Nat King Cole was appearing at the hotel in the Copa Room as the star.

████████████████████████████ Nat King Cole discontinued his engagement at the Sands for personal reasons.

It will be recalled that in April, 1956, while appearing in Birmingham, Alabama, Cole was attacked by a group of men, reportedly members of the North Alabama Citizens Council. The attack took place in Municipal Auditorium and the assailants were prosecuted in local court and sentenced to one hundred eighty days in jail.

By personal letter to the Director dated October 8, 1957, SAC Salt Lake City advised as follows.

Nat King Cole is presently performing at the Sands ████████

████████████████ there were many complaints received from citizens and suggestions that The Sands be closed. (100-379380)

The "New York Herald Tribune" of May 4, 1960, contained a story concerning the "Committee to Defend Martin Luther King." The committee was described as a group formed to raise money to help Dr. King fight an income tax evasion indictment in the state of Alabama. A pretext telephone call by Agents of the New York Office ascertained that this committee was at 372 West 125 Street and that Nat King Cole was the treasurer. (100-40377-326)

RECOMMENDATION:

None. For information.

An informant who has furnished reliable infor
in the past reported on February 21, 1955, that an empl
the Sands Hotel, Las Vegas, Nevada, who was a gambler f
east coast, had advised the informant that Jack Entratt
owner of the Sands Hotel and who was in charge of the S
Copa Room, found Nat King Cole and Dorothy Dandridge to
in Cole's room at the hotel. Cole was appearing as a s
the Copa Room at the time. The informant stated that E
became furious with Cole for having an "affair" with Do
Dandridge and threatened him. Dandridge reportedly tol

Entratter to forget the whole matter as she was Cole's c
too. The informant further advised that Entratter was j
manager and part owner of the Copacabana in New York Cit
has reportedly spent a great deal of time and money prom
Dandridge's career and that Entratter considered her his
friend. (CI SU-293-C; 62-75147-44-591)

Two scenes from the television classic Sounds of Music.

Left to right in the top photo: Lester Young, Coleman Hawkins, Gerry Mulligan and Ben Webster. Lower photo: Billie Holiday

Cut III
Billie Holiday:
The Motherless Child

No one in Billie Holiday's (Eleanora Fagan) life ever pointed out to her the danger of crossing the street against a red stoplight, hence, her life was overwhelmed by partaking of fruit from the forbidden trees of our society.

 Her mother Sadie Fagan, was a 19 year-old female, without rudders. She gave birth to a baby who never had an opportunity to be a child. The male person who fathered the baby was a seventeen year-old boy, who answered to the name

Clarence Holiday of Clarence Holiday.

Billie Holiday first saw the light of day in Baltimore, Maryland on April 17, 1915. The girl grew up in a topsy-turvy lifestyle on the streets of Baltimore,

Maryland. Nobody to this date has been able to produce a bonafide birth certificate or any other document that might validate her birthdate. The Maryland Division of Vital Statistics forbids anyone other than blood relatives to see or make copies of birth, death and marital records.

Bessie Smith

Since education was not high on the agenda for the shapely Miss Holiday, she scrubbed floors, ran errands, and turned tricks at a neighborhood whorehouse. The only salvation that came out of her brothel experience other than earning a percentage of the small trick money she had earned was the opportunity to rest between sexual bouts in the front parlor where she listened intently to the Victrola recording of her two music idols, Louis *"Dipper Mouth Blues"* Armstrong and the great blues singer Bessie *"Give Me A Pigfoot And A Bottle of Beer"* Smith. Billie's childhood environment no doubt caused her to become one of the original baby dolls. In every song that she later sang as a professional, she paid silent homage to both Louis Armstrong and Bessie Smith.

Following the harrowing experience of being brutally raped at age thirteen, by a "white" john, she was sent to a Catholic reformatory by the police and charged paradoxically with "seducing" the rapist. The institution where she was confined was run by a Catholic order. The hallowed sisters never went outside of the four walls of the reformatory, but they managed to put the fear of God in the physically attractive Billie Holiday. The first night that the thirteen year-old child was incarcerated they locked her up in a semi-dark closet size room with a buck naked dead Colored girl who had been laid out on a long, cold, white slanted slab.

Billie described her rape episode, in detail to her co-author William Dufty in her autobiography the *"Lady Sings The Blues"*. She revealed to Dufty the following: *"One day when I came home from school my mother was at the hair-dresser and there was nobody in the house but Mr. Dick, one of our white neighbors who was shacking up with a Colored woman next door. He told me that my mother had asked him to wait for me and then take me to a good time house a few blocks down the street where she was suppose to turn a trick.*

Without me thinking anything about it, he took me gently by the hand and led me to this stranger's house, I went along willingly... As the time got later and later I began to get sleepy. Mr. Dick saw me dozing and took me to a back bedroom to lie down... He then crawled up on top of me in the bed with his private part erected upright like the branch of a tree. He started doing to me what my cousin Henry had tried. I started to kick and scream like a wild-cat. The noise caused the madam of the house to come into the room and assist Mr. Dick in holding my arms down so he could penetrate my private parts... The next thing I knew, my mother and a policeman were breaking down the door of the room. I will never forget that night. Even if you are a whore, you don't want nobody to rape you...

But that wasn't the worst of it. The cops dragged Mr. Dick off in handcuffs to the police precinct. I was cry-ing and bleeding in my mother's arms, and they made the two of us come along in a second paddy wagon to the sta-tion house.

When we arrived at the police station they started treating me and my mom like criminals who had killed somebody. They would not release me and let my mother take me home in spite of the fact that Mr. Dick was in his forties, and I was only thirteen.

After a couple of days in the bullpen they dragged me down a long corridor into the courtroom where Mr. Dick was sentenced to five years in jail and I was sentenced to five months in a Catholic institution."

Billie Holiday

After serving jail time Billie Holiday returned to the world's oldest profession prostitution without having a pimp to bail her out. On the day that she was finally sprung from the jail house by her mother, she had acquired a New York City frame of mind in that her mother had sent her a ticket to come to Long Branch, New York to live with her. However, when her maternal grandfather put her on the train, she immediately ripped the big yellow tag that read Long Branch, New York off her outer garment because she had made up her mind that she was going to see what the "Big Apple" and the New York City's Harlem Renaissance was all about.

The year that Billie made her maiden trip to New York City must have been 1928 because Charles "Lucky Lindy" Lindbergh had made that solo nonstop flight across the Atlantic Ocean in "The Spirit of St. Louis" from Roosevelt Field in Long Island, New York to Paris, France.

When Billie and her mother finally got hooked up in Harlem, the mother arranged to get her daughter a room in a fancy walkup elaborately furnished apartment that was run by Florence Williams on 141st Street just off of Seventh Avenue and just North of Strivers Row where many Black professionals like Fletcher Henderson and Madam C. J. Walker the first Black female millionaire lived.

Florence Williams, was one of the biggest madams operating in a district just below the famous Sugar Hill district in

Harlem. Billie's mother had asked Florence to take good care of her only child. Underneath Billie's well developed teenage façade was a cocky hip chick schooled on the side-walks of Baltimore's Pennsylvania Avenue, hence she felt streetwise enough to teach Madam Florence some new tricks.

Billie and Florence were like the song *"Tight Like That"* in that all of her regular customers were white men. She absolutely refused to turn any tricks with the brothers because Negro men early in the game had kept her working all night trying to live up to the myths of their manhood in the bed. On the other hand her white clients were usually well heeled married men who were satisfied with a couple of rapid hip twists in sync with wham, bam, and thank you ma'm. Whereas the Colored brothers wanted to talk a lot of horse dung and asked such silly questions as: "Was it good baby?" and "Don't you want to be my lady?" Some of the brothers actually believed that they had been endowed with a goldenrod with a goose feathered tip.

Bill "Bojangles" Robinson

Billie Holiday ulti-mately found working on her back in the world's oldest profession boring. She wanted to be famous like Bill "Bojangles" Robinson, Willie "The Lion" Smith and Florence "Shuffle Along" Mills. She walked up and down Seventh Avenue looking for a dancing gig doing the Charleston, the Black Bottom and the Shimmy, but found no takers until she stumbled into Jerry

71

the saloonkeeper and owner of Preston's Log Cabin. Her good looks got his attention along with her plea for a job as a dancer. Jerry the saloonkeeper sent her to the back of the cabaret section of the club where the piano player was practicing some new numbers. The piano player was interrupted when Jerry shouted: "Music man play something and let me see what this broad can do." In addition to the Charleston, The Black Bottom and the Shimmy she only knew two other dance steps and they were the Time Step and the Crossover. After watching her for a few minutes Jerry growled: "Young lady you are wasting your time and mine." She continued pleading to Jerry for a break. The piano player showing a sign of sympathy asked her if she could sing. She replied: "Yes! I have been singing all my life."

Billie asked the keyboard man to play *"Traveling All Alone"* in the key of C. Her unique style of singing captured the mood of the barflies that afternoon. When she finished singing two choruses, the hip cats and fly chicks in the joint were literally moved to tears. She had reached down and touched their intestines with her voice. She netted $58.00 in tips that afternoon. During the 1930's Depression, $58.00 was three weeks salary for a Colored common laborer.

John Hammond

The bonafide musical story of Billie's life really starts with the fact that she was discovered by a rich white boy named John Hammond who was related to the late Cornelius Vanderbilt the railroad and steamship tycoon. Hammond just happened to be slumming up Harlem way at Monette Moore's place on 133rd and Seventh Avenue that night where he had come to hear Monette, a local blues singer. As luck would have it, young Billie Holiday was substituting for Monette because she had gotten a bit part in a Broadway Show starring the deft and debonair Clifton Webb. In less than a decade later Webb starred with Gene Tierney in the 1944 movie block buster Laura. Billie's accompanist that night was Dot Hill, and among the first songs that Hammond heard her sing was *"Wouldja For A Big Red Apple."*

The planet was in the right position for Billie that night because beside being rich, Hammond was a cheer-leader for Black artists. He had become the wind under the wings of such stars as Count Basie, Lionel Hampton, Teddy Wilson and his future brother-in-law Benny Goodman, the clarinet player who by 1936 had become "the king of swing" in the eyes of the general public.

In addition to being an impresario Hammond was a newspaper critic, talent scout and record producer. In the fall of 1933 on December 12th Hammond arranged a record session with Columbia Records for Billie Holiday and

Billie sings the Blues.

73

Benny Goodman. Goodman assembled a small group of musicians, including Shirley Clay, trumpet; Jack Teagarden, trombone; Art Karle, tenor sax; Joe Sullivan, piano; Dick McDonough, guitar; Artie Bernstein, bass; and Chicago's Gene Krupa, drums. The titles that they recorded were *"Riffin the Scotch"* and *"Your Mother's Son-In-Law."* That was Billie's first recording session and also the first time that Benny had recorded with a Negro musician, who happened to be Shirley Clay one of Don *"Chant Of The Weed"* Redman's orchestra trumpet players.

On July 2, 1935 Billie was called back into the recording studio by Hammond and backed up by an orchestra led by Teddy Wilson who was a member of the Benny Goodman Trio. The lineup for this set was Roy Eldridge, trumpet; Benny Goodman, clarinet; Ben Webster, tenor sax, Wilson, piano; John Trueheart, guitar; John Kirby, bass; and Cozy Cole, drums. The group recorded songs that became Billie Holiday classics. Specifically *"I Wished On The Moon"; "What A Little Moonlight Can Do" "Miss Brown to You"* and *" Sunbonnet Blue."*

Zinky Cohn

As Billie Holiday moved up the ladder in the jazz world, it was observed by some of this writer's older friends such as Zinky Cohn, the pianist for Ethel Waters, violinist Eddie "The Black Angel" South and clarinetist Jimmie Noone that her beauty surpassed her disposition, the latter being like a revolving door. You never knew whether you were going to get the sometimes I am happy Billie or the Billie that was in a deep blue funk. Smoking marijuana, opium and drinking booze did not help her disposition. She was accused of being tempermental,

Teddy Wilson and Billie Holiday preparing for a recording session.

hot tempered, and wild. You mix those traits in a glass with substance addictions and you have got a person who is shakingly undependable.

Billie first met Norman Granz in the early 1940s. He found it difficult to deal with her inharmonic moods. Thus, their friendship was played in both major and minor keys. The simplest way to describe the relationship would be to say at best it was restrained. She could fall out with you faster than you could strike a match and revive a relationship equally as fast.

On August 15, 1942 Billie got a three month gig playing at the Sherman's Garrick Showbar on Randolph Street in downtown Chicago. On the same show bill was trumpeter Henry "Red" Allen and a sextet.

While in Chicago Billie landed in jail for leaving the scene of an accident although she was not driving the car. Her first reflex when it appeared that she was going to be questioned by the Men In Blue was flight. This kind of reaction could be attributed to some of her early life experiences with the law.

Henry "Red" Allen

She ended her Chicago stay at the Regal Theater where it was reported in the Downbeat Magazine that the show was a rip roaring success. She and the Lionel Hampton Orchestra figuratively blew the roof off of the 3200 seat Regal Theater located in the heart of Bronzeville at 47th and South Parkway (Martin Luther King Drive.)

During her stay in Chicago she met Dorothy Donegan, the piano wizard. Donegan describes an early episode with Billie as follows: *It was during the early World*

The Regal Theater on 47th and South Parkway in Chicago, Illinois.

War II period that I met Billie Holiday, who used to come around to see me at Elmer's when she was working at the Garrick Lounge in Chicago, Illinois. It appeared that we

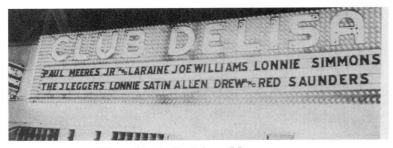

The Club DeLisa Marquee

were going to become very fast friends, and then one morning after work we decided to go out to the Club DeLisa at 5521 South State Street to catch the Monday morning breakfast dance. After we were seated ringside in the Club DeLisa, Billie lit up a giant size reefer, I told her I didn't think she should do that.

She said, "Well, if you don't like it, go home!"

I said, "Well, bye!"

I loved Billie, but I just didn't like that habit. I always thought that she should have spent more money on buying clothes instead of pot. Billie used to give me advice about men, and I learned a lot from her. I remember one thing in particular she told me.

She said, "Never give a man twenty-five percent of your money unless he's sleeping with you."

So I told her I didn't intend to give any of my money away if I could help it. Billie had some hip street ideas which I guess she must have picked up early in her life.

Although Billie and Norman Granz had known each other prior to World War II they could not put anything meaningful together because she was so unpredictable. Thus, a decade passed before she was comfortable enough to enter into a recording deal with Granz's Clef Label.

Songs that she recorded with Granz were what we call standards in the music business. All of the songs had memorable lyrics.

"Yesterday" was one of the first recordings she did for Granz with Oscar Peterson on organ. She also did a remake of "He's Funny That Way", and also Duke Ellington's "Do Nothing Til You Hear From Me."

On Clef Records she recorded "I Only Have Eyes For You," "These Foolish Things" "You Turned The Table On Me", and "Autumn in New York", she was burning on this gig. The musicians backing her were Charlie Shavers, trumpet; Flip Phillips, tenor sax; Oscar Peterson, piano; Barney Kessell, guitar; Ray Brown, bass; and Alvin Stoller, drums.

Things went well for Billie until she was busted for

Holmes "Daddy-O" Daylie and Billie at a veteran hospital benefit.

possession of drugs while literally lying on her deathbed in a New York hospital.

Holmes "Daddy-O-Daylie" said: *The first time I met Billie Holiday was in the 1940's when I was tending bar at the DuSable Lounge. I believe every Black jazz artist in the world came to the DuSable Lounge at some time or anoth-*

er. One morning about four o'clock I told Lady Day while she was sitting at the bar getting a "taste" before she went to waste that I was taking a show out to Hines Veteran Hospital in Hines, Illinois to do a benefit.

Lady Day said, "Daddy-O, I don't do benefits because they are all so crooked, Mike DeLisa volunteered the entire Club DeLisa show, which included Slim Gaillard and Timmy Rogers. The troupe didn't arrive at the hospital until about three p.m. but I started trying to get Duke Ellington ready around noon. Duke Ellington would give you a heart attack with any attempt to get him up and out of the bed. I succeeded in getting him up without performing mouth to mouth resuscitation. Duke played the piano

Coleman Hawkins, Billie Holiday and a friend.

accompaniment for Billie Holiday without the benefit of his orchestra. When I called for Billie Holiday to come out to the mike and do her number, she stepped up there with her little dog, and said: "Daddy-O, what is that thing up there?"

I looked up and it was the sun.

She said, "I'm never up this early in the day." And all of the veterans rolled over in unison laughing.

Billie went on "I'm going to do one tune, because it's too early for anybody to be singing and you got me way out here in Hines, Illinois, which is a thousand miles from nowhere."

The vets showed so much enthusiasm and warmth for her singing that she actually sang forty minutes after that first number and I had to ask her to come off because there were other acts that had to go on. But from that time on, Billie and I became fast friends. The last time I saw Billie was in early 1959, shortly before she became desperately ill. She came to Chicago and called me and suggested that we have a three p.m. breakfast and talk. I took her up to my place after we finished eating and we listened to records. I attempted to play her records but she wouldn't let me. She was very critical of her own work. She would always say she didn't want to hear herself, she wanted to hear "Pres." She loved Lester Young. As you know, Lester Young was the one who named her "Lady Day," and she, in turn, called him the "President," which was ultimately abbreviated to "Pres."

For some reason, Lester and Billie had a terrible falling out and everybody tried unsuccessfully to get them to patch it up. Pres. died March 15, 1959. Billie was terminally ill. About that time, Billie's Chicago friends called me and said: "Dad, you know Lady Day is very, very sick." I started telling my radio fans to write Lady Day because she had given us all of these beautiful years of entertainment, and now she needs us, so while she's still here, send her flowers and cards. I had no idea what kind of response she would receive. Lady Day passed away on July 17, 1959, almost four months to the day after Pres. left us. One week after she died, some fellow whom I didn't know came to radio station WAAF while I was on the air and handed me a pair of rhinestone sunglasses. He said, "Lady Day wanted you to have these." The fellow said before he left, "Lady Day told me to thank you, because she received bags and bags of Chicago mail in that New York hospital as a result of your request on the air." The shaded green sunglasses had a cracked left lens. I will always keep them as a constant reminder of the great Lady Day.

Billie Holiday was under constant police and FBI surveillance most of her adult life. This was particularly true after she made the song ***"Strange Fruit"*** feature num-

81

ber in her nightclub and theater appearances. The lyrics of the song enraged FBI Director J. Edgar Hoover.

Louis Armstrong and Billie Holiday in a scene from the movie "New Orleans."

Federal Bureau of Investigation

Freedom of Information/Privacy Acts Section

Subject: <u>Billie Holiday</u>

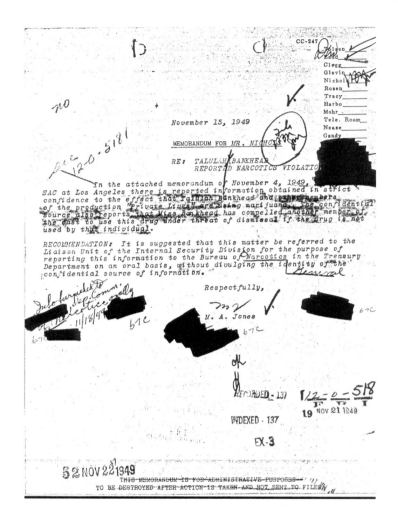

CC-247

Wilson
Ladd
Clegg
Glavin
Nichol
Rosen
Tracy
Harbo
Mohr
Tele. Room
Nease
Gandy

November 15, 1949

MEMORANDUM FOR MR. NICHOLS

RE: TALULAH BANKHEAD
REPORTED NARCOTICS VIOLATION

In the attached memorandum of November 4, 1949,
SAC at Los Angeles there is reported information obtained in strict
confidence to the effect that Talulah Bankhead and other members
of the production "Private Lives" are using marijuana. The confidential
source also reports that Miss Bankhead has compelled another member of
the cast to use this drug under threat of dismissal if the drug is not
used by that individual.

RECOMMENDATION: It is suggested that this matter be referred to the
Liaison Unit of the Internal Security Division for the purpose of
reporting this information to the Bureau of Narcotics in the Treasury
Department on an oral basis, without divulging the identity of the
confidential source of information.

Respectfully,

M. A. Jones

RECORDED - 137

INDEXED - 137

EX-3

19 NOV 21 1949

52 NOV 22 1949

THIS MEMORANDUM IS FOR ADMINISTRATIVE PURPOSES
TO BE DESTROYED AFTER ACTION IS TAKEN AND NOT SENT TO FILES

84

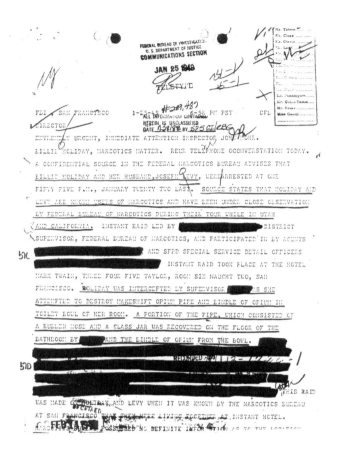

PAGE TWO

OF ANY NARCOTICS IN THEIR POSSESSION BUT PRESUMED THAT SINCE
THEY WERE TOGETHER THEY PROBABLY POSSESSED SOME NARCOTICS,
AND ACCORDINGLY THEY REQUESTED THE ASSISTANCE OF THE SAN FRANCISCO
POLICE DEPARTMENT IN CONDUCTING THIS RAID BECAUSE OF MORE LIBERAL
STATE LAWS COVERING SEARCHES AND SEIZURES. THE SOURCE STATES THAT
BECAUSE OF THE IMPORTANCE OF HOLIDAY IT HAS BEEN THE POLICY OF HIS
BUREAU TO DISCREDIT INDIVIDUALS OF THIS CALIBER USING NARCOTICS,
BECAUSE OF THEIR NOTORIETY IT OFFERED EXCUSES TO MINOR USERS. SOURCE
STATES THAT RAID WAS A LEGITIMATE RAID BASED ON ABOVE AND THAT CLAIMED
QUOTE FLAME UP UNQUOTE WAS AS MUCH FOR PUBLICITY PURPOSES AS IT
WAS TO AVERT THE SUSPICION OF GUILT FROM HER INASMUCH AS SHE WAS
CAUGHT IN POSSESSION OF THE MAKESHIFT PIPE. ███████████████ HEAD
OF SPECIAL SERVICES DETAIL, TOGETHER WITH OFFICER ███████████
WERE CONTACTED AND THEY ADVISED SUBSTANTIALLY THE SAME INFORMATION
AS SET FORTH ABOVE. HOLIDAY IS CHARGED WITH POSSESSION OF OPIUM AND
IS BEING TRIED IN MUNICIPAL COURT. HER HEARING IS SET FOR FEBRUARY
TWO NEXT. NO FURTHER ACTION BEING TAKEN.

b7c

KIMBALL

END AND ACK PLS

1015PM OK FBI WA LS

CC Rosen

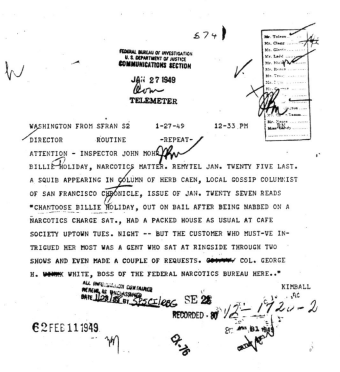

Hotel Elysee
60 East 54th Street
New York, N. Y.
February 9, 1949

J. Edgar Hoover
Federal Bureau of Investigation
Washington, D. C.

Dear Mr. Hoover:

I am ashamed of my unpardonable delay
in writing to thank you a thousand times for the kindness,
consideration and courtesy, in fact all the nicest
adjectives in the book, for the trouble you took re
our telephone conversation in connection with Billie Holiday.

I tremble when I think of my audacity
in approaching you at all with so little to recommend me
except the esteem, admiration and high regard my father
held for you. I would never have dared to ask him or you
a favor for myself but knowing your true humanitarian spirit
it seemed quite natural at the time to go to the top man.
As my Negro mammy used to say - "When you pray you pray to
God don't you?".

I have met Billie Holiday but twice in
my life but admire her immensely as an artist and feel
the most profound compassion for her knowing as I do the
unfortunate circumstances of her background. Although my
intention is not to condone her weaknesses I certainly
understand the eccentricities of her behaviour because she
is essentially a child at heart whose troubles have made her
psychologically unable to cope with the world in which she
finds herself. Her vital need is more medical than the
confinement of four walls.

However guilty she may be, whatever penalty
she may be required to pay for her frailties, poor thing,
you I know did everything within the law to lighten her
burden. Bless you for this.

Kindest regards,

Tallulah Bankhead

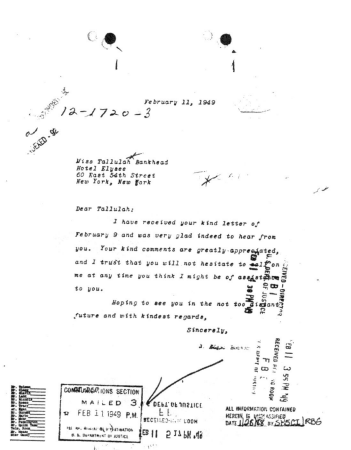

February 11, 1949

12-1720-3

Miss Tallulah Bankhead
Hotel Elysee
60 East 54th Street
New York, New York

Dear Tallulah:

I have received your kind letter of February 9 and was very glad indeed to hear from you. Your kind comments are greatly appreciated, and I trust that you will not hesitate to call on me at any time you think I might be of assistance to you.

Hoping to see you in the not too distant future and with kindest regards,

Sincerely,

J. Edgar Hoover

COMMUNICATIONS SECTION
MAILED 3
FEB 11 1949 P.M.
FEL BUREAU OF INVESTIGATION
U. S. DEPARTMENT OF JUSTICE

ALL INFORMATION CONTAINED
HEREIN IS UNCLASSIFIED
DATE 1/26/68 BY SP5CI RBG

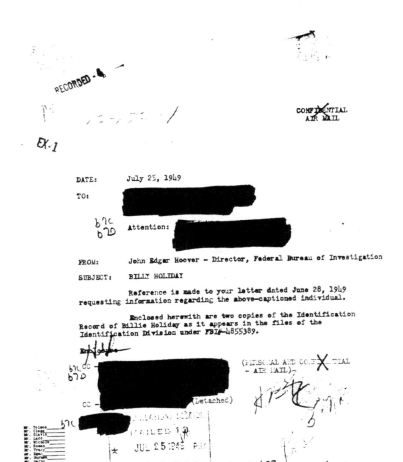

RECORDED -

CONFIDENTIAL
AIR MAIL

EX-1

DATE: July 25, 1949

TO:

Attention:

FROM: John Edgar Hoover - Director, Federal Bureau of Investigation

SUBJECT: BILLY HOLIDAY

Reference is made to your letter dated June 28, 1949 requesting information regarding the above-captioned individual.

Enclosed herewith are two copies of the Identification Record of Billie Holiday as it appears in the files of the Identification Division under FBI# 4855389.

(PERSONAL AND CONFIDENTIAL - AIR MAIL)

CC   (Detached)

MAILED 18
JUL 25 1949 P.M.

#289,487

Billie Holiday, Singer, Held In Coast Dope Raid

SAN FRANCISCO, Jan. 22 (UP). Dusky blues singer Billie Holiday and her agent were arrested in a Tenderloin district hotel room in downtown San Francisco today and charged with possession of opium.

The 29-year-old star of radio, night clubs and recordings was booked at the Hall of Justice with John Levy, 40, of New York and Los Angeles, and both were released on $500 bail each.

Charge Opium Found

Police charged a vial of opium was found in her apartment. Both promptly denied they knew the opium was there.

A five-man squad of officers, including federal agent Gene White and four police from a special San Francisco detail, raided her apartment in the Mark Twain hotel in San Francisco's night life area.

White said the detail found the colored song enchantress in the bathroom, washing her hands beneath the medicine cabinet where they located a small vial of opium.

Took "Cure" in New York

Miss Holiday, only recently released from a federal institution at Alderson, W. Va., as "cured" of drug addiction, appeared at the city prison for fingerprinting and booking in a black dress beneath $7,000 blue mink coat.

She wore high heels and a perky hat and was flanked by Levy, hatless and coatless in the mild San Francisco weather. Throughout the proceedings Miss Holiday remained virtually silent.

But Levy indignantly denied the charge.

"We both deny everything," he said. "She didn't even sleep in her room last night."

Claims Friend Used Room

Levy said Miss Holiday "lent" the room to a girl he knew only as "Mandy," a Negro girl friend of the singer.

He charged the officers "apparently were tipped" and said they went "directly to the bathroom and took the vial out of the chest."

Levy said he first got suspicious "something was up" when he got a call from the lobby downstairs that said: "Are you the Levy who is a stocking salesman?" He said "No", and hung up and a few minutes later police knocked on the door and he admitted them.

Sang at Night Club

The chubby Negro songstress, whose record albums feature smoky, world-weary numbers, has been appearing at the Cafe Society Uptown in San Francisco's "Harlem" district along Fillmore Street.

Levy said he had just arrived in San Francisco on the Coaster, an overnight passenger train from Los Angeles, and that he had been in his client's room only about an hour before the law burst in.

Immediately after the booking, the pair left for the cafe with the words, "The show must go on." Since the death of her acknowledged model and mentor, Bessie Smith, the husky-voiced Miss Holiday has generally been rated tops in her line. Her albums are best-sellers and her recording of "Strange Fruit," the weird, minor-key lament of a Negro lynching, has become her virtual trademark.

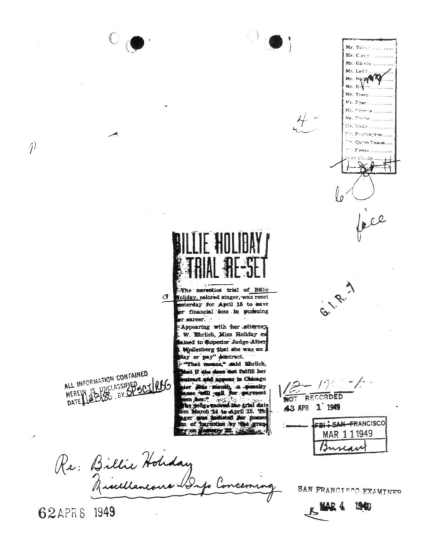

BILLIE HOLIDAY TRIAL RE-SET

The narcotics trial of Billie Holiday, colored singer, was reset yesterday for April 15 to save her financial loss in pursuing her career.

Appearing with her attorney, J. W. Ehrlich, Miss Holiday explained to Superior Judge Albert C. Wollenberg that she was on a "play or pay" contract.

"That means," said Ehrlich, "that if she does not fulfill her contract and appear in Chicago later this month, a penalty clause will call for payment from her."

The judge moved the trial date from March 14 to April 15. The singer was indicted for possession of narcotics by the grand jury on January 22.

SAN FRANCISCO EXAMINER
MAR 4 1949

FBI — SAN FRANCISCO
MAR 11 1949
Buscard

Re: Billie Holiday
Miscellaneous Info Concerning

62 APR 8 1949

ALL INFORMATION CONTAINED
HEREIN IS UNCLASSIFIED
DATE ____ BY ____

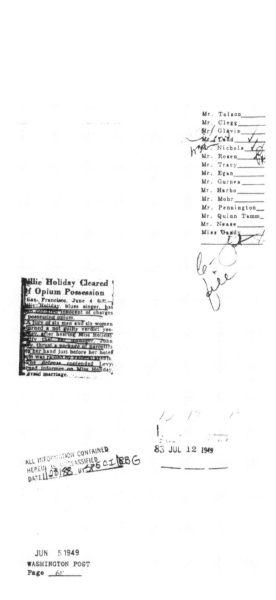

John Birkes "Dizzy" Gillespie at age seventeen.

Cut IV
John Birkes "Dizzy"
Gillespie: A Musical Genius

"Dizzy" was born in Cheraw, South Carolina on October 21, 1917. He was the last of nine children begotten by his parents James and Lottie (Powe) Gillespie, they christened him John Birkes. His father James was a brick mason. As a young man he had been a musician. In fact, the first bass fiddle "Dizzy" ever saw belonged to his father. The old man played several other instruments, including the clarinet, the mandolin

Dizzy's parents.

95

and piano. However, back in his hometown of Cheraw, South Carolina, a Colored man with nine kids could not make an adequate living wage as a musician or sharecropper to support a large family. An intinerant musician in the ragtime era was very low on the economic totem poll.

My father died when I was nine years old. Papa made an effort to get my older sisters and brothers interested in music. He failed. The only thing that my siblings were interested in doing was getting away from home because my father was what you might call an extreme authoritarian and disciplinarian. He was the epitome of that breed of parents who believed in meting out

Dizzy tells his story to *heavy discipline on their*
Dempsey Travis. *children's behind, even*

when they had not knowingly done anything wrong. As a matter of fact, every Sunday that God sent, my father would give me and my brother Wesley a beating. I can still hear my father's voice now and I sometimes tremble with the thoughts of that period. I guess I was only about five or six years old when Dad began meting out punishment every Sunday. He would say, "John Wesley! Go and get the razor strap hanging on the back of the bathroom door." With the strap in hand, my dad would beat the living daylight out of us every Sunday afternoon - rain or shine, snow or sleet, high or low water. And the funny thing about it, we hadn't done anything. He just beat us because he didn't have anything better to do before sundown on Sunday - at least that's what I thought as both a boy and man.

    I remember the day my father died. My older brother Wesley had left the house to pick blackberries, and then suddenly turned around after he got about halfway to the field and went back home, as though he had had a premo-

nition of some sort. My brother Wesley and I were both in the house when my father died from a fatal heart attack. Dad had suffered with a severe case of asthma most of his adult life and he was only forty-two years old when he died. I'm not ashamed to say I didn't shed a tear. In fact, I didn't even cry until I found that razor strap and a razor to cut that bugger into a hundred pieces, it was then that I felt sorry for the old man. But until I destroyed that strap, I felt no pity about his dying.

John Wesley, age 8 and Dizzy at age 5.

    My mother was just the opposite of my dad in temperament. I guess I could best describe her as having the milk of human kindness. Looking back, my father may have had more insight into my character and personality than my mother. I say that because I was a devil when I was a little guy and as strong as an ox. I could whip all the guys my size and bigger in the neighborhood. In fact, when some of the larger boys in Cheraw saw me coming down the street, they actually crossed over to the other side of the street in order to avoid a possible whipping. Sometimes I would sneak up on them and start a fight or hit them in the stom-

*ach as I passed them, if you were losing a fight in the part
of the country that I came from, you would pick up a stick
and defend yourself. I never really hurt anyone but I always
felt a need for combat. My father's harsh methods of punishment might have stimulated that spirit into my mind-set.*

*My interest in music began at Robert Small
Elementary School in Cheraw when the state purchased
instruments for distribution to the various Colored elementary and high schools throughout the state. I was one of the
first ones to get in line in an effort to obtain an instrument
from the teacher, but he passed me by in favor of some of
the larger boys in the class. I was only about twelve years
old then. After the teacher had passed out all but one
instrument, and that was a trombone, he said, "John Birkes,
you can take this one."*

*My arms were too short to get down to the last posi-
tion on the trombone, but I still wanted to get in the band,
so I decided I would mess around with that horn until I
could do better. My next door neighbor, James Harrington,
also attended Small Elementary School. His father bought
him one of those long trumpets. One day I asked Jimmie if
he would let me practice on his horn and he said, "Why not?
We can practice together."*

*I literally lived over at his house because I was in
love with his horn. In a relatively short period of time I
became pretty good at playing the trumpet. Since I was
showing that kind of development without any practical
training on the instrument, the principal of the school gave
me a trumpet to play in the band. I remember that all the
songs we played in the Small Elementary School Band were
in the key of B-flat. Frankly, I thought that was the only key
on the scale.*

*I never had a trumpet of my own until I was seven-
teen years old. I moved to Philadelphia, Pennsylvania, following my mother and brother who had moved there a year
earlier. They left me behind, thinking that I could finish*

high school and then come to Philadelphia, but I just could-n't get my mind on regular books. My primary interest was music and, specifically, the trumpet. My brother-in-law bought me a second hand horn from a local pawn shop. He didn't purchase a case for the horn, so I carried it around in a paper bag, it was then that the guys started calling me "Dizzy". First, I was the dizzy trumpet player with the paper bag, and later they shortened it to Trumpet Dizzy, and then to Diz. Now there are at least four or five guys around who say they gave me that nickname. To this day, I'm not exactly sure which one of the four should get credit, but the name has stuck with me for more than fifty years.

Roy "Little Jazz" Eldridge was Dizzy's mentor.

I didn't make the ninety-mile trip from Philadelphia to New "Big Apple" York, until 1937. My first big job there was with Teddy Hill's band at the Savoy Ballroom. The home band there at the Savoy was headed by Chick Webb featuring Ella Fitzgerald as the canary. I had heard Teddy Hill's orchestra on the radio, broadcasting from New York's Savoy Ballroom on 140th and Lenox Avenue in 1935, and I listened especially to skyscraping solos of Roy "Little Jazz" Eldridge his ace trumpet player. When I joined Teddy Hill's band myself and sat in Roy's chair, I could play all of Roy's solos exactly as he had played them. There is no question about "Little Jazz" being my musical father. Roy Eldridge influenced me more than

99

any other single trumpet player on the scene. People often ask whether Louis Armstrong is my musical father, I admit that there is a definite connection between Louis and myself, but in between the two of us there is Roy Eldridge.

It's difficult to explain how one's style evolves. You start out as a rule playing like somebody else, and then your style evolves and you play less and less like the guy that you started imitating... You build on what you have learned from him into something that is very unique in you.

In 1939 my friend Mario, who was then playing with Cab Calloway, suggested that I come over and visit with him at the Cotton Club because they were looking for a solo trumpet player. About a week after my visit, Mario called me and said he wasn't feeling well. He asked me to go down to the Cotton Club and sit in his chair. He said I should let Lammar Wright take all the first trumpet parts and then when the time came for a solo I should really do my stuff. Cab Calloway didn't know me. In fact, I didn't even formally report that night. I just put on the uniform and went up and sat in Mario's chair. I wasn't afraid of Cab Calloway, one of the most famous band leaders in the United States. I had no fear in Cab's orchestra because at the country music school I had attended in Cheraw, South Carolina, I had been taught how to read a speck on a fly's wing and my ears permitted me to hear the sound of an ant pissing on cotton. In other words I could hear and read anything in the Calloway book.

While I was with Teddy Hill's band I had polished up my playing and sharpened my reading. So when I took a solo in a Cotton Club floor show that night in 1939 everyone's head turned toward me, as if to say "Who the hell is that playing?" Back in those days whenever a tap dancer like Bill "Bojangles" Robinson did his number, he was always backed up by the trumpet player. I stood up and blew the accompaniment for Mr. Robinson as he tapped across the stage and all the musicians and entertainers in the club that night were flabbergasted at my technique as well as my tone.

Despite all that, the only thing that came out of that evening was an increase in my self-confidence. I felt I could play with ease with the best of them. Cab at that time had one of the best bands in the country. Both he and Duke Ellington were the interchangeable regulars at the Cotton Club.

Lorraine, a chorus girl and Dizzy's wife.

Several weeks later my wife Lorraine, who was a chorus girl playing five to seven shows nightly, decided she was too tired to keep up that pace. She had a friend named Rudolph who was Cab Calloway's valet, and she asked him if he could do something to help me get a regular gig. A couple of weeks passed after my wife asked for help he called me for a one week gig at the Apollo Theatre. A week following the Apollo gig Rudolph called me again and said, "Hey Pops, I think you should come down to the Cotton Club."

"Yeah?" I said. "What for?"

"Man, come on down. Don't be no fool and bring your horn."

I went down to the Cotton Club that night. I had not yet met Cab Calloway, but there was a vacant chair in the

The Cab Calloway Orchestra with Dizzy shown playing trumpet and standing third from the left.

*trumpet section. I was ecstatic over the chance to play with Calloway's Cotton Club orchestra. There were some difficult numbers in Cab's book, and that night he called for the orchestra to play a new arrangement on the **"Cuban Nightmare"**, which was a particularly hard song to play. However, I ate up that song like a whale eating a minnow. Cab liked the way I handled that complex number, and that was the beginning of a two year association with Cab's orchestra. And during those two years he let me do a lot of soloing. That was a real break when you consider how tightly the Cab Calloway arrangements were written. There was not much solo work for anybody besides Cab. After all he was the star.*

I left Cab's band because somebody threw a spitball on the stage during a performance at the State Theater in Boston. I was accused of doing it, I didn't, but I refuse to plead the Fifth.

My early work with Cab reflected Roy Eldridge's influence. He remained the main influence on me, although later I was certainly influenced by Charlie "Yardbird" Parker, and the work of Art Tatum, Coleman Hawkins and Benny Carter also had some effect on my work.

The Brass section of Earl Hines Orchestra in 1945. (l to r) Dizzy, Berry Harris; Howard Scott, Trombone; Gail Brockman, Trumpet; Shorty McConnell, trumpet; Eugene Chappel, Trombone; Earl Hines at piano and Benny Green, Trombone.

I am often asked about bebop. Actually we were playing around with bebop ideas in New York at Minton's Playhouse on 7th Avenue back in the late '30s and early '40s, but the whole thing came together when I was with the Earl Hines band, out of Chicago, which I joined in 1943. Billy Eckstine was vocalist, Shadow Wilson was on drums, Scoops Carey and Goon Gardner, on alto; Thomas Crump, on tenor sax; and Johnny Williams, on baritone sax; and Sarah Vaughan was the vocalist. And it was there in the Hines band in 1943 that the whole bebop movement took shape. In 1943 the Hines band was doing things that were ahead of the time. I don't think people realize the kind of contribution Earl Hines made, not just for piano-players, but to music in general. Hines would have gotten more credit for his work if there had not been a union ban on orchestral recordings because the material used to make records was needed for army equipment during World War II from 1943 to September 1945. Therefore, some musical things that were not recorded during that period have been lost forever.

The Hines band was the incubator of the bebop

Charlie Parker and Dizzy being Dizzy.

school and its leading exponent until 1944. Men from the Hines band formed the nucleus of Billy Eckstine's bebop band. I was in the first Eckstine band with Charlie Parker, Gail Brockman, Miles Davis, Fats Navarro and some other bebop players. I would say that Charlie Parker stands head and shoulders above everybody else as the prime mover among instrumentalists of the bebop style. He played the same notes everybody else played but his unique style contributed to the development and acceptance of bebop in no small way.

I first met Charlie Parker in Kansas City in 1940, and he was no shortstop then. A trumpet player by the name of Buddy Anderson brought the "Yardbird" by my room in the Booker T. Washington Hotel. (Charlie Parker got the nickname "Yardbird" because of his love for fried chicken.) The young cat pulled out his alto sax and started blowing ideas and concepts that I couldn't believe. "Bird" would be playing one song and slide right into another song with the same chord structure, perfectly and never miss a note. Man, I could not believe my ears.

*Let me tell you a little story about **To Be Or Not To Bop,** which is the title of my latest book. I was in London on a gig and staying at the Mayfair Hotel. I took a walk one day in Hyde Park and you know they have all these quaint boutiques with paintings, sculptures, books and everything handsomely displayed. I stopped at a little shop to browse and saw all of these little paintings about two inches in diameter. The object that caught my eye was a painting of Shakespeare. Just above it was one of those little English hats with a small question mark protruding out of the top, resembling an ornament, and under the bottom was the phrase: "To Be Or Not To Be." I told the saleslady I had an idea. "If you will change the last word for me on that sign, I will buy all of those ornaments that you have on that shelf."*

She said, "You come back in half an hour and I

105

believe I can fulfill your wishes.   How do you want it changed?"

I said I wanted it to read: ***"To Be or Not to Bop."***

So when I came back she had changed the last word to "Bop" in very tiny writing.   Of course I kept my promise and bought all the trinkets on that particular shelf and that is how my book got its title, ***To Be Or Not to Bop.***   *I took the idea to the editors and publishers but they didn't look on this title too kindly.   They had another in mind and wanted to call it The Movement or something like that.   Another editor wanted to call it Gillespie - A Legend in His Own Time.   But I said without blinking an eye that I wouldn't accept anything except* ***To Be Or Not To Bop.***   *I wanted "To" printed small, a large "Be," and then further down a small Bop," but when you look closer you see the full title. I thought it was a clever idea.   However, the book has not sold well.*

Whenever I travel abroad, I try to keep my eyes and

Dizzy's friends right to left: Dr. W. E. B. DuBois, Paul Robeson and a person unknown to the author.

106

ears open and I have found more jazz in some parts of Europe than you could find anywhere in the United States. I attribute that to the fact that our country is culturally young and we are not up to the European standard because we deal in commercialism and they look upon jazz as an art form. Of course, Europeans love our artistry and our music. When I think of artistry and music, I always remember Paul Robeson, whom I loved. Paul traveled throughout Europe and the Soviet Union giving concerts and spreading the good word. At the same time that Robeson was idolized in Europe, he was figuratively crucified in his own country.

In late 1949 or early 1950, I was playing at the Apollo Theater and received a telegram from Paul Robeson that read: "I enjoyed your performance, but I didn't want to create any heat or anything on you so I didn't come backstage."

I called Paul and asked what he meant. "You are

Congressman Adam Clayton Powell and Dizzy.

me, man," I told him. I sincerely meant that. Paul Robeson was a great human being. It's too bad that there were those among us who did not appreciate the contribution that this great citizen of the world made to mankind.

Paul Robeson was a forerunner of Dr. Martin Luther King and Malcolm X. Teddy Wilson, Dr. W. E. B. DuBois, Adam Clayton Powell, Pete Seeger, and Marian Anderson. All of them recognized the importance of the position that Robeson took on Civil Rights.

The dues that Robeson paid for his unwillingness to bend were higher than the dues paid by Martin and Malcolm and they paid with their lives. Robeson paid more and suffered longer because he stayed alive until he was 78 years old whereas Martin and Malcolm were killed before their 40th birthdays.

Robeson was an incorruptable soul. Thus, Dizzy was most proud when he was presented the Paul Robeson Award by the Rutgers Institute of Jazz Studies at the 1973 Newport Jazz Festival.

On another occasion, when we were touring the Far East, a human tragedy took place in Japan. When we arrived in Japan, Sonny Stitt who had been in trouble earlier with the FBI, was not permitted to enter the country. He had to stay in a room at the airport, and we had to use a Japanese fellow named Sleepy Motzumoto to replace Sonny. Although Sleepy was a good saxophonist, it was unfortunate that Sonny had traveled such a great distance thinking he would be able to work. It appears to me that when he applied for his visa and passport, they should have informed him of the problem and thereby avoided the hangup. I remember on another occasion when I went through customs, there was a Japanese fellow who searched my bags frantically, looking through underwear, socks and everything. I simply tapped him on the shoulder and said, "Look, man, if you tell me what you are looking for, maybe I can help you find it," and that's the way I left it.

The Japanese are very interested in jazz. Their love for jazz almost equals the Europeans'. One Japanese fellow said to me, "You are a very fast trumpet player, the fastest." That's not true. There have been many fast trumpet players. I am thinking of Rex Stewart, who played with Duke for many years and, of course, my mentor, Roy Eldridge. There were also Fats Navarro, Clifford Brown, Lee Morgan and many others that you have never heard of who are equally as fast.

I believe my harmonic knowledge of the piano has always helped me with the horn. In fact, I am a piano nut. I cannot pass a piano without touching it, so when someone writes something for me, or when writing myself, it's as though I am writing for a symphony. In other words, someone might elect to write a melody for trumpet in B-flat, but I tell them to write for me as if it were a concert. When I open my ears, I hear a concert; I don't only hear a single note.

The Monk and Dizzy.

As I explained to this Japanese fellow in analyzing style and what one hears, one can hear not only a certain amount of creativity, but also training and experience. My style did not develop as a sudden flash of genius but was the result of an accumulation of hard-earned ideas from many artists. To mention a few, I would say Thelonius Monk, Lester Young, Buck Clayton and my close friend and partner, Charlie Parker. We all spent a lot of time down at Minton's Playhouse in New York City during our formative years.

One misconception is that bop employs whole tone scales. That's true. But it also extends the chords in an unorthodox manner, which gives it its totally different sound. Often these are substitute chords, such as a minor 7th with an associated minor 9th, or occasionally an aug-

mented or diminished 11th. There is no definite pattern to the chord structures I use. I use them as I feel them and that is probably where the difference comes in. I advocate every musician learn as much about the piano as he or she can. I found that all good singers know something about piano. Carmen McRae is an excellent pianist and Dinah Washington could sit down and play piano as well as most people who do it for a living. Sarah Vaughan does that too, and Ella Fitzgerald is not a slouch at the piano. That also applies to trumpet players,

Ella and Sarah in song.

saxophone players, trombonists, bass players, guitar players - the more familiar they are with the piano, the better they perform on their respective instruments.

Speaking of performers, Duke Ellington once told me, and I will never forget it: "Birkes, you should never have let them name your music bebop. You should have insisted on it being known as Gillesienna," he said, "because you are dated with a name like bebop, and you shouldn't date yourself at any time. I hope my music will always be remembered as Ellingtonian."

Travis, I think your idea of writing about our music

is important. The time for Blacks to write about their own music is long past due. It's time for us to do it ourselves and tell it like it is. Whites have given a whitewashed look to our music. Naturally, they are going to ooze off as much as they can to other whites. That is why it is so important to document our own history for the Black generations to come.

Norman Granz did not whitewash jazz he brought it down to the front row when he first employed Dizzy to play in his Jazz at The Philharmonic concert in Los Angeles on

(L to R) Dempsey J. Travis, Marthann Campbell, Dizzy and Noor Halani.

January 27, 1946. The other musicians on the gig with Dizzy were Mel Power, piano; Willie Smith, alto sax; Lester Young, tenor sax; Charlie Ventura, tenor sax. This group blew their heads off playing multiple solos on *Crazy Rhythm.* The music set had a duration of 8:41 minutes.

The Krupa Trio included Gene Krupa, drums; with Charlie Ventura, tenor sax; and Teddy Napoleon piano; they played **Stompin At the Savoy** and **Idaho.** They received thunderous applause behind each solo. Their set lasted 13 minutes.

Other show stoppers were **Blues For Norman** played by Arnold Ross, piano; Howard McGhee, trumpet; Charlie Parker, alto sax; Willie Smith, alto sax; Arnold Ross, piano; Billy Hadnott, bass; and Lee Young, the brother of Lester Young on drums. Playing time for this number was 8:34 minutes.

Another show stopper that night was **Oh, Lady, Be Good!** by George and Ira Gershwin. The musicians on this set were the same as those on the previous number. The playing time for this number was 11:13 minutes.

One of the other killer diller numbers played that night was **Crazy Rhythm** as played by Mel Powell, piano; Willie Smith, alto sax; Lester Young, tenor sax; Dizzy Gillespie, trumpet; Charlie Ventura, tenor sax; the set lasted an intense 8:41 minutes and the audience was left screaming and applauding wildly.

Charlie Parker, Dizzy's partner was the first of the JAPH group to die. He died at the Stayhope Hotel in the apartment of Baroness Pannonica "Nica" de Doeningswarter on March 12, 1955 in New York City at the age of 34. The body was taken to a funeral home and the undertaker refused to release the body without a valid life insurance policy or money on the barrel head. Dizzy intervened in the dilemma of whether to bury the body in New York where all of his known three women including his lawful wife lived or in Kansas City where his mother lived. The decision was made to send the body to Kansas City.

Everything was in order but the money; thus, Dizzy called Norman Granz and told him there was not enough money to get the body released for burial. Norman said, *"I will tell you what, you call and find out if his mother wants the body, and if she does I will pay the cost for releasing the body. In addition, I will pay for the shipping of the body by plane and also the gravesite and burial. The body was sent to Kansas City and buried and as promised, Granz picked*

Dizzy and four of his bandsmen at Charlie Parker's gravesite in 1961.

up the entire tab.

Seven years before Parker died he began recording almost exclusively with Norman Granz. In 1947 Granz recorded two studio sides featuring Parker for a special album of 78s called The Jazz Scene.

The new recording arrangement came at a time when Parker and his manager were trying to make Parker more acceptable in the jazz marketplace. Parker was covertly jealous of Dizzy Gillespie's critical and popular success. Parker's lack of fame and fortune was caused by his need to carry a gorilla "cocaine"on his back as opposed to a monkey "marijuana" in addition to his love of swimming in alcohol for a very large portion of his short life span. Dizzy treated Parker like a brother to the very end of his life in spite of his faults.

Gillespie's support of the civil rights movement earned him the following FBI File.

FEDERAL BUREAU OF INVESTIGATION

FREEDOM OF INFORMATION/PRIVACY ACTS SECTION

COVER SHEET

SUBJECT: <u>JOHN BIRKS GILLESPIE</u>

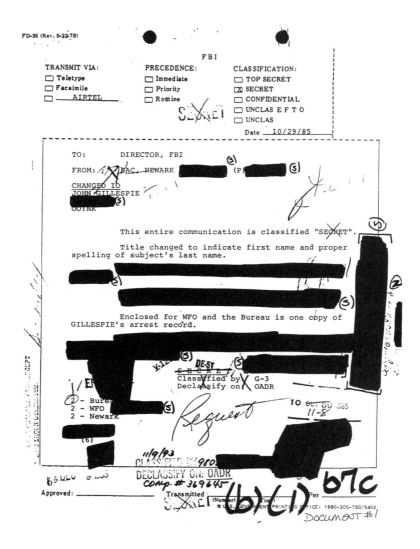

FD-36 (Rev. 5-22-78)

FBI

TRANSMIT VIA: PRECEDENCE: CLASSIFICATION:

☐ Teletype   ☐ Immediate   ☐ TOP SECRET

☐ Facsimile   ☐ Priority   ☒ SECRET

☐ ___AIRTEL___   ☐ Routine   ☐ CONFIDENTIAL

☐ UNCLAS E F T O

☐ UNCLAS

Date ___10/29/85___

TO: DIRECTOR, FBI   (S)

FROM: SAC, NEWARK ▮▮▮▮▮ (P) ▮▮▮▮▮ (S)

CHANGED TO

JOHN GILLESPIE (S)

OO:NK

This entire communication is classified "SECRET".

Title changed to indicate first name and proper spelling of subject's last name.

Enclosed for WFO and the Bureau is one copy of GILLESPIE's arrest record.

SECRET

Classified by G-3

Declassify on OADR

2 - Bureau

2 - WFO

2 - Newark

(6)

CLASSIFIED BY 980

DECLASSIFY ON: OADR

COMP. # 369645

Approved: _____ Transmitted _____ Per _____

(b)(1) b7c

DOCUMENT #1

S E C R E T

NK ████ (S) b1

Investigation conducted at Newark is as follows:

Telephone 201-569-4875 is listed to JOHN GILLESPIE, 477 North Woodland Ave., Englewood, N.J.

Englewood, NJPD, furnished arrest sheet listing subject with DOB 10/21/7, and POB Charew, South Carolina. FBI number is 378675B.

DMV negative in New Jersey.

Newark credit check still outstanding.

REQUESTS OF THE BUREAU

b1
        1. Bureau is requested to grant an extension ████ ████████ so that Newark and WFO can obtain FBI (S) records and credit check.

        2. Furnish WFO and Newark with copy of arrest record on JOHN GILLESPIE, FBI #378675B.

LEADS

    WFO

        AT WASHINGTON, D.C: Will review material on GILLESPIE and furnish any additional information concerning b1 possible relationship between ████ and GILLESPIE.
        (S)
        2. Advise Newark if an interview of GILLESPIE would have negative impact.

    NEWARK

        AT NEWARK, N.J: Will furnish credit check when available.

        2. Will await Headquarters and WFO response before conducting interview.

S E C R E T

2*

WFO ▮▮▮▮▮▮ (S) b1

The above is furnished for the information of Newark Division.

WFO interposes no objection to subject's interview under suitable pretext if Newark feels it worth the attempt.

No other contacts between ▮▮▮▮▮ (S) and GILLESPIE are known. b1

REQUEST OF THE BUREAU

Bureau is requested to furnish subject's identification record to both WFO and Newark as set out in Newark's airtel of 10/29/85.

3*

☆GPO : ☆U.S. GOVERNMENT PRINTI ICE : 1966 O - 154-590

MASTER MASTER MASTER
1-4b (Rev. 7-19-77)

2

UNITED STATES DEPARTMENT OF JUSTICE
FEDERAL BUREAU OF INVESTIGATION
IDENTIFICATION DIVISION
WASHINGTON, D. C. 20537

Use of the following information from FBI record, NUMBER 378 675 B , is REGULATED BY LAW.
It is furnished FOR OFFICIAL USE ONLY and should ONLY BE USED FOR PURPOSE REQUESTED.

Description and Related Data:

Race: Black

Sex: Male

Height: 5'10

Weight: 195

Hair: Black

Eyes: Brown

Date and Place of Birth: 10-21-17 Cheraw SC

Scars and Marks: Unknown

Address: 477 N Woodland St Englewood NJ(In 1972)

Occupation: Musician(In 1972)

Social Security Number: 083 14 0442

-3 -

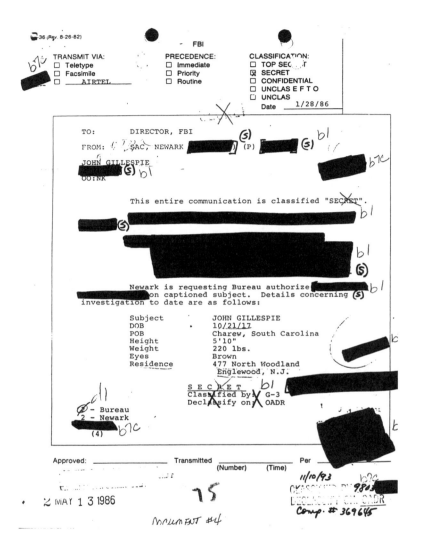

-36 (Rev. 8-26-82)

- FBI

TRANSMIT VIA:
- [ ] Teletype
- [ ] Facsimile
- [ ] AIRTEL

PRECEDENCE:
- [ ] Immediate
- [ ] Priority
- [ ] Routine

CLASSIFICATION:
- [ ] TOP SECRET
- [x] SECRET
- [ ] CONFIDENTIAL
- [ ] UNCLAS E F T O
- [ ] UNCLAS

Date 1/28/86

TO: DIRECTOR, FBI   (S)

FROM: SAC, NEWARK   (P)   (S)

JOHN GILLESPIE   (S)
OO:NK

This entire communication is classified "SECRET".

(S)

Newark is requesting Bureau authorize   (S)
on captioned subject. Details concerning
investigation to date are as follows:

Subject   JOHN GILLESPIE
DOB   10/21/17
POB   Charew, South Carolina
Height   5'10"
Weight   220 lbs.
Eyes   Brown
Residence   477 North Woodland
                Englewood, N.J.

S E C R E T
Classified by: G-3
Declassify on: OADR

Ø - Bureau
2 - Newark
(4)

Approved: _____ Transmitted _____ Per _____
                                      (Number)   (Time)

2 MAY 1 3 1986   75   11/10/93

                                             Comp. # 369645

DOCUMENT #4

U. .TED STATES DEPARTMENT OF /STICE
FEDERAL BUREAU OF INVESTIGATION
IDENTIFICATION DIVISION
WASHINGTON, D.C. 20537

The following FBI record, NUMBER   378 675 B   , is furnished FOR C
Information shown on this Identification Record represents data furnished FBI by finge
WHERE DISPOSITION IS NOT SHOWN OR FURTHER EXPLANATION OF CHARGE C
DESIRED, COMMUNICATE WITH AGENCY CONTRIBUTING THOSE FINGERPRINTS.

CONTRIBUTOR OF FINGERPRINTS	NAME AND NUMBER	ARRESTED OR RECEIVED	CHARGE
Police Department New York New York	John Gillespie B-242650	May 18, 1946	rape
Identification Division Allegheny County Detective Bureau Pittsburgh Pennsylvania	John Gillespie 76018	June 18, 1953	fail to support child born out of lawful wedlock
Police Department Englewood New Jersey	John Gillespie 3839-28	January 26, 1972	possession of heroin 3512 poss of marijuana less 25 grams 3562

R&E CD 3666

121

Mary Lou Williams: Miss Music To You.

Cut V
Mary Lou Williams: The
Lady Who Swings The
Bands

Mary Lou Williams (née Scruggs) was born in Atlanta, Georgia on May 8, 1910. The little girl was a contemporary of Earl Hines (1903), Duke Ellington (1899), Fats Waller (1904) Roy Eldridge (1911) and Art Tatum (1909). In the spring of 1914 she moved to Pittsburgh, Pennsylvania (The Smoky City) with her mother and sister Mamie along with her other siblings prior to celebrating her fourth birthday. She had begun pecking on the piano keys shortly before her third birthday. Her real fascination with the piano came while she was sitting in the parlor on her mother's lap and watching the Upright Grand piano keys move up and down like jumping jacks. The piano keys were activated by a perforated piano paper roll propelled by her mother physically pumping the foot pedals like riding a

123

bicycle. The byproduct of these mechanical and physical interactions caused their front parlor to be filled with the sounds of hymns, spirituals, and ragtime music. Her mother was a party girl and a trained musician who had vehemently refused to give her daughter formal musical training because she sincerely believed that it would contaminate what she hoped were her God-given gifts.

It was on her mother's lap that little Mary Lou Williams began playing ragtime and religious melodies by ear on the Grand Upright Piano keyboard. This was early

Ahmad Jamal

evidence that little Mary Lou might be within a razor's edge of becoming a child prodigy. The thought of her baby's success both pleased and delighted Mrs. Scruggs in that it marked the beginning of what was to become an extraordinary musical career.

The Scruggs' newly adopted hometown was commonly known among Negroes as "the Mississippi of the North" because of its flagrant racism. Even in its stifling discriminating climate Pittsburgh managed to turn out more than its share of musically talented people such as: Earl Hines, piano; Errol Garner, piano; Ahmad Jamal, piano; Billy Strayhorn,piano; Roy Eldridge, trumpet; Art Blakey, drummer extraordinaire; and then there was Maxine Sullivan and Billy Eckstine both of whom were world class jazz singers.

While still a pre-teenager at the Westinghouse Junior High School, Mary Lou was able to get gigs playing

Mary Lou at the age of eleven.

Mary Lou sitting at the piano in the middle of an all male orchestra. Andy Kirk extreme left.

house rent parties for one dollar per hour in the Duquesne area which was heavily populated by Blacks. She also played at social events in the upscale Squirrel Hill district of Pittsburgh which was primarily inhabited by upper class Jewish families. During this period her legs were not long enough to touch the piano pedals without her sitting on the very edge of the piano bench.

During the summer of 1925 at fifteen she went on the road working for The Theater Owners Booking Association Circuit which was commonly known by Colored entertainers as the T.O.B.A. (Tough On Black Ass's). On her first Vaudeville tour she traveled with a show that starred Buzzi Harris and Arletta, a triple threat song, dance and comedy team. However, at the end of the summer school vacation she left the show and resumed her studies at the Westinghouse Junior High School in Pittsburgh.

John O. Williams, Mary's first husband.

In 1926, at the age of sixteen she dropped out of school and rejoined the Harris show and became the regular piano player of (the eighty-eight) with the Holder Orchestra, which was directed by John Overton Williams. Within the same year she married Williams who in addition to directing the orchestra he played the alto and baritone saxophone in the reed section. John quit the Terrance Holder Band to join Andy Kirk and his newly organized Twelve Clouds of Joy.

**Jimmie
Lunceford**

Mary Lou assumed John's leadership position with The Holder Group. She hired Jimmie Lunceford to direct the orchestra for the balance of the engagement. Some years later after Lunceford had become one of the nation's topflight bandleaders she reminded him with a girlish grin and giggle that she had hired him when she was still a teenager.

The Andy Kirk band left the Oklahoma territory and moved to Kansas City, Missouri, a twenty-four hour wild and wide open mid-western city controlled by Johnny Lazia, a gangster whose reputation as a Jazz Slave Master paralleled that of Chicago's Al Capone, and New York's Owney Madden of

Second from the left is Andy Kirk, Mary Lou Williams, Pha Terrell and some friends.

the Cotton Club. Lazia was also the silent boss of the Kansas City police department which enabled him to control the bootleg liquor, gambling and prostitution operations. The political overlord of Kansas City dating from the roaring twenties through the forties was Tom Pendergast, one of President Harry S. Truman's primary political spon-

127

sors. Pendergast almost single-handedly set the tone for the "everything goes crowd" in that he made it into the Twentieth Century's Sodom and Gomorrah of the mid-west.

Through Mary Lou Williams' mind's eye: *"Kansas City was such a ball when you made the jazz scene every night, and participated in the jam sessions that lasted way past dawn. It was in a jam session that I first met Count Basie, Thelonious Monk and Ben Webster.*

Left to right: Drummer, Ronnie Free. Singer Mose Allison. Tenor Saxophonist, Lester Young and Mary Lou Williams. Tenor Saxophonist, Charles Rouse. Bassist, Oscar Pettiford.

In April 1930 at the age of twenty, Mary Lou auditioned along with several other pianists for a permanent chair in the Andy Kirk organization. Mary Lou Williams won the piano cutting contest and joined her husband John Williams as the regular piano player with Andy Kirk's Twelve Clouds of Joy. During her residency with the Kirk orchestra between 1930 and 1942 she became invaluable to Kirk as an arranger, principal pianist and composer.

In a very short period she was taught how to sight read and arrange music by Andy Kirk, Don Redman, and

128

Mary Lou, a master pianist, arranger and composer.

Edgar Sampson were considered top-drawer musicians and arrangers by both Blacks and whites in the music industry. Mrs. Williams soon became a member of an elite group of composers and arrangers in that she produced many of the Andy Kirk Orchestra's biggest hits, such as: **"Froggy Bottom," "Walking and Swinging"** and **"Little Joe from Chicago"** and **"Rolling"** for the Benny Goodman Orchestra. Henry Wells a trombonist and vocalist in the Kirk Band (co-composed **"Little Joe"**).

In 1942, Mary Lou left the Andy Kirk Band and also divorced John Williams. She subsequently met and married trumpeter Harold "Shorty" Baker. When Baker joined the Duke Ellington Orchestra in

Harold "Shorty" Baker, Mary Lou's second husband.

129

1943, Williams toured for six months with the Ellington orchestra as a staff arranger. It was during this period that she also did arrangements on the side for other orchestra leaders such as Louis Armstrong, Earl Hines, Benny Goodman, Tommy Dorsey, Jimmy Dorsey, Jimmie Lunceford and Cab Calloway. This group of orchestra leaders were on top of the swing world in the 1930's and 40's.

In 1948 she wrote and played briefly with the Benny Goodman Orchestra. In 1949, she composed what became the national anthem for the beboppers. It was entitled **"In The Land of Oo-Bla-Dee."** She also composed for Duke Ellington in 1946 **"Trumpet No End"** which was a recomposition of **"Blue Skies"** a 1927 popular music hit written by Irving Berlin.

Duke Ellington said: *"Mary Lou Williams was a major figure in the history of jazz. She played an important role in both the establishment of the Kansas City Big Band style and the emergence of bebop, while at the same time maintaining a position as one of the premiere creative artists of her time... Her writing was perpetually contemporary, and her performance was always ahead of its time throughout her career. Moreover her music retained a standard of quality that is timeless."*

Ellington further noted: *"Mary Lou Williams made a special contribution to his organization during the time that she and Shorty Baker were married. They brought Al Hibbler to my attention for a second time when we were playing at the Hurricane Club on Broadway in New York City on Saturday, May 15, 1943."*

The Bakers had no knowledge of the fact that Ellington had auditioned Hibbler in Little Rock, Arkansas in 1935 and found him to be an alcoholic. On that occasion Duke said: *"He had no problem hiring a blind man but a blind drunk was a bit more than he could tolerate."*

On another occasion Ellington stated: *"Mary Lou did not have a style of her own like Earl Hines, Errol*

130

Garner and Teddy Wilson." She considered Ellington's statement a left handed compliment in that she retorted: *"...Everyone with ears can identify my work without any difficulty... What happens to so many good pianists is that they become so stylized that they can't break out of the prison of their styles and absorb new ideas and new techniques."*

Duke Ellington also found a place for her in his autobiography **"Music Is My Mistress"** therein he wrote*"Mary Lou Williams, is perpetually contemporary. Her writing and performing are and have always been just a little ahead... And it maintains a standard of qualities that is time-less. She is like soul on soul."*

Art Tatum, a pianist with the fastest hands in the land. When he showed up on a gig other musicians would say " God is in the house."

This writer remembers vividly when he first saw Mary Lou Williams and the Andy Kirk Orchestra perform in September 1936 at the Savoy Ballroom in Chicago. She actually blew my mind with her ability to sound like Earl Hines, Art Tatum, Willie "The Lion" Smith, James P. Johnson, Claude Hopkins and Fats Waller. She was able to put them all in one neat package. There was a group of young piano players that attended DuSable High School with me. Among that group was Dorothy Donegan, Nat

131

Fats Waller, pianist, composer and arranger.

Cole, Martha Davis and Thomas Rigsby. We were all standing at the edge of the bandstand with our mouths gape wide while we listened to this wizard of the keyboard.

The jumping but relaxed piano style of Mary Lou Williams was mind boggling. I concluded that night that she indeed deserved to be known as "The Lady Who Swings The Bands," because that is what she actually did. The other attraction of the Kirk Band that evening was Pha Terrell who sang his version of a hit ballad entitled **Until The Real Thing Comes Along** (originally known as **The Slave Song.**)

Mary Lou changed her harmonic chords in 1945 and wrote the **"Zodiac Suite"** - 12 separate semi-classical compositions. She premiered the suite on 12 consecutive radio

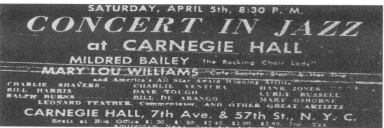

shows, which she hosted on what was known as the Mary Lou Williams Piano Workshop; **The Zodiac Suite** was also performed in New York City at Town Hall in a special arrangement written by her for a Chamber Orchestra and

Mary Lou entertains at the Cafe Society.

her Piano Trio.   In addition she also premiered a three-movement version of **"The Zodiac Suite"** with the Carnegie Pops Orchestra.   She was featured on piano with that orchestra in Carnegie Hall.

Mary Lou Williams' musical career became a mixed bag for the next thirty-five years.   Norman Granz persuaded her to record for his label and appear in a mini J.A.T.P. jazz concert with her downtown Café Society Trio at Carnegie Hall.   At the same time she was composing Jazz Masses and other liturgical music after converting to Catholicism in 1956.   The lady composed **"Mary Lou's Mass"** which was adapted to a ballet, and performed by the Alvin Ailey American Dance Theater, in 1971...   She was invited by President Jimmy Carter to perform at The White House in 1978.

Mary Lou Williams died from cancer of the bladder three years later on Friday May 28, 1981 in Durham, North Carolina at the age of 71.   Miss Williams spent the last decade of her life before she became fatally ill touring worldwide, performing, recording, making radio and television appearances, and taking part in workshops on college and university campuses.

At the time of her death she was working on a piano concerto designed to reflect the history of jazz. Her efforts were being funded by a grant from the National Endowment for the Arts.

Left to right: Dizzy Gillespie (standing), Mary Lou had a love gaze in her eyes for Jack Teagarden who once proposed marriage to her.

A requiem mass was held for Miss Mary Lou Williams on Monday June 1st at 2 P.M. at St Ignatius Catholic Church, at 84th Street and Park Avenue in New York City. From there her body was flown to Pittsburgh where a burial mass was held at St. Peter and St. Paul Cathedral at 9:30 A.M. on Tuesday morning June 2, 1981. She was buried in Pittsburgh where a graveside burial mass was also held. Her burial in the Pittsburgh hills was fitting in that it was the place where her meteoric musical career began.

Title of Composition	Year	Composers

<u>COMPOSITIONS</u>

A Partial list of Mary Lou Williams' compositions are listed on the next pages in chronological order:

PIANO

Little Joe From Chicago	1936	Mary LouWilliams and Henry Wells
Walkin' and Swingin'	1936	Mary Lou Williams
Toadie Toddle	1938	Mary Lou Williams
Twinklin	1938	Mary Lou Williams
Scratchin' in the Gravel	1940	Mary Lou Williams
Scratchin' in the Gravel	1941	Mary Lou Williams
Six Original Boogie Woogie	1944	Mary Lou Williams
Twinklin'	1944	Mary Lou Williams
The Zodiac Suite	1944-1945	Mary Lou Williams
The Duke and the Count	1984	Mary Lou Williams
Special Freight	1984	Mary Lou Williams

JAZZ ENSEMBLE

Cloudy	1929	Mary Lou Williams and Ted Brinson
Corky Stomp or Corky	1929	Mary Lou Williams and Andy Kirk
Lotta Sax Appeal	1929	Mary Lou Williams and John Williams

Messa Stomp	1929; revised 1938	Mary Lou Williams
Drag Em	1930	Mary Lou Williams
Getting' Off a Mess	1930	Mary Lou Williams
Mary's Idea also arranged as "Just an Idea."	1930	Mary Lou Williams
Nite Life	1930	Mary Lou Williams
Corny Rhythm	1936	Mary Lou Williams
Bearcat Shuffle	1936	Mary Lou Williams
Clean Picking	1936	Mary Lou Williams
Froggy Bottom	1936	Mary Lou Williams and John Overton Williams
Isabelle	1936	Mary Lou Williams and Earl Hines
Mary's Special	1936	Mary Lou Williams and Lester Young
Overhand (New Froggy Bottom)	1936	Mary Lou Williams
Roll Em	1936	Mary Lou Williams
Steppin' Pretty	1936	Mary Lou Williams

Swinging for Joy	1936	Mary Lou Williams
Camel Hop	1937	Mary Lou Williams
I Went to a Gypsy	1937	Mary Lou Williams
Keep It in the Groove	1937	Mary Lou Williams
A Mellow Bit of Rhythum	1937	Mary Lou Williams
Dunkin' a Doughnut	1938	Mary Lou Williams
Ghost of Love	1938	Mary Lou Williams and Jack Lawrence
The Rocks	1938	Mary Lou Williams
Sweet (Patootie) Patunia with Regan and Alexander	1938	Mary Lou Williams
What's Your Story Morning Glory	1938	Mary Lou Williams, Paul Francis Webster and Jack Lawrence
Big Jim Blues	1939	Mary Lou Williams
Close to Five	1939	Mary Lou Williams
Big Time Crip	1940	Mary Lou Williams
Mary Lou Williams Blues	1940	Mary Lou Williams
Why Go On Pretending?	1940	Mary Lou Williams and Roy Jordan

Riffs	1941	Mary Lou Williams
Shorty Boo	1943	Mary Lou Williams and Milton Orent
Trumpet No End or Trumpets No End	1943	Mary Lou Williams
Carcinoma or Cancer Mood	1944	Mary Lou Williams
Eighth Avenue Express	1944	Mary Lou Williams
Gjon Mili Jam Session	1944	Mary Lou Williams
Man o' Mine or Sweet Juice	1944	Mary Lou Williams and Don Byas
Mary's Boogie	1944	Mary Lou Williams
New Drag Em Blues	1944	Mary Lou Williams
Satchel Mouth Baby	1944	Mary Lou Williams
Song in My Soul	1944	Mary Lou Williams
Yankee Doodle Blues	1944	Mary Lou Williams
Yesterday's Kisses	1944	Mary Lou Williams
You Know Baby	1944	Mary Lou Williams
Lonely Moments	1945	Mary Lou Williams
Boogie Misterioso	1946	Mary Lou Williams

or Flunga

Fifth Dimension or Dunga	1946	Mary Lou Williams
Fragments en dessous or DU	1946	Mary Lou Williams
Harmony Grits	1946	Mary Lou Williams
Hesitation Boogie	1946	Mary Lou Williams
Timmie Time	1946	Mary Lou Williams
Waltz Boogie	1946	Mary Lou Williams
Kool	1947	Mary Lou Williams
Whistle Blues or Whistle	1947	Mary Lou Williams and Milton Orent
Benny's Bop	1948	Mary Lou Williams
Blue Views	1948	Mary Lou Williams
In the Land of Oo-Bla-Dee	1949	Mary Lou Williams and Milton Orent
Knowledge	1949	Mary Lou Williams
Tisherome	1949	Mary Lou Williams
Walkin' or Walkin' Out the Door or I'm Walkin' Out the Door	1950	Mary Lou Williams
Bobo	1951	Mary Lou Williams

In the Purple Grotto	1951	Mary Lou Williams
Koolbonga	1953	Mary Lou Williams
Melody Maker	1953	Mary Lou Williams
New Musical Express or N.M.E.or Musical Express or Express	1953	Mary Lou Williams
Chicka Boom Blues	1954	Mary Lou Williams
Nickles	1954	Mary Lou Williams
Nicole	1954	Mary Lou Williams
O.W.	1954	Mary Lou Williams and Orlando Wright
Swingin' Till The Guys Come Home	1954	Mary Lou Williams and Oscar Pettiford
Twylight or Twilight	1954	Mary Lou Williams
Army	1955	Mary Lou Williams
Easy Blues	1955	Mary Lou Williams
Fandagle	1955	Mary Lou Williams
I Love Him	1955	Mary Lou Williams
My Mama Pinned a Rose On Me	1955	Mary Lou Williams
Chunka Lunka Jug	1959	Mary Lou Williams

or Chunka Lunka

Po-Ta-Be.	1959	Mary Lou Williams and Melma Doretta Liston
Dirge Blues	1963	Mary Lou Williams
A Fungus Amungus	1963	Mary Lou Williams
Miss D.D.	1963	Mary Lou Williams
Misty Blues	1963	Mary Lou Williams
The Watchers or Joycie	1965	Mary Lou Williams
Laddle Leedle	1967	Mary Lou Williams
Who Stole the Lock off the Henhouse Door	1969	Mary Lou Williams
Blues for John	1971	Mary Lou Williams
For the Figs	1971	Mary Lou Williams
Gemma	1971	Mary Lou Williams
Let's Do the Froggy Bottom	1972	Mary Lou Williams and Juanita Fleming
Willis	1972	Mary Lou Williams
Intermission	1973	Mary Lou Williams
Medi II	1973	Mary Lou Williams

Also arranged for big band as
"Busy, Busy, Busy - New York."

Zoning Fungus II	1973	Mary Lou Williams
Play It Momma	1974	Mary Lou Williams
Rosa Mae	1974	Mary Lou Williams and Larry Gales
Blues for Peter	1975	Mary Lou Williams
Blues for Timmie	1975	Mary Lou Williams
JB's Waltz	1975	Mary Lou Williams and Milton Suggs
Ode to Saint Cecilia	1975	Mary Lou Williams
The Blues Never Left Me	1977	Mary Lou Williams
Back to the Blues	1977	Mary Lou Williams
Basic Chords	1977	Mary Lou Williams
The Blues	1977	Mary Lou Williams
Good Ole Boogie	1977	Mary Lou Williams
K.C. Twelfth Street	1977	Mary Lou Williams
The Lord Is Heavy: 1 Spiritual II and Spiritual III	1977	Mary Lou Williams
Turtle Speed Blues	1977	Mary Lou Williams
Baby Bear Boogie	1978	Mary Lou Williams
Concerto Alone at Montreux	1978	Mary Lou Williams

Exit Playing	1978	Mary Lou Williams
Love Roots	1978	Mary Lou Williams
N.G. Blues	1978	Mary Lou Williams
No Title Blues	1978	Mary Lou Williams
Old Fashioned Slow Blues	1978	Mary Lou Williams
Rhythmic Pattern	1978	Mary Lou Williams
Shafi	1978	Mary Lou Williams and Shafi Hadi
Shoo Be Doo Be Doo	1978	Mary Lou Williams and Cynthia McCrea Tyson
Space Playing Blues	1978	Mary Lou Williams

CONCERT BAND

The History of Jazz	1981	Mary Lou Williams

CHORAL MUSIC

Elijah Under the Juniper Tree	1948	Mary Lou Williams
The Devil	1952; revised 1962	Mary Lou Williams
Anima Christi	1962	Mary Lou Williams

Black Christ of the Andes	1962	Mary Lou Williams
Mass or Mass I or The Pittsburgh Mass	1966	Mary Lou Williams
Pater Noster	1967	Mary Lou Williams
Thank You Jesus	1967	Mary Lou Williams
Mary Lou's Mass	1967-1971	Mary Lou Williams
I Have A Dream	1968	Mary Lou Williams
Mass for the Lenten Season or High Mass in Jazz	1968	Mary Lou Williams
Tell Him Not to Talk Too Long	1968	Mary Lou Williams

Clark Terry

Cut VI
Clark Terry: The Man Who Made The Trumpet and Flugelhorn Mumble at Each Other.

IN THE BEGINNING IT WAS HELL!

Clark "Shorty" Terry, Sr. was born in a shotgun shanty on the outskirts of Fort Scott, Kansas in 1888, however he was reared in Dallas, Texas by his maternal grandparents both of whom had been slaves. In 1903 at the age of 15 "Shorty" hoboed on a freight train from Dallas, Texas to St. Louis, Missouri carrying a grand total of 75 cents in the right hand pocket of his faded blue overalls. His northbound odyssey was prompted by a weathered, tan skinned, blue eyed Texan who told him about the possibilities of finding employment in the booming railroad yards and factories in St. Louis, a city on the west bank of the Mississippi

River. St. Louis subsequently became immortalized in 1914 by W.C. Handy's musical composition entitled **"The Saint Louis Blues**." Failing to gain employment in either of the two recommended industries, he took a job as a "Fire Feeder" stoking the coal hungry mouths of blast furnaces at the Laclede Light and Coke Company.

In 1907 he met, courted and married little Mary Scott. Neither he nor his bride measured five feet in height. Mary had migrated to St. Louis from Crystal Springs, Missouri in search of a $2.00 per day domestic job. The young married couple pooled their money and rented a small three room love nest for $15.00 per month in the Colored section of the Carbondale Area on the South Side of St. Louis at 6207 South Broadway. The four flat frame apartment building in which they resided was just a stone's throw from the west bank of the muddy Mississippi River. The floor plan in their approximately 500 square feet of living space included a front room, middle room and kitchen. The only lighting in the entire apartment was furnished by portable kerosene lamps. In the center of the kitchen there was a Sears Roebuck and Co. ACME coal fired cooking stove. The young couple took their once a week Saturday night baths in a #2 galvanized tin tub which sat directly behind the nickel plated stove. Since there was no inside plumbing they used purple thunder mugs to relieve themselves at night.

The Terrys' first born was Ada Mae who was delivered by a midwife in their tiny abode on May 3, 1909. Her birth was trailed by ten more siblings, the second in line being Marguerite who was nicknamed "Mollie O", she first saw the light of day during the Christmas holidays on December 29, 1910, their next bundle of joy was Virgil Otto "Bus" born on March 16, 1913, seventeen months before the outbreak of World War I in Europe between France and Germany, their fourth born was Charles Edward "Shorts" who arrived at twenty minutes after 12 o'clock on time

January 1, 1915, then came Lilly Edda "Sugar Lump" who arrived on January 16, 1917 the year of the St. Louis race riot and also the year that the United States entered World War I on the side of the French against Germany. Mable Myrtle "Sug" dropped out of heaven on November 22, 1919, ninety days after the bloody Chicago race riot. Then came Clark "John" Terry their seventh child born on December 14, 1920, the year that women won the right to vote. Clark's birth was followed by Juanita "Neet" on May 30, 1923 and the twins Mary and Mattie who brought in the New Year at 12:01 A.M. on January 1, 1926. They were followed by Marion Odessa "Dess" on May 30, 1927, the year that Charles Lindbergh flew the Spirit of St. Louis nonstop from Roosevelt Field in New York to Paris, France. All of the children and their parents camped in that small 3 room apartment on South Broadway until they either got married or felt that their wings had become strong enough to fly away.

Clark Terry's mother, Mary died at age 39 on May 30, 1927 during the delivery of her eleventh child. Her death reduced the family income by more than thirty percent. In addition to Clark Terry Jr. losing his mother he lost his childhood. It was snatched from him by Clark Terry Sr. who would not allow any of his children to enjoy the pleasures of childhood with new toys of any kind like other children their age. The old man was angry because he had lost his wife and tired because he had to take on two additional part time jobs in order to fill eleven empty bellies including his own. Their diet was strictly low calorie in that it was restricted to chicken necks, feet and hog intestines, better known in some circles as chitterlings. Clark states he was not introduced to the drumsticks and breast of the bird until he was a teenager and he was twenty years of age before he tasted a pork chop. On special occasions like Thanksgiving and Christmas the kids would be served a large hot buttered biscuit and honey for dessert.

Clark Sr. demanded that Clark Jr. at the age of seven learn to earn his own keep. Little Clark was introduced to junking in the alleys and squalid streets of his and adjacent neighborhoods in search of scrap metal, discarded newspapers, empty Coca Cola bottles, old rags and iron, in addition to tinfoil from empty cigarette packages discarded by human chimneys. He scavengered anything of value that could be sold to the local junk dealers. Every penny that young Clark Terry earned was turned over to his dad who was a mean disciplinarian who found it easier to slap his kids around rather than smile or pat them on the head. The only time that old man Clark displayed any milk of civility was when "Bus" his oldest boy by demand, played the movie star Dorothy Lamour type of Hawaiian tunes on his ukulele to soothe the old man's jangled nerves. Simultaneously, young Clark or one of his other siblings would massage and sandpaper the old man's heavily callused feet.

The only time that the Terry kids could get more than a grunt, a groan or a barrage of expletives to flow from the old man's lips was when they begged him to talk about the 1917 East St. Louis, Illinois Race Riot. He would sometimes oblige them. His ritual then was as follows: first he would lean way back in his secondhand rocking chair, he would fill the bowl of his pipe with tobacco and light it while making a sucking noise on the tube, once it was lit he would close his eyes, and clear his throat as if he was preparing to sing **"Don't Forget The Sabbath."** He would then break the cadence of his ritual and mumble some obscenities about white folks and pause briefly before stating: *"The bloody race riot in East St. Louis started in the steaming heat of the midmorning on Monday July 2, 1917, nine whites and approximately forty Negroes were killed and hundreds of Negroes were injured on that extremely hot and bloody day. The killings were ignited because of politics and jobs."*

The Negro population had tripled in East St. Louis between 1900 and 1910 to 59,000. Most of the Negroes were employed as laborers on the dirtiest, stinkiest, back-breaking jobs you could imagine in the large stockyards and packing plants of Swift, Armour, and the Morris Companies. Negroes represented cheap labor and white folks were in fear of their jobs. The other problem was political in that the Democratic leaders accused the Republican Party of recruiting and colonizing southern Negroes for the sole purpose of swinging the Abraham Lincoln votes to their side of the ticket. (Negroes voted decisively for the party of President Lincoln up until 1936 when they switched to President Franklin Delano Roosevelt and his "Happy Days Are Here Again" Democrats).

In the wake of the riot young Terry saw a multitude of Negroes abandon their burnt-out homes and flee for their lives on foot across the Mississippi River via the Eads Bridge and the Free Bridge, the two bridges that tied East St. Louis, Illinois and St. Louis, Missouri together. *"Some of the families found refuge on the South Side in our neighborhood. Some of the parentless children became river people. That period in our history was memorialized with the blood of colored people."*

The tired old man would sometimes drop his head as if to nod. We kids would then yell: *"Tell us some more Daddy, tell us some more."* It was entertaining and spellbinding to listen to the old man talk about the olden days.

Clark Terry like his father is endowed with excellent recall and an uncanny talent for rekindling the experiences of his early childhood. He said the following: *"My first school was the Delaney Elementary School located at Bowen Street at Michigan in the Carndolette area. My first teacher was Mrs. Jordan, a kindhearted "Roly-Poly" shaped lady."*

Clark enjoyed the schoolroom environment but he caught hell trying to get there. Kids use to pick on him because he wore his sister's "hand me down clothes" such as her Buster Brown shoes, black bloomers and white lace blouses. His undergarments were first discovered by outsiders when he tore his pants climbing over a fence. Frank Woodson, a neighborhood bully, called him a sissy because of his female underwear. He physically punched on Terry daily. One day Woodson really beat the daylights out of Clark and the lad ran home crying. His brother Ed who was a rough and tough little cat like his dad, told him that if he let Woodson beat him again that he was going to finish the job when he got home. Two whippings in one day would be more than Clark could take. Therefore, the next day Clark beat the devil out of Woodson. He left that cat lying on the pavement with a bloody nose, and two black eyes. The fallen warrior had a look of fear in his eyes that Clark never forgot. Clark left the battle feeling like he was badder than Leroy Brown, the toughest cat in town.

The Terry family belonged to the Corinthian Baptist Church which was more straight-laced than the New Covenant Sanctified Church located right down the street from their home. The sanctified people played tambourines throughout their services. They played with a beat and a rhythm on the tams that Clark can still feel in the marrow of his bones. He recalls how the neighborhood kids would congregate outside of the sanctified church on hot summer evenings and dance with deep respect to the beat of the tambourines. The rhythm of the spiritual songs still envelops him. He cannot escape that beat. Clark said: "I get mad with myself today if I miss a single beat during my performances."

THE ANATOMY OF A TRUMPET PLAYER

The tiny apartment in which the Terry family lived metaphorically shrunk as the kids began to mature. In an effort to give laughing room to his blossoming sisters Clark

Terry at the age of 9 moved into a house with his oldest sibling, Ada Mae, who had married Silas "Sy" McField a professional tuba player.

Dewey Jackson and the Jazz Ambassadors rehearsed at the McField house at least once every week. Young Terry was fascinated with the sound, pulsating beat and the rhythms that glued Jazz, Blues and Gospel together. Clark would stand in the shadow of the living room and listen with great intensity and fascination to the band during rehearsals.

Louis Caldwell, the trumpet player with the Dewey Jackson Orchestra would bring Clark several pieces of Mary Jane caramel candy wrapped in yellow waxed jackets every time the band rehearsed. As a bonus, Mr. Caldwell frequently gave Clark several shiny copper colored pennies to watch his horn when the band took a 15 minute break. One day Caldwell returned from his break sooner than expected and caught Clark red handed huffing and puffing on his trumpet in an effort to get a sound. Caldwell smiled and patted Clark on the head and said: *"Son, some day you are going to be a great trumpet player."* That compliment was the skeleton upon which Clark Terry hung his musical dreams.

Since Clark could not afford to buy a horn he constructed a homemade instrument by coiling on old water hose and attaching a kerosene funnel on one end to simulate the bell of a trumpet and he affixed a small water pipe on the other end for a mouthpiece. Admittedly the contraption did not look like a musical instrument, but it actually produced a trumpet like noise, according to Terry.

Clark Terry didn't get a musical instrument in his hands that he could temporarily call his own until he reached Vashon High School, a school for "Colored Students Only." Vashon was located on Garrison and McLead. Clark registered for the band on his first day in high school. He was anxious to learn how to play a real trumpet. Clarence Hydon Wilson, the bandmaster, said to him, *"I understand you want to play the trumpet. I'm sorry, we don't have a single trumpet left. But I've got an old valve trombone hanging over there on the wall that you can use."* Mr. Wilson assured young Terry that the fingering on that instrument was exactly like a B-flat trumpet. *"You can make a lot of noise with it."* He added: *"Take it and those big pleading eyes of yours out of my face."*

To Clark Terry's high school principal, Mr. "Fess" Williams the word "Jazz" meant, "Kill". Unlike the principal, many of Clark's classmates loved Jazz music as much as he did, hence they organized a clandestine jazz orchestra. Some of the men in the Dewey Jackson band had anted up enough money to buy Clark a secondhand trumpet.

The other young men in the orchestra were James Barr on guitar, the drummer was O.C. Reese. Benny Nelson was the clarinet player and the kid on the piano "88" was Walter Ray. The group met at different members' homes to rehearse after school. They called themselves "The Vashon High School Swingsters."

One of the most popular nationally known small bands during Clark's high school years was Fats Waller. The Vashon Swingsters learned most of the songs in the Fats Waller Band library note-for-note including Waller's own compositions such as **'Ain't Misbehaving', 'Black And Blue', 'I'm Crazy About My Baby', 'I've Got The Feeling I Am Falling'** and the ever popular **'Honeysuckle Rose'**.

The Vashon Swingsters piano player Walter Ray could play the piano exactly like Fats Waller. He was a very talented young man, and reputedly had the highest I.Q. of any student in the entire St. Louis school system at that time.

Poverty forced Clark to create ways to learn more about the techniques of trumpet playing. One of his vehicles for learning was Edwin Batchman, a fellow student in

154

the high school band. Batchman was from a middle class family that could afford to pay $2.50 a week for a half hour lesson with Gustov the German trained musician who taught trumpet at the St. Louis Instrument Company downtown. Gustov was also the first trumpet player in the section of the St. Louis Symphony Orchestra.

Clark's father only earned 40 cents per hour, therefore $2.50 for a half-hour music lesson was beyond comprehension. Hence Clark covertly got his music lessons by proxy from Edwin Batchman, whose nickname was "Batch". *Everytime "Batch" returned from his trumpet lessons with Gustov, he would brag, "Awe man!! You should hear what I learned today!" Clark, like the sly fox that he was, would say, "Well, what did you learn today?" Batch would retort: "Well, you can't do it, but it goes something like this..."*

Then Clark would side up to "Batch" and say: *"You didn't learn that! And if you did you probably can't do it right!"*

"Yes I can! Watch me!" "Batch" responded.

While "Batch" was displaying his new found knowledge, Clark was all eyes and ears. Everytime Batch would go downtown for his lesson, Clark would question him about what he had learned and "Batch" would braggartly spill his guts.

Clark Terry said to the writer: *"I don't think "Batch" had a clue that he was giving me Gustov's lessons by proxy. He was too busy showing me what he had learned and needling me because I couldn't afford to take lessons like him."*

Miles Dewey Davis who was six years younger than Clark also took lessons from Gustov while he was a student at Lincoln High School in East St. Louis. Davis' father was a wealthy dentist with a thriving practice across the Mississippi River in East St. Louis, Illinois.

Clark stated: *"There was a force inside me that compelled me to seek further knowledge about my instrument, therefore I would frequently ask older musicians questions. The older cats gave me a lot of misinformation because they feared the possibility of a younger cat taking their chair. For instance, I asked an old timer how I could improve my tone in the lower register."*

He replied: *"Son, you go home and sit in front of a mirror while you are practicing. And at the same time you wiggle your left ear. Not the right one! You also must grit your teeth as tight as you possibly can. The results you get will amaze you."*

Terry made the following observation: *"Being a naïve kid, I went home and practiced what the old cat had told me. It didn't help my tone, but I became a novelty. People began to remark, "Did you see that kid wiggle his left ear? Wow!"*

During his Junior year in high school, Clark Terry got an opportunity to play jazz with older professional musicians. Unfortunately, the kid's timing was bad because principal "Fess" Williams kicked him out of high school for impregnating Mayola Robinson, a classmate who he subsequently married. Clark's marriage prompted his brother-in-law "Sy" to take him on his first "Big Time" gig. "Sy" later introduced Clark to another maestro whose orchestra was known as Dollar Bill and His Small Change. Clark initially was one of the Pennies. He eventually worked his way up to be a Nickel. Later he played with Fate Marable, a piano and calliope player who was considered a giant among musicians in the St. Louis area.

Terry's first road gig was with Willie Austin, a trombone player and bandleader from St. Louis who had a job traveling with the Rueben & Cherry Carnival Show. Carnival and medicine shows during the big economic depression of the 1930's were a means of survival for many musicians. Both Roy Eldridge and Harry James got their early professional experience working with carnival shows in the 1920's. Eldridge worked with the Greater Sheesley

Carnival Band in 1927. James worked with his father Everett who was the leader of the band with a traveling circus.

The Reuben & Cherry Carnival Show was second heaven for Clark until it went bankrupt in Hattiesburg, Mississippi. There they were, stranded without any money in the middle of cotton country where most of the sharecroppers traded at plantation owned stores using scrip in lieu of dollars. As late as the 1960's, 100 years after emancipation, Dr. Martin Luther King, Jr., discovered that many of the plantation sharecroppers had never seen U.S. currency in their cotton-picking lives. They did not need to because they did all of their business at the plantation owner's store.

Luckily for Clark, a fellow with the Rueben and Cherry carnival who had a monkey act also owned a truck, the carnival band leader, Willie Austin, duped the "monkey man" into letting him and his lady friend ride in the cab of his truck, Clark and a couple of the other musicians rode in the rear of the truck with 15 active monkeys for 750 miles. Clark recalls, that ride was a real experience. During the course of the trip, band members learned to know the monkeys by their names and Clark swears that the monkeys knew them by theirs.

The next time Clark Terry hit the road it was with a big-time blues singer by the name of Ida Cox who headed the "Dark Town Scandal Revue". It was a great experience for a young musician. The revue traveled in an old, broken-down bus and every time they came to a hill everybody had to get out and push. A midget called "Prince" in the show just sat in the bus while the rest of the guys pushed their behinds off. One day Ida Cox asked the midget, *"What are you doing sitting in the bus while we are all out here pushing?"*

He answered: *"I'm too small to push."*

Ida retorted, *"We've got a tiny place for you to push*

here at the back of the bus. Follow me."

Clark has never forgotten that. Ida's sense of humor always cracked him up. When the Cox show terminated in St. Louis, Clark got a regular gig with Fate Marable who had one of the most celebrated riverboat bands of his day. Marable employed as guest stars such luminaries as Louis Armstrong. Fate himself was quite a character who had changed his name from Marble to Marable. *"Whenever Fate was going to fire a person,"* Terry recounts, *"he'd take one of the fire axes from the wall of the boat and put it in that cat's seat. When the guy came on board, we would start playing. Naturally the cat would figure he was late, and as he ran up to the band, we would break into playing* **'There'll Be Some Changes Made.'** Clark believes to this day that "getting the axe" an expression for getting fired, was actually coined by Fate Marable of St. Louis.

"I worked with Fate, not on the boat, but years after he came off the River. He was notorious for playing in difficult keys. He liked to play the song **"Cherokee"** *in F sharp which is a difficult key. He would watch you scuffle as you laboriously tried to make it through a few measures, he would then double up in laughter, because he got a big kick out of seeing people sweat.*

Marable carried a chain full of housekeys, he would throw them on your music stand to let you know when you were playing in the wrong key. He was both funny and diabolical", Clark Terry observed.

One of the last gigs that Clark Terry played before he volunteered to go into the Navy was with Benny "Peg Leg" Reed's Orchestra at the Spinning Wheel, a nightclub in Carbondale, Illinois. During that engagement the band got an afternoon gig to play for the high school's athletic May Day interscholastic program.

Miles Davis, a student at Lincoln High School, came down there with the Lincoln High Band which was under the direction of Elwood Buchanan, the bandmaster.

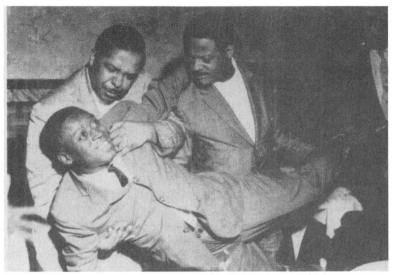

Horse playing backstage at the Club DeLisa in Chicago are Miles Davis, Lonnie Simmons and Clark Terry.

Clark Terry and Buchanan were drinking buddies. Clark describes Miles Davis at their first meeting as a kid so skinny that if he turned sideways you would mark him absent.

In spite of his size Miles was not shy. He was bold enough to walk right up to Clark Terry and asked him if he was a trumpet player.

Clark snapped: *"How did you know I was a trumpet player?"*

"I could tell by your embouchure and the hip way you are dressed with your bad coat, butcher boy shoes, and a bad hat cocked ace-deuce and wearing that beautiful scarf around your neck like a cobra", Miles retorted.

During that brief meeting Miles attempted to ask Clark Terry something about playing trumpet, Clark blew Miles away indicating that he did not want to talk about horns with all those pretty girls prancing around him.

Several months later Clark stopped by the Elks Club on Ewing Avenue in St. Louis. When he entered the foyer he heard a fantastic trumpet sound unlike anything he had heard before floating down from the second floor. He dashed up to the second floor and there sitting at the end in the trumpet section of the Eddie Randle band was little Miles Dewey Davis. Clark walked over to Miles and said: *"Hey! Man aren't you?"* Davis interrupted, *"Yes! I am the cat you brushed off down in Carbondale."*

In spite of their bumpy beginning, Clark became Davis' idol. Davis made the decision at the initial meeting that he would be as hip if not hippier than Clark as a trumpet player and a clotheshorse when he got his act together.

THE COLORED EXPERIMENT AT THE GREAT LAKES NAVY INSTALLATION

Clark Terry was among the initial guinea pigs of color to become part of the Camp Robert Smalls musical experiment in August of 1942. The manpower shortage during World War II and an order from President Franklin Delano Roosevelt

Clark Terry the sailor boy. to recruit Colored musicians was the springboard for the experiment. The National Association for the Advancement of Colored People and Negro newspaper publishers such as the Chicago Defender's John H. Sengstacke and Robert L. Vann publisher of the Pittsburgh Courier were the agitators behind the idea.

Camp Robert Smalls was a fenced in, isolated, Navy facility built in 1942 for "Colored Sailors Only." It was located within the perimeter of the greater Great Lakes Training Center on the North Shore approximately forty miles due north of Chicago, Illinois. Before they built Camp Smalls it was said that white recruits were men among men and Colored men were the cooks, waiters, and dishwashers.

Prior to 1942 people of Color were only permitted to serve in the United States Navy in the basement of the ships as mess stewards, waiters and orderlies. On land most were assigned to duties as stevedores loading and unloading hazardous supplies and ammunition.

On August 20, 1942, Leonard L. Bowden entered the United States Navy with the blessings of the Secretary of the Navy Frank Knox and the support of NAACP and Colored newspaper publishers. There was a prior verbal agreement that if he convinced some professional musicians to volunteer, he would be their bandmaster at Camp Robert Smalls, and director of the concert orchestra, the military marching unit and the swing band.

Leonard L. Bowden, was very qualified in that he was a professional musician of high standing in the St. Louis circle of the craft. He had played as a side man at the famous "for whites only" mob controlled Club Plantation in St. Louis with both the Eddie Randle Orchestra and the George Hudson Orchestra, the two top-flight jazz bands in that territory. In addition he had served as the Tune Town resident arranger, and conducted performances fronting the Mark Doyle and Boyd Raeburn Bands, both were lily-white organizations. He was also a warrant officer, having completed ROTC training at Tuskegee Institute in Tuskegee, Alabama where he had gained experience as the first student director of the band in the absence of the regular conductor.

Bowden recruited and brought with him to Camp Robert Smalls from St. Louis musicians such as Clark Terry, the Batchman Brothers, Edwin and Clifford, Charles Pillars from the Jeter-Pillars band, an orchestra best known in the Midlands for its 1937 Vocalion recording of **"Lazy River"**. Also in his entourage of recruits from St. Louis were the Wilkins Brothers, Jimmie and Ernie, after the war

161

Ernie became one of America's best jazz orchestra arrangers, he played and arranged for both the Count Basie and Tommy Dorsey Orchestras.

Clark Terry during his tour of duty in the Navy from 1942 to 1945 emerged as one of the most prominent of all the Great Lakes bandsmen. Some of the other musicians who accompanied Bowden to Camp Smalls had performed with some of the best known Colored jazz bands in the 48 states during the 1930's and early 1940's. The roster of bands that the new Navy recruits played with included: Duke Ellington, Count Basie, Cab Calloway, Jimmie Lunceford, Baron Lee, Nat "King" Cole, Lucky Millinder, Earl "Fatha" Hines, Andy Kirk, Fats Waller, Fletcher Henderson, Don Redman, Claude Hopkins, Benny Carter, Louis Armstrong, Louis Jordan, Chick Webb and Jay McShann.

Within nine months, after Bowden entered the Great Lakes Training Center in August 1942, both Camp Lawrence and Camp Moffet were turned over to the large influx of Colored recruits. Each of the camps had a 45 piece resident band. Camp Smalls Ship's Company Band "A", was directed by Bowden, at Camp Lawrence the Ship's Company Band "B", wing band was led by Eddie Penningar and at Camp Moffett, Ship's Company Band "C" swing component performed under the baton of Edwin Batchman, Clark Terry's high school classmate.

Clark Terry was in Band "A", along with Willie Smith the great first alto player with the internationally renown Jimmie Lunceford Orchestra. Camp Smalls "A" band was the best of the bands at Great Lakes, it was the musical representative of the Ninth Navy District and performed wherever official functions or special occasions required music.

The "A" band was so good that visiting bands such as Jimmy Lunceford, and Earl Hines would stipulate that the "A" band could not appear with them on the same program, the exception to the rule was Louis Jordan's Tympany Five, he always said: *"Let The Good Times Roll."*

Camp Smalls was named in honor of Robert Smalls, a Negro slave and Civil War hero who joined the crew of the Planter a Confederate transport ship in 1861 in Charleston Harbor, South Carolina. In 1862, in the still of a moonless night, he escaped with his family and piloted the Planter into the hands of the Yankee forces. The Union Navy made him a pilot in the United States Navy with the rank of Captain. He was later promoted to the rank of Commander. During the Reconstruction Period he was elected to the House of Representatives in South Carolina and later became a State Senator. In 1875 he was elected to the United States Congress where he served until 1887.

The Commander of Camp Smalls was Lieutenant Commander D.W. Armstrong, the son of General Samuel C. Armstrong, the founder of Hampton Institute in Hampton, Virginia, the school was built for Colored Freedmen in 1869. Hampton was the springboard for such Colored trailblazers as Booker T. Washington, the founder of the Tuskegee Institute; and Robert S. Abbott founder and publisher of the Chicago Defender. Abbott's nephew John H. Sengstacke also a Hampton graduate picked up the torch when Robert S. Abbott died in 1940. Sengstacke transformed the Chicago Defender weekly into a daily in 1957 and it subsequently grew into a national newspaper chain.

The success of the Great Lakes Experiment aided in opening the Navy Music School doors to Colored sailors at its Hampton, Virginia installation in 1944. The roads that led to and from the Great Lakes Training Center were not paved with "Good Times" and "Happy Hours", the thoroughfares were punctuated with potholes and barricades. Several events illustrate the point. Cab Calloway and his orchestra were invited to travel up the highway from Chicago to Camp Smalls at the Great Lakes by bus to entertain the sailors during a "Happy Hour" one Wednesday evening. Griff Williams the former orchestra leader who became a Naval officer shortly after the outbreak of World War II opened the show with some distasteful antebellum dialogue spewing from the exaggerated snow white lips of some charcoal painted puppets. Cab Calloway did not think his act was funny. Thus he said to the audience: *"If I had known I was going to be confronted with this kind of symbolic racism, I would not have shown. However, since I am here I will entertain the servicemen, but I will not accept any future invitation."* However, among the many others who entertained the sailors during "Happy Hours" were Lena Horne, Dorothy Donegan, Jimmie Lunceford, Ethel Waters and Louis Jordan.

To make bad matters worse, Eddie Peabody the famous banjo player who was also a commissioned officer in the Navy, decided that he would put on a minstrel show during a Sunday afternoon "Happy Hour". He wanted all the Colored musicians to smear their faces with black grease paint and enlarge their lips with white makeup in the fashion of Al Jolson the famous white jazz singer who frequently performed in black face when he performed such Dixie songs as **"Swanee"** and **"My Mammy"**. The sailors refused to kneel down on their knees to that level to follow his order. Peabody threatened to court-martial them for a mutinous act. However, cooler heads decided that such a serious charge would send a wave of disenchantment across the Colored communities and damage the war effort. (The Naval Counterintelligence officers during World War II ranked "Negroes" as a primary suspect group among subversives right behind the Japanese. The author thinks that their notions were racist in that we were at war also with Germany and Italy, but German and Italian American ethnics were not incarcerated like the West Coast Japanese Americans.)

Clark Terry said: *"The degrading of the Blue Jackets a Negro singing group, was orchestrated by a Negro First*

164

Class Petty Officer named Wayman Hatchcock who was in charge of preparing them for President Franklin Delano Roosevelt's visit to Great Lakes. *Prior to the President's arrival Hatchcock ordered the Blue Jackets to take off their whites and don blue denim overalls, work shirts and wrap their heads with red and blue handkerchiefs like those worn by southern cotton-pickers.* *He further ordered them to stand at attention on both sides of the road with rakes, hoes and shovels at their side.* *When they were signaled that the President was minutes away, they were to start raking non-existing leaves while singing and humming* ***"When It's Sleepy Time Down South"*** *as the presidential motorcade passed through.* *It was humiliating, but we did it and smiled through gritted teeth because we did not want to see the brother get busted."* *(Hatchcock was the former head of the Music Department at Morris Brown College in Atlanta, Georgia).*

Clark Terry said: *"Serving with hundreds of great musicians in the Navy was a great education for me and I am also certain that applies to many others.* *I learned the chord changes to most of the jazz tunes during the many jam sessions that I participated in while in the service.* *Fifty-three years after being discharged from the Navy those chord changes are still at my fingertips when I feel the need to call on them."*

Leonard L. Bowden with all of his musical experiences before and during his Navy service could not find a decent job outside of the Post Office after the war. His job at the Post Office was on the platform handling small bags. While working evenings for the government he enrolled in the Chicago Conservatory of Music where he earned a degree and started teaching school at Prairie View A & M and Florida A & M Universities in that order.

During World War II the bottom began to drop out of the big band jazz business. There was not much for Colored Army and Navy musicians to march home to. By the 1950's Count Basie, Louis Armstrong and Cab Calloway were fronting five and six men musical groups. The long 8 to 26 week hotel engagements never existed for Colored bands. Therefore, their livelihood was made riding buses and staying on the road 48 to 50 weeks per year if they were lucky. Ellington, Calloway and Basie kept their organizations on the road during the best of times throughout the 1920's, 30's and 40's.

Five thousand Colored musicians passed through Great Lakes between 1942 and 1945. It is projected that less than ten percent worked at their craft full time after being discharged from the Navy.

THE NORMAN GRANZ JAZZ EXPERIMENT

While Clark Terry was in the service of the "Jim Crow" United States Navy, Norman Granz was busy trying to integrate the jazz scene in Los Angeles, California. Granz was a businessman whereas, John Hammond who discovered and recorded Benny Goodman, Billie Holiday, Count Basie and other stars was satisfied with the cultural status quo, in that he was an establishment cat and the heir to the Vanderbilt fortune. He treated his jazz and blues music activities as a hobby, plus he got his cookies listening to it.

On the other hand, Granz had to borrow money to stage a jam session that turned out to be a very successful Jazz venture at the Philharmonic. Norman displayed his genius when he cut a deal with the Armed Forces Radio Service to record his first show which was beamed to American G.Is all over the world. Face up the event was very patriotic. On the back side of the event it was strictly business in that Granz was able to get possession of the sixteen inch celluloid acetates of the show and it laid the ground work for his subsequent recording venture. His next step was to get the G.I. show recorded commercially by

Moe Asch and distributed on the Asch Label.

The Asch Label had a very poor distribution system. Therefore, Granz made a deal with Mercury Records and they in turn distributed Granz's recordings on their label. This comfortable arrangement stayed in place for five years. Granz subsequently formed his own record label known as the Clef.

Following Clark Terry's discharge from the Navy he did not hook up with Granz because they were unknown to each other. Thus, he started working with George Hudson at the Club Plantation in St. Louis and while still working with Hudson, Clark received a call from Charlie Barnett, the millionaire orchestra leader who played music just for kicks in the Los Angeles area.

During a telephone conversation with Clark Terry the wealthy band leader said: *"Our mutual friend Gerald Wilson the trumpet player recommended you highly and I want to know if you would be interested in joining my orchestra which is now playing at Hermosa Beach in Los Angeles, California?"*

Clark responded: *"I would love to."*

Charlie retorted: *"Do you want to drive, fly or take the train?"*

Clark snapped back: *" I would dig taking the train because that will give me time to think about the gig while traveling across the country; moreover, it won't seem to me like I am rushing into some things too fast. Barnett sent me the ticket by airmail special delivery. I had a three-day train ride in which to contemplate my future."*

Gerald Wilson met me at the Union train station and whisked me right out to Hermosa Beach where Charlie's band was performing. The orchestra was on the air when we walked up to the bandstand. They were in the middle of a coast-to-coast radio broadcast; Charlie Barnett signaled that I should take my horn out of the case. He then announced, "And now, here is our new trumpet player Clark

Terry." I had to go right into a solo on an old standard. I don't remember the name of the tune, but I know it was a number that had a standard set of chord changes like maybe **"Lady Be Good"**, *so once I heard the verse there was no pain. That was Charlie Barnett's style of doing things. Charlie Barnett was a beautiful human being. In fact, we remained the best of friends right to the end. His mother Charlotte owned the controlling stock of the New York Central Railroad, and when she passed, of course all of the money went to Charlie. He used to give the guys in the band Buicks, Cadillacs, Packards and what have you for Christmas. Of course when I joined the band he was only giving out fifths of whiskey. That's the story of my life. Some of the guys who had been with him earlier said that Charlie ran through a million dollars in a very short time with his first orchestra. In addition to giving big gifts, he paid astronomical salaries.*

In 1948, Count Basie asked me to join his band, and

Count Basie, the piano man.

I jumped at the opportunity. I had not worked with the Count very long before he began to encounter financial problems. His managing agent in New York told him that he had to reduce the size of the band immediately. I cut out for St. Louis but I was only there for a short time when I received a call from the Count asking me to rejoin him at the Brass Rail on West Randolph Street in Chicago, and he asked me to bring along a good tenor sax man. I brought a young white boy named Bob Graff with me. The other guys in the

168

group were Freddie Green on guitar, Gus Johnson on drums, Jimmy Lewis on bass, and Buddy DeFranco on clarinet. When Bob Graff was recruited by Woody Herman, we replaced him with Wardell Gray. Basie had apparently been able to resolve his financial problems because in less than six months he started reorganizing the big band. While we were playing at the Strand Theater in New York City Basie said he needed another alto sax player. I told him I had a friend in St. Louis who could fill the bill. Count said, "Call him up."

I went directly to the phone and called Ernie Wilkins, who had never played an alto saxophone in his life, so I whispered to him via telephone, "Can you get an alto? Do you want to come and join Basie?" So Ernie borrowed one of those silver-colored high school students' saxophones (we used to call them the "grey ghosts") and came to New York the next day. The Basie band was still playing the old Kansas City book and I suggested to Basie that he let Ernie Wilkins write some new material. That might have been the best suggestion I ever made, because from that point on the band's reputation simply skyrocketed. Ernie wrote all of that great material for Joe Williams the singer from Chicago. And just think-all of those good things came as a result of a whispered telephone call.

In 1951 Duke Ellington dropped in on one of Count

Basie's Club dates to scout the band. Duke subsequently had his managing agent work out a deal where I would leave Count Basie because I was supposed to be tired, sick and needed a rest - he agreed to pay me $200 per week while I rested in St. Louis. This ploy was used because Duke wouldn't dare lift a guy out of his good buddy's band. Incidentally,

Duke Ellington

169

Count had just given me a ten dollar raise which made my salary a grand total of $125 per week, Count immediately took back that raise when I handed in my two week notice.

Duke Ellington made a big boy out of me because he literally threw me smack dab in the middle of one of the most awesome trumpet sections in the nation: William "Cat" Anderson, Harold "Shorty" Baker, and Ray "Little Dipper" Nance. All of those cats had their act together. Duke never wrote parts like first, second, third and fourth trumpet. He simply wrote Anderson, Nance, Baker, and Clark. Those were parts. You didn't know whether or not it was first, second, third or fourth until you actually played it. He started this system way back in the early days of his orchestra, because he found that Rex Stewart had an uncanny way of playing an E-natural on his horn. Stewart used to play it with a semi or suppressed valve, which is called a cock-valve. Therefore whenever that note appeared in a chord, Duke automatically gave it to Rex Stewart. It didn't matter if it was first, second, third or fourth, therefore your part could jump all over the arrangement. I'm sure you've heard many times that Duke's band was his instrument. It's true. Duke surrounded himself with talented musicians that he dug, and he used them to extend his feelings musically.

Let me tell you about Duke. He had a way of getting things out of you that you didn't realize you had in you. Let me give you an example. We were doing an album called "The Drum is a Woman", and Duke came to me one day and said: "Clark, I want you to play Buddy Bolden for me on this album."

I said, "Maestro, I don't know who the hell Buddy Bolden is!" Duke said, "Oh, sure, you know Buddy Bolden. Buddy Bolden was suave, handsome and a debonair cat who the ladies loved because he was so fantastic! He was fabulous! He was always sought after. He had the biggest, fattest trumpet sound in town. He bent notes to the tenth degree. He used to tune up in New Orleans and break

170

glasses in Algiers! He was great with diminishes. When he played a diminished, chord change he bent those notes, man, like you've never heard them before!"

By this time, Duke had me psyched out! He finished by saying: "As a matter of fact, you are Buddy Bolden!" So I thought I was Buddy Bolden.

Duke said, "Play Buddy Bolden for me on this record date."

I played the part and at the conclusion of the session, Duke came up to me and put his arms around my shoulders, and said, "That was Buddy Bolden."

Duke Ellington was a genius. His black skin prevented him from earning top dollar during his lifetime. There was a glass ceiling on where and how he could work. You wouldn't believe it, man, but there was a time, in the 1950's when we played the Hotel Flamingo in Las Vegas, that Duke had to walk through the kitchen in order to get to the bandstand, that was, in spite of the fact that his name was the top billing on the marquee. It was bigotry. It had a lot to do with blatant racism. They would not give this man an opportunity to play his music in the establishment venues. They wouldn't let him reach the height of his glory until he was dead and no longer a contender. He had to hustle and go out on the road and do one nighters right up until the end. He never had an opportunity to do a radio or television show like Benny Goodman or Tommy Dorsey and many other less talented musicians. They kept him scuffling and batting his head against brick walls. He had to be a courageous man to stand tall under the nonsense. He believed in his music and himself and he kept his band together until his health took its toll. Count Basie was caught in that same exploitive trap.

*Clark Terry left the Duke Ellington band in 1959 to join Quincy Jones in Europe in the Harold Arlen Blues Opera - **Free and Easy.** This show flopped thus Quincy and his orchestra were stranded and needed work. Norman*

Standing on the extreme left Budd Johnson; center standing second left on the staircase Clark Terry; extreme right with trombone is Melba Moore; sitting at the bottom of staircase second from the left is Quincy Jones.

Granz heard about their plight and put Quincy Jones in touch with Nat King Cole who was touring Europe, Nat in turn hired Quincy and his entire orchestra to back his show in Sweden, Denmark, Germany and Switzerland.

Terry returned to New York City in 1960 and became the first Black staff musician at NBC. That job was a by-product of an Urban League Affirmative Action campaign against NBC for not employing more minorities. The staff band subsequently became the Johnny Carson Tonight Show regular band. It would be difficult for me to categorize that band because we had to swing, we played classical music, and in fact, we had to play any kind of music that came along. It was a unique band to say the least.

After Skitch Henderson left the show by special request, NBC received many letters asking that I be made the bandleader. The management people at NBC thought that a Black leader would affect their southern market strategy... that was the reason they wouldn't give me the job. I also had the first shot at becoming the bandleader on the David Frost Show. But I turned that down because they wanted the band to play behind a screen out of sight of the television audience.

Some people might say that I'm picky. That's true - I won't play music if I have to sacrifice my integrity. My television exposure has led to my ongoing involvement in education. Listeners would write in requests for different members of the Tonight Show band to appear at various high schools and colleges. The instrument companies would sometimes sponsor these appearances and I soon found myself involved in the music clinic circuits full blast. It has really given me an opportunity to stay involved with jazz education and I love working with kids, so I get around to the universities and colleges, high schools and grammar schools all over this country and in other parts of the world, just to stay involved with the perpetuation of my craft. It's refreshing to me and it keeps me on the ball. I know that my craft is in good hands because the kids are getting into it.

One of the many things that I have found disturbing is the fact that Black kids are letting our music slip right through their fingers like sand on a beach. And it really worries the hell out of me that Black people are not interested in perpetuating their own cultural contribution to the arts scene which is jazz America's only original art form.

In 1982 Shin Watanbe one of the largest music publishers in Japan decided to commemorate the thirtieth anniversary of the 1953 Jazz at the Philharmonic concert by inviting the group back to perform at the Yoyogi National Stadium in Tokyo, Japan.

Many of the cats who made that 1953 gig had made their transition: Charlie Shavers, trumpet, died in New York City on July 8, 1971; Ben Webster, tenor sax, died in Amsterdam, Holland on September 20, 1978; Bill Harris, trombone, died in Coral Gables, Florida on August 21, 1973; Gene Krupa, drums, died in Yonkers, New York on October 16, 1973; and Willie Smith, alto sax, died in Los Angeles, California on March 7,1967. Roy "Little Jazz" Eldridge the great high register trumpet player and one of my mentors had retired because he was tired and his chops were gone.

Therefore, in an attempt to maintain the spirit of the 1953 jazz jam session Norman Granz selected as replacements such greats as: Harry "Sweets" Edison and Clark "Mumbles" Terry on trumpets; J.J. Johnson and Al "Talk to Me" Grey on trombones; John "Zoot" Sims and Eddie "Lockjaw" Davis on tenor saxophones; Joe Pass on guitar, Niels Henning Orsted Pederson on bass and Louis "Thunder" Bellson on drums. The headliner of the show was the great Ella **"Tisket-a-Tasket"** Fitzgerald, plus her trio which included Paul Smith at the piano, William "Keter" Betts on bass and Bobby Durham on drums.

When Clark initially signed up to work for Norman Granz he did not have the foggiest notion that he had

174

hooked up with a financial angel. Norman paid all the musicians a minimum that was double the stateside union scale plus travel, lodging and food.

Clark decided he wanted to take his new lady along with him on the tour, but he didn't have the bread for the ticket. Therefore, he asked Norman Granz if he would advance the money to buy her ticket with the understanding that he would pay him back out of his paycheck. To Clark's surprise when he finished the tour Granz was so pleased with his work he refused to accept the money for the ticket he had advanced for Terry's new sweetie.

In October 1991 Clark Terry had a serious hernia operation while in Switzerland. Granz got word about it and called Clark in the hospital to see if he needed anything. Clark assured Granz that everything was cool because he had insurance. However, when Terry returned home to the States from his hospital stay overseas there was a small envelope in his mailbox with a $5,000 check along with a note from Granz saying please use this bread as backup money.

The late Norman Granz is a man that Clark Terry will always hold in the highest esteem.

Left to right: Billie Holiday, Lester Young, Coleman Hawkins and Gerry Mulligan.

Cut VII
Lester "Prez" Young: The
Coolest of the Cool Cats

The "Prez" was born in Woodville, Mississippi on August 27, 1909 and he died at age 49 in New York City on March 15, 1959. The woman that he affectionately called "Lady Day" made her final transition on July 17, 1959 at age 44. Both of them were victims of an over abundance of wet and dry narcotics.

Both of Young's parents Willis and Lizetia were schoolteachers in a local one room frame potbelly heated sharecroppers' elementary schoolhouse in Woodville, Mississippi. His father was a college trained musician. He had studied at Alabama State College in Montgomery and also at Booker T. Washington's Tuskegee Institute in Eastern, Alabama near Montgomery.

Willis Young gave all of his children music instructions on the drums, trumpet, violin and alto sax. At the age of ten Lester was playing the bass drums like an old pro in the family orchestra. In 1923 at the age of thirteen he turned his attention and energy to the alto saxophone.

In 1926 the Young family escaped to the north in double time in an effort to catch up with the great post World War I Black migration. They moved north by train from New Orleans, Louisiana to Minneapolis, Minnesota "The State With a Thousand Lakes." They took up residence in a two story frame house located at 573 Seventh Avenue North which was smack dab in the middle of an integrated community. Shortly after the Youngs settled in that most Northern mid-western city they got a gig at a local dance hall that paid them ten dollars for a couple of hours work. Ten oversized greenback one dollar bills was considered big dough for country bumpkins of Color in the mid 1920's.

Charles "Truck" Parham, a friend of the writer's, a former semiprofessional boxer and tuba player who subsequently turned to playing bass fiddle at the suggestion of Sy Oliver. Oliver was the trumpeter and arranger for what later became the famous international Jimmie Lunceford "Jazz Express" Orchestra. Truck, who passed on June 5, 2002 at age 91 played his fiddle over the years with such musical stars as pianist Art Tatum, star trumpeter; Roy Eldridge, bandleader Jimmie Lunceford, and Earl "Fatha" Hines, the musical director at of the Grand Terrace Café Orchestra. He also gigged with Franz Jackson, a tenor sax combo leader, Dorothy Donegan, a pianist extraordinaire, and her trio, King Oliver, Louis Armstrong's mentor, Fats Waller and numerous other stars.

Truck passed the word to the Young boys that Minnesota was unlike Mississippi in that Black men could date white blue eyed, blond women without fear of being whipped or lynched. It was commonplace to see Black men on public streets with white female companions from time

Lester Young

to time, however, the Minnesota police with the force of a Billy Club would not let Colored brothers forget that they were still Black.   The twin cities of St. Paul and Minneapolis were many light years ahead of the rest of the country in that they accepted integrated couples as a given.

During the carnival season the Young family traveled with a minstrel show in which their father played trumpet and Lester played the drums and saxophone on tours that took them through the states of Minnesota, North and South Dakota, Kansas, Nebraska, and New Mexico.

Lester was unwilling to tour the deep south because of some of the horrid racial things like a lynching he had witnessed as a child before coming North, thus, he left the family band in New Mexico, and moved back east to Salina, Kansas which in reality was just two steps ahead of Woodville, Mississippi in race relations. While in Salina he met Art Bronson the orchestra leader, Bronson gifted Lester with his very first tenor saxophone. From January 1928 to January 1929 he toured the western territory with Bronson. He left the Bronson band in late January 1929 and returned to the family band in snow covered Minnesota. For reasons unknown to the writer he rejoined the Bronson orchestra in June 1930 and stayed with that jazz group for several months until the band ran out of gigs because the money began to dry up in tandem with President Herbert Hoover's economic depression.   The Bronson orchestra died in Wichita, Kansas and was respectively buried there.

In the summer of 1931 Lester Young was seen by Jabo Smith, the great jazz trumpeter who for years was Louis Armstrong's only musical challenger, Lester was playing both the alto and baritone saxophone with Eugene Schuch's Cotton Club Orchestra at the Nest Club in Minneapolis, Minnesota. Early in 1932 Lester signed on with the original Blue Devil Orchestra in Oklahoma City, and from that home base he did an extensive amount of barnstorming. Later, because of a financial misunderstanding he and several other members of the Blue Devil members cut out from the Devils and moved to Kansas City, Missouri where they joined the orchestra of Bennie Moten the great piano player and the composer of **Moten Swing.** Moten died in 1935 after having his throat cut by a jealous lover. The remnants of the Moten band was taken over by Count Basie who had been the number two piano player behind Bennie Moten with his organization.

While Lester was working with Basie in a small group he received an offer to join the very popular Fletcher Henderson band as a replacement for the great Coleman Hawkins who had left Fletcher for a much better gig in Europe. Young's stay with the Henderson Orchestra was

Standing at the extreme left is Count Basie and Lester Young is seated at the right.

short-lived because he was viciously criticized by other members of the band for not having a big round blustering tenor sound like the "Hawk."

Lester's next gig was with the Andy Kirk Orchestra featuring Mary Lou Williams at the piano, that gig aborted in less than six months, thus he rejoined Basie who was still working at the Reno Club down on Twelfth and Vine Street in Kansas City.

One very cold and windy night in January 1936 John Hammond the record producer and promoter was tooling around Chicago in his Rolls when he accidentally tuned in on his Motorola Golden Throat radio and picked up the sounds of a red hot and low down jazz band broadcasting from the Club Reno in Kansas City. They were playing some of the best jazz music that Hammond had ever heard. That jazz was emanating from Count Basie's nine-piece band, however they were blasting with the energy of a twenty piece orchestra.

Hammond's schedule would not permit him to get out to Kansas City until March of 1936. Upon entering the Reno Club he was immediately escorted to a seat at a ringside table next to the bandstand because it was the custom of that period to give white folks the best seats in the house whenever they visited nightclubs located in the Black community. That preferential white seating arrangement stayed in place for the first fifty years of the 20th century. Mrs. Rosa Parks and Dr. Martin Luther King and others led the battle against Jim Crow seating preferences for whites on the Montgomery, Alabama bus line in the mid 1950s.

In 1936 members of the Count Basie band personnel were Oran "Hot Lips" Page who was an incredible topnotch trumpet player, Joe Jones, a drummer who had no peers but had never been heard of outside of KC, Basie was at the piano, in the reed section were Jack Washington on the baritone, Lester Young on tenor and Buster Smith on alto, Joe Keyes played first trumpet and Dan "Slew Foot" Minor was playing the slide trombone. Let's not forget Little Jimmy "5 by 5" Rushing who handled the blues vocals for Basie like the pro that he was. The rhythm section was top cabin with Basie on piano rationing the ivories like gold nuggets, Joe Jones was wailing on drums and Walter Page was plucking his bass like chicken feathers. There was not another rhythm section in the country that could touch these three guys with a twenty foot pole. Although they all have made their transition I can still hear and feel their well synchronized steady as we go rhythmic swinging beat.

The Reno Club was located several feet below street level, its plate glass windows were decorated with signs advertising a shot of domestic Scotch for 10¢ a shot glass and imported Scotch for 15¢ a shot glass. Cold beer was 5¢ a mug. Hot dogs were 10¢, hamburgers 15¢ and 25¢ per sandwich if it was served at your table. There was no cover charge, and no minimum, however, they put on four floor shows, nightly that included eight beautiful chorus girls, plus Jimmy Rushing and Hattie Noels the vocalist. The full Count Basie band furnished the music for dancing and the stage shows nightly from 8:30 P.M. to 4:00 A.M.

The members of the band were paid $15.00 per week. Basie, the leader got $18.00. It was a seven night a week gig. Basie made extra money playing the Hammond organ at a local theater during the afternoon. He shared some of the extra money with two key players in his band.

John Hammond

Willard Alexander deserves as much credit as John Hammond in helping the Basie band escape from the low paying jobs in Kansas City. Willard performed a difficult task in getting the Music Corporation of America (MCA) organization to represent Basie who was literally unknown. The same plight had confronted Willard and the MCA people earlier when they brought the unknown Benny Goodman Orchestra into their stable. The Goodman group turned out to be a box office dream for MCA. Hence, they

183

decided to roll the dice with Basie.

After playing their final Kansas City date at the Reno, the Basie band boarded a chartered bus for the Grand Terrace nightclub at 3955 South Parkway (Dr. Martin Luther King Drive) in Chicago, which was the home base for both the Earl Hines and the Fletcher Henderson Orchestra.

The Grand Terrace had an elaborate floor show that would challenge the very best bands in the land. The promoter's real nightmare with the Basie group raised its ugly head on opening night when the band attempted to play the music arrangements for the top-flight floor show. It was then that Ed Fox the club manager discovered that half of the Basie band sidemen could not read a note as big as the Tribune Tower. Count Basie was included in that group of nonreaders. On the other hand, Buck Clayton read beautifully, Caughey Roberts, who was first alto was replaced with Buster Smith who was a top-flight sight reader. Herschel Evans could not read at all, Lester Young's father had taught him to read a speck on an ant's back. Jack Washington was also a good sight reader. Keyes a horn player was a non-contender because he was a drunk. Thus Basie had to cut him a loose. Jo Jones' natural born rhythm instincts were his saving grace. Walter Page and Charlie Williams were able to cut the mustard on their instrument.

Walter Fuller, Hines' former trumpet player and some of the other Hines cats actually played the show for the Basie bands while they were at the Grand Terrace. Following the Grand Terrace gig in the "Windy City" the band headed east by bus to New "The Big Apple" York for a debut at the Roseland Ballroom in December 1936. The Roseland was located in midtown Manhattan between Seventh Avenue and Broadway on West 52nd Street.

The jazz critics were waiting on the sideline salivating and gritting their teeth in anticipation of chewing up Count Basie and his orchestra like cotton candy in their

Lester Young, blew with wings.

The President's porkpie hat was his signature.

opening night reviews. Lucky for Basie the reviews were mixed with the exception of George Simon the prominent music critic who said: "The band was the most out-of-tune bunch of horn blowers that he had ever heard." Several nights later he recanted his story and admitted that his first impressions were wrong. Only the dead could refuse to pat their feet when they heard the Basie band swing out on **Moten Swing, <u>One O'clock Jump</u>**, and other Kansas City style blues numbers.

In 1937 at the suggestion of John Hammond, Freddie Green, the guitar player joined the Basie band as they were going through a reorganization process. It was then that recognition was given to the Basie band, following their residence at the Savoy "Home of Happy Feet" Ballroom in uptown Harlem in January 1938. The new sidemen who made a difference in the band were Freddie Green, guitar; Earl Warren, on alto; Buck Clayton and Harry Edison on trumpets; Benny Morton and Dickie Wells on trombones. However, their final stamp of approval came

Lester Young and Roy Eldridge, uptown in Harlem.

during a six month gig at the Famous Door nightclub in midtown Manhattan. The Famous Door was the hangout for the white boys and girls with the heavy Wall Street bread.

According to Douglas Henry Daniel's book entitled **Lester Leaps In**, Lester Young and Billie Holiday shared a dislike for John Hammond because of his not so covert arrogance and manipulative business methods. On the other hand, Hammond was Billie's number one booster in that he gave Billie her first big break and also advanced Count Basie the money he needed to hire her for his band. Hammond felt that Basie needed a female soloist to compliment Jimmy Rushing.

Lester flies again

In 1939 Billie made the following comments about Lester's musical influence on her performance. She said: *"I don't think I am singing, I feel like I am playing a horn. I try to improvise like Lester Young and Louis Armstrong... Lester sings with his horn. When you listen to him closely you almost hear the words."*

J o h n n y Griffin a friend of the writer and a former fellow Chicagoan said: *In 1957 I started gigging with Gene Ammons and Lester Young in Chicago at the Stage Door and the Crown*

Propeller Lounge. Both were located on East 63rd Street, and were owned by the same white people. Lester was a humorist, a quiet, soft, gentle man. He always called me Lady Griffin and when Sonny Stitt was around, he called him Lady Stitt. Lester had a peculiar habit of speaking of himself in the third person. For example, if he was telling you that he fell down the stairs he would say, "The Pres fell down the stairs and hurt himself." Pres was always anoth-

er person. Lester called everybody Lady. If he knew you, he made you a lady. Pres was always acting effeminate anyway, but he always had a woman

Lester Young and Jo Jones in the army.

on his arm, and the only skypiece I ever saw on his head was a pork-pie hat. Working with Lester Young was a gas when he was in good health and good spirits.

I had the unpleasant experience of working with Lester during his last days while he was here in Chicago. He was staying at the Pershing Hotel at 64th and Cottage Grove, and we couldn't get him to leave his room, except when we picked him up to take him on a gig in the evening. He would just lie in bed all day and listen to his old Count Basie records. Pres was so weak when we got on the job, we had to get him out the bed for a gig in the evening. We also had to almost lift him out of a chair up to the microphone. He had been into drugs earlier, but he also liked to drink gin. In his final days, he switched to a weird concoction of bourbon and wine. He seemed to want to drink himself to death. He had a death look in his eyes, like Coleman Hawkins. I saw the same look in Billie Holiday's eyes, and she died just a couple of months after "Pres" had passed on. It's a sad commentary on our lifestyle that people prefer to die rather than wrestle and laugh at life.

Laughing at life is impossible when you have been knocked off a pedestal after having been labeled the most photographed jazz musician in America by Ebony Magazine. "Prez' was drafted into the Army and then incarcerated in a Jim Crow U.S. Army jail at Fort McClellan, in Alabama and fed horsemeat and shit on the shingles as part of a daily diet. Buddy Tate, a Count Basie saxophone player contended that Young was being detained under some terrible conditions until Norman Granz intervened, insisting, that you got to let this man out of this dungeon..

The war ended in August 1945 and Lester Young was discharged after serving fifteen months. He became popular again but he never regained his pre World War II self-esteem.

Lester and Billie saying a last goodbye.

Ray Brown, Oscar Peterson and drummer in front of the London House on the corner of Wacker Drive and North Michigan Avenue in Chicago, Illinois.

Cut VIII
Oscar Peterson: The Pianist
With Forty Fingers

Oscar Peterson was born on August 15, 1925 in Montreal, Quebec, Canada. He was the fourth of five children to be created from a marital union between Daniel Peterson, a native of Tortola one of the British Virgin Islands, which is geographically located just to the east of Cuba and the Dominican Republic. Daniel married Kathleen Olivia John a West Indian girl from St. Kitts one of the Leeward Islands located southeast of San Juan, Puerto Rico. The couple had five children, all of whom were born in Canada and answered to the given names of Fred, their first born, followed by Daisy, Charles, Oscar and May the fifth and the Omega of the bloodline.

Oscar's father's skin pigment was charcoal Black. He came to Canada as a merchant marine and also a self-

Oscar Peterson and his father Daniel in Montreal, Canada checking their finger spread.

taught amateur organist. The old man insisted that all of his children take formal music lessons because he saw it as a means of breaking the yoke of a racial serfdom. Father Peterson was initially their music teacher. The second piano teacher was Oscar's oldest sister Daisy. Both Oscar and his sister Daisy Peterson Sweeney also studied with Paul de Marky, a Hungarian concert pianist trained by Franz Liszt, the piano virtuoso and composer. Young Peterson's classical training was both comprehensive and extensive.

When Papa Peterson came home from his ten to twelve day runs on the Canadian Pacific Railroad where he worked as a sleeping car porter, his first order of business was to have his children line up like little soldiers chronologically from the youngest to the oldest and play the music lessons that they had practiced during his absence. Oscar always passed the piano test without getting a whack across the knuckles even though he never had to practice as frequently and hard on the instrument as his siblings. The boy had a perfect ear for music in that he could play any song that he had heard once and certainly not more than twice.

Oscar cut his childhood teeth on classical music. He also played both the trumpet and the piano with some competence when he was only six years old. Some years later he learned that most good jazz pianists have a modicum of classical training. He could discern the European musical exposure or lack of it after hearing eight bars of any given jazz performance.

Oscar Peterson at the age of fourteen won a local piano contest and got a job playing on a weekly radio show.

At the age of seven Peterson was sidetracked from music with a serious bout of tuberculosis. He was confined in the Children's Memorial Hospital in Montreal for a period of thirteen months. Although the doctor that discharged him from the hospital told his parents he had been cured, his father demanded that the boy give up blowing the trumpet because in his opinion his lungs were too weak to handle a wind instrument.

According to Oscar his oldest brother Fred was the

best piano player in the family and his sister Daisy became a very gifted music teacher. As a matter of fact Daisy was Oscar's mentor. The question of who would have been the best jazz pianist in the Peterson clan will never be known because Fred died in 1934 at the age of fifteen, after being afflicted with a lung disease known during the early nineteen thirties as galloping consumption. Oscar was only nine years old at the time of his brother's death.

At age 14 Oscar won a prize in a local amateur piano contest and soon thereafter was offered a gig on a local weekly radio show where sometimes the white announcers would introduce him in what he later considered a racially demeaning manner.

At age 19 Oscar was invited to join the all white Johnny Holmes Band, one of the most popular white jazz orchestras in Canada. Peterson's red hot piano licks soon caused him to be billed as a feature attraction in the Holmes Orchestra.

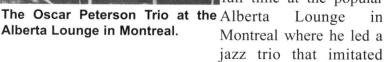

Oscar was permitted to drop out of high school in his senior year when he convinced his father that he would not simply be a jazz piano player but the best using Art Tatum's piano skills as a measuring tool. Since he was out of school he went to work full time at the popular Alberta Lounge in Montreal where he led a jazz trio that imitated

The Oscar Peterson Trio at the Alberta Lounge in Montreal.

America's Nat "King" Cole ensemble. The lounge was about the same size as the London House in Chicago which seated approximately 100 elbow bending patrons. Oscar's trio personnel included Clarence Jones, on drums, and Ozzie Roberts, on bass, and the big (250lbs. 6ft. 1 ½ inches tall) guy himself at the piano. Radio Station CJAP in Montreal did a 15 minute remote broadcast from the Alberta Lounge featuring the Oscar Peterson Trio every Wednesday night. That engagement lasted for approximately three years.

According to Norman Granz, he first heard the Oscar Peterson Trio on one of those remote radio broadcasts while enroute to Montreal's Dorval Airport in a taxicab. Granz originally thought he was listening to a disc jockey playing records until the cabdriver told him it was a live remote radio program coming from the Alberta Lounge. Granz with the snap of his fingers told the cabbie to forget the airport and take him directly to the place where that music was being hatched.

Norman Granz was immediately overwhelmed with the technical skills of Oscar Peterson. As a matter fact that night the tall collegiate looking white man in the white buckskin shoes and thick, bushy eyebrows extended Oscar an invitation to participate in a **Jazz at the Philharmonic** concert at Carnegie Hall in New York City. The event was scheduled to take place in September 1949 and Oscar was to appear as his surprise guest at the JATP event. Having a surprise celebrity guest at these gigantic jam sessions had become a tradition in that Granz had had Lionel Hampton as a special guest at the Hall in 1948 and Billie Holiday a year earlier.

Oscar Peterson who was accompanied only by Ray Brown* on bass. He opened his set that September evening playing *Tenderly* and tore the 57th and Seventh Avenue hall down. The crowd clapped, screamed, hollered, cheered and stomped. Peterson was taking his initial approval bows when he got a signal from Granz standing in the left wing of the stage to play three more numbers.

*Ray Brown was born in Pittsburgh, Pennsylvania

on October 10, 1926 and he apparently died in his hotel room while sleeping on Tuesday July 2, 2002 in Indianapolis, Indiana. A week prior to the Indiana gig he had completed a five day run at Joe Segal's Jazz Showcase in Chicago, Illinois.

Dizzy Gillespie paid a deserving tribute to Brown some years ago when he said. "Ray played the strongest, most fluid and imaginative bass lines in modern jazz during the 1950s and 60s with the exception of Oscar Pettiford. Ray's sounds were so deep and true you could hear the wood."

Brown has been featured on more than 2,000 recordings including some with his ex-wife Ella Fitzgerald, Frank Sinatra, Dizzy Gillespie, Charlie

Oscar Peterson and Ray Brown on stage at Carnegie Hall in New York City.

Parker and Duke Ellington. It was the twenty-two year old Jimmy Blanton, Duke Ellington's bass player that influenced Brown the most.

The late Ray Brown, 1926 to 2002.

In the October 21, 1949 edition of the Downbeat Magazine, its New York Editor Mike Levin reported, *"A Montreal citizen, Oscar Peterson, stopped the Norman Granz "Jazz at the Philharmonic" production cold in its tracks here at Carneige Hall. Oscar had balanced his large and bulky body on the* **The late Jimmy Blanton,** *piano stool much in the fash-* **1918 to 1942.** *ion of Earl "Fatha" Hines,*

199

and Nat "King" Cole. Peterson displayed a flashy lightning fast right and left hand. In addition he displayed a load of bop and (George) Shearing ideas, as well as a good sense of harmonic development. Moreover, he scared, some of the local minions by playing bop ideas with his equally fast left hand, which is distinctly not a common practice... Whereas some of the bop stars conceive good ideas but had to sweat to make them work. Peterson ripped them off with an excess of power which leaves no doubt about the technical excess (sic) he has in reserve."

Peterson had been inspired by most of the great piano players that came before him such as Art Tatum, Earl Hines, Fats Waller, Errol Garner, Willie "The Lion" Smith, Nat Cole and Mary Lou Williams. His contemporary pianist, Dorothy Donegan from Chicago had appeared in

The great Art Tatum, the piano player's player.

200

Fats Waller, the joyful keyboard tickler.

several movies and with Cab Calloway on Broadway and was as bad as she wanted to be but Art Tatum had set the pace for them all.

In turning the calendar back we discovered that during Oscar's teenage years his father brought home an Art Tatum record for him to hear. Young Peterson thought he was listening to four piano players. It blew his mind when he was told he was listening to just one man playing the piano. Oscar did not touch the piano keyboard for two months after that baptism in jazz piano playing. Many years later, Peterson met and watched Tatum work out on the piano and was mesmerized by what he saw and heard. Oscar's piano style can best be described in one word and that word is Tatumeque.

Following that September 1949 Carnegie Hall Concert Oscar Peterson became an integral part of the JATP Family in that Norman Granz became his personal business manager the same as he was for Ella Fitzgerald.

In addition to being a serious jazz artist he was a fun guy to work with according to Dizzy Gillespie who said: *"Oscar Peterson and I had a recording date, using just piano and trumpet. Knowing that I had to work hard because Oscar was there, I got to the recording studio early, to warm up properly. When Peterson came into the studio*

Mix two giants of Jazz with a pair of the music's greatest producers and the recording executive who got them all together and--mop!--you've a jazz summit. Shown here (L-R) are impresario Norman Granz, RCA Records President Ken Glancy, alto sax titan Benny Carter, piano master Oscar Peterson and Newport's George Wein at an RCA hosted gala at Carnegie Hall celebrating Granz's Pablo Jazz Festival concerts. RCA Records distributed Granz's Pablo jazz line.

I was lying down on my back with my horn across my chest pretending to be asleep. It was all planned in that I told the studio people to let me know when he arrived. Oscar said to me when he walked into the studio and saw me on the floor, 'Ain't no use trying to get your rest now, brother, you are in trouble today.' Gillespie retorted, Wait a minute before you go any further. I just want you to know the significance of what you saw. I have not been asleep; I stayed here all night waiting for you! You better be ready! I started popping my fingers for a rapid tempo for the first number. Oscar Peterson cracked up."

The Following Is How Oscar Peterson Was Seen And Heard By Others

The author with Wynton Marsalis.

Jazz Musicians

In 1998 Wynton Marsalis played a fund-raiser with Oscar Peterson.
Wynton's charm and lack of pretension
gave way to his sweating hands.

Miles Davis

He was truly awestruck by Peterson.

Miles Davis said Oscar Peterson is a bad
mother##…

Carmen McRae…Oscar Peterson happens to
be my favorite all-around pianist… Oscar is
the best.

When Earl Hines first heard Oscar
Peterson play his jawbones became
unhinged.

Nat Cole saw Peterson as a faster and seven year
younger edition of himself.

Norman Granz as a special novelty act
would put Oscar & Count Basie in duet mode for a concert.
Basie would play a few bars and Oscar would follow with
the same bar by bar. Basie said he was happy when the tour

was over because he could not go on the stage face to face with the dynamic Oscar Peterson every night without possibly having a nervous breakdown.

When Oscar Peterson first came thundering into the "Big Apple" with his dazzling piano technique a group of New York's best piano players gathered around the baby grand piano listening intently with both ears and waiting for the cutting contest to begin. That was not to be because when Oscar finished his exhibition Art Tatum said, *"Young man that was very nice. Now I would like to play a song for you."* The song that Tatum played for Peterson was: ***"Little Man You Have Had A Busy Day"***.

Coleman "Body and Soul" Hawkins

Cut IX
Coleman "Bean" Hawkins:
Mr. Body and Soul

Hawkins at 6 months.

Hawkins was born on November 21, 1904 in St. Joseph, Missouri which is a small college town located in the northwest section of the state of Missouri approximately 50 miles north of Kansas City. He was the only child of Wil and Cordelia Hawkins. His father was a skilled electrical worker and his mother was a public schoolteacher. The senior Hawkins was crushed to death in a freak acci-

W.C. Handy composer of the St. Louis Blues receives the key to the city from the mayor of St. Louis.

dent in 1922 while working on the edge of a Missouri River dock. Coleman was eight years old at the time that his dad made his premature transition.

Young Hawkins had been bathed in jazz blues and the ragtime sounds of Scott Joplin, "the Father of Ragtime". At age nine he thought that W.C. Handy's *St. Louis Blues,* composition was the Negro National Anthem.

His mother was an organist. Music floated around in his brain like an ant in a warm cup of milk. Teaching music to Coleman "The Bean" Hawkins was tantamount to releasing a fox in the henhouse.

The talented lad was made to study and practice the cello and piano for several hours daily. At the age of nine

Hawkins was gifted by his mother with a tenor saxophone for his birthday. The instrument was not popular nor was it in season. Serious music composers turned up their collective noses at the mention of the saxophone because it was thought of as a novelty marching band toy. Some music makers rated the saxophone several steps above a juice harp. The Hawkins family was out of sync with the music establishment's opinion about the saxophone in that period. By the age of 12, young Hawkins was making more money than a shoeshine boy playing the sax at college and high school dances with mature seasoned jazz musicians.

Some years later Hawkins also boasted that his musical training at the Washburn College in Topeka, Kansas and the Chicago Conservatory of Music put him light years ahead of his peers. Unfortunately up to this date, no records have been found to validate Hawkins' claim of having been enrolled as a student at either one of the aforementioned institutions.

At the age of sixteen, he could be found playing background music for silent motion picture films in the orchestra pit of the Twelfth Street Theater on Vine Street in Kansas City, Missouri. Headlining the Vaudeville act on the theater's double bill was Mamie Smith who was a special attraction because she was eating high on the hog as a result of the popularity waves that were generated by her unexpected hit record entitled **The Crazy Blues.**

Mamie Smith's clarinetist, Garvin Bushell suggested that the "Blues Queen" make Hawkins a regular member of her orchestra. The members of the Smith band were known as the Jazz Hounds. Bushell had recommended Hawkins because of his superior ability in cutting through difficult music scores. When Miss Smith offered the Hawk a regular gig he jumped at the opportunity and immediately agreed to go on the road with her act which was crisscrossing the country.

A year later in New York City Joseph "Kaiser"

Sixteen year old Coleman Hawkins is standing second from the right next to Mamie Smith with her Jazz Hounds.

Marshall, the drummer with Fletcher Henderson's recording ensemble that accompanied Ethel Waters, the blues singer, on the Black Swan Records. Again Bushell suggested that Hawkins be given serious thought in his plans for expanding the band. In the winter of 1923 Fletcher began the process of organizing an eleven piece jazz orchestra. In the spring of 1924 Hawkins became a member of the Fletcher "Smacks" Henderson Orchestra. The Henderson band by all musical standards was the best Colored jazz band in the United States. Duke Ellington's five piece combo was not even a speck on the music scene at that time. On the other hand, it was being quietly said among show business people that Henderson in fact was the Colored Paul Whiteman.

The Fletcher Henderson Orchestra, 1924. Left to right, Howard Scott(trumpet), Coleman Hawkins (tenor saxophone), Louis Armstrong (cornet), Charlie Dixon(banjo), Fletcher Henderson (piano and leader), Kaiser Marshall (drums), Buster Bailey (clarinet and saxophone), Elmer Chambers (trumpet), Charlie Green (trombone), Bob Escudero (tuba), and Don Redman (arranger and alto saxophonist).

White America's music establishment had already crowned Paul Whiteman the King Of Jazz basically because of the many star musicians he had employed. The 'King' premiered George Gershwin's, *Rhapsody In Blue* in February

1924 at Aeolian Hall in New York City.

On the other hand, the Fletcher Henderson group won out over 20 other band entries Black and white who auditioned for a steady gig at the "for whites only" Club Alabam which was located in Midtown Manhattan on 44th Street. The Henderson Orchestra furnished the music for the stage show which was billed as the "Creole Follies", the entertainers in the production were Mulattos and Octoroons all of whom were very light skin Colored individuals who out of costume frequently passed for Caucasian.

The Roseland Ballroom in New York City, New York.

By the middle of the roaring twenties Coleman Hawkins had mushroomed into an extraordinary talented musician. In fact, he was a man for all seasons in that he was very proficient in playing several instruments including the piano.

In the early fall of 1924 Fletcher Henderson's orchestra was selected for a highly prize gig playing six nights a week at the beautiful "for whites only" Roseland Ballroom. The dance palace was located on 51st Street between Seventh Avenue and Broadway in Midtown Manhattan. The expanded Henderson Roseland Orchestra included the following musicians: On trumpets were Elmer Chambers, Howard Scott, and Louis Armstrong who Henderson personally sent for in Chicago, in the reed section there was Buster Bailey, Don Redmond, and Coleman Hawkins; on trombone: was Charlie Green. In the rhythm section there was: Fletcher Henderson, piano; Charlie Dixon, banjo; Ralph Escudero, bass tuba; and Kaiser Marshall, on drums.

Shortly after Louis Armstrong joined the Henderson band Hawkins went out of his way to personally make fun of him and his countrified ways. The college trained Hawkins actually turned his nose up at the lower bred Louis Armstrong because he considered him to be a low life New Orleans urchin from Jane Alley. In the Crescent City Jane Alley was known as the bucket of blood because it was the stomping ground for Jack The Knife type characters. Coleman treated Armstrong like a leper who had been contaminated with HIV virus.

Louis Armstrong, the original king of the high "C" in jazz.

Louis Armstrong was a very proud, creative, and sensitive man who managed to keep his cool during Hawkins' verbal attacks. Thus, it would have been difficult, if not impossible, for Louis to ever forget or forgive Hawkins for both the personal and professional put-downs.

Although Armstrong only played with the Fletcher Henderson Orchestra for a little less than one year, his return to Chicago on November 9, 1925 was that of a hero when he joined his wife Lil Armstrong and her band at the Dreamland Café located at 3518-20 South State Street, which was commonly known as "The Stroll" by the brothers and sisters of the hood. However, before Armstrong left Henderson he

213

had influenced almost every cat in the "Big Apple" who heard him play including Coleman Hawkins. Hawkins became a better tenor sax man because of "Pops". Some years later "The Bean" admitted that most of his music ideas came from non-reed players like trumpet players and keyboard plunkers.

While playing in Toledo, Ohio near the end of the Roaring Twenties the local cats told Hawkins about a young seventeen-year-old partially blind pianist who literally made piano keys talk. Hawkins and several other sidemen from the Henderson band decided to drop by this after hour joint where the teenage wizard wiped the keyboard like creamed white potatoes. The whiz kid was Art Tatum. Hawkins lost his socks without removing his shoes while listening to Tatum's lightening fast techniques. He dug the way that the young genius used the harmonic underpinning of a tune as opposed to its melody as a basis for improvisa-

Art Tatum

tion. Tatum's approach to adlibbing shortly became evident in Hawkins' playing.

One afternoon in the late fall of 1934 at Local 208, the Colored Musicians Union Hall at 3934 South State Street in Chicago, Fletcher Henderson told, George Dixon, a trumpet and sax player with the Earl Hines Orchestra the following:

"You know Coleman Hawkins is leaving the band."

"Leaving?" George retorted, *"You have got to be kidding! Where's he going?"*

214

Coleman Hawkins deep in his element.

"To Europe," Henderson replied.
Dixon snapped back: "I've got just the man
for you, read this letter."

George had just received an airmail special delivery letter that morning from Lester Young asking him for help in finding a new gig. He further indicated in the missive that he was ready to leave Kansas City, Missouri on the first train smoking. Without mincing any more words the two men both headed straight to the public phone in the hallway of the union hall where George made a collect phone call to Lester.

Fletcher Henderson made arrangements during the telephone conversation for Lester to meet him in Detroit at

In flight with Lester Young.

the Greystone Ballroom on Saturday, December 29, 1934. Henderson hired Lester sight unseen via the telephone. However, the guys in the Fletcher Henderson Band did not like Lester Young's style of playing. They were accustomed to Hawkins' big broad tone and they couldn't adjust to Lester's light and airily sweeping style. Finally Lester got tired of the bull and left the Henderson band in disgust and joined the Count Basie Orchestra.

George Dixon had first met Lester Young in 1932 in a cutting contest at an after hour joint called the Subway in Kansas City. That after midnight jam session went on non-stop to shortly before noon. Cutting contests were a common practice in those days whenever a group of cats got together after their regular gigs.

Seventy years later I cannot erase the memory of seeing musicians in tuxedos and their ladies in long evening dresses going home during my elementary school lunch break.

A little more than a decade after the Henderson gig

Count Basie standing on the extreme left and Lester Young is seated on the extreme right.

"Satchel Mouth" Armstrong and Coleman Hawkins were invited to participate in a star studded "Battle of Horns". It was a Jack Hylton promotion. Hylton was a famous English bandleader and concert promoter before World War II. Louis said, "He did not believe that Hylton who had been a friend had acted in his best interest." Thus, he severed his relationship with Hylton in 1935 because he felt that Hylton's primary interest was raking in the gold and secondly making a weak attempt at building a bridge over the troubled waters that had separated him and Hawkins. Unfortunately, the depth of the troubled water was too deep and much too salty for the twains to ever reconcile.

This writer got an earful of Hawkins' updated sax style when he caught him in the late fall of 1939 on a gig at Whites Emporier in Chicago shortly after he had returned

A Blues - Jazz jam session. Left to right: Ben Webster, Benny Carter, Leon "Chu" Berry and Coleman Hawkins.

from Europe. The cabaret where the Hawk appeared was on the second floor at 309 East Garfield Boulevard in Chicago. It was jammed tighter than sardines in a can. It was the Hawks' first gig in the Middle West following his return to the United States from Europe where he had lived from 1934 until the late summer of 1939. His tenancy as an expatriate was cut short by World War II when the Germans invaded and subsequently occupied Poland in September 1939.

Whites Emporier nightclub was packed tighter than gunpowder in a canister while musicians waited to welcome the Hawk. In the meantime, America slept as President Franklin D. Roosevelt secretly prepared our country to join Britain in the war against Nazi Germany and her allies. The great Coleman Hawkins opened his first set that night playing his version of the immortal *"Body and Soul"* written by John Green in 1930. The only sounds in the room other than the sound of his gold plated tenor saxophone were the soft sighs of joy emanating from the salivating zoot suit wearing cats and kittens. Otherwise, you could hear a fly piss on cotton. The general public could not get near Whites Emporier for the first week, because every musician in Chicago and its environs who could lift a horn or plunk a piano keyboard was there early every night gawking in amazement at the performance of this genius and his tenor saxophone.

Hawkins did not invent the tenor sax, but he single-handedly turned it into a jazz solo instrument. He was a formidable technician with a natural talent that he had taken the time and patience to develop. There is not a tenor saxophonist living or dead who ever attained the full, rounded power of the great Coleman Hawkins' instrumental tone. Some contenders for his throne in those days were Ben Webster a Duke Ellington star; Leon "Chu" Berry, who was an ace for both the Fletcher Henderson and Cab Calloway orchestras. Bringing up the rear were Herschel Evans and

Lester Young, both of whom starred in the Count Basie band.

In 1941 Coleman Hawkins came back through Chicago enroute to the Fox Head Tavern in Cedar Rapids, Iowa, where he had been booked to play a seven week gig. He stopped off in Chicago long enough to find a good alto sax player and luckily met Delores Sheridan who became his first and only wife. Someone recommended Johnny Board an alto sax man who had attended DuSable High School with the writer.

In a mellow mood Coleman Hawkins' light brown eyes shine through.

An opportunity to work with the great Hawks sextet was every musician's dream. The Hawkins group worked at the Cedar Rapids nightclub six nights a week, and when they finished playing the last set on Saturday night, Johnny and the Hawk headed back to Chicago because the Hawk

Left: Bud Freeman, a founding member of the all white Austin High School Gang Band observes Coleman Hawkins during a break in a recording session.

did not want to spend his entire weekend in a hick town which he considered the pits.

Coleman and Johnny Board would travel back to Chicago alone; the other fellows in the band always stayed over. The Hawk bought a brand-new Chrysler Imperial

Johnny Board, second from the left and Coleman Hawkins at the extreme right; at the Fox Head Tavern in Cedar Rapids, Iowa.

every year up until they stopped making them during World War II, he considered the Cadillac too vulgar and the Rolls Royce too conspicuous. As the two men glided along the road, (there were no super highways) Hawkins would sip from his quart whiskey bottle of Old Grand-dad. By the time they reached Chicago the Hawk would have consumed an entire quart of liquor by himself. The roads were narrow, some sections were dirt filled in those days, but the Hawk drove between eighty and a hundred miles an hour. On the other hand, for some strange reason with the Hawk behind the wheel, Johnny Board never worried about anything going wrong.

Hawkins' real reason for returning to Chicago every weekend was to spend some time with Delores Sheridan, a pretty little southwest side Irish girl. She had recently graduated from a Catholic high school. He subsequently married her in New York City on June 21, 1943. They had three children, Collette in 1945, Mimi in 1947 and a son Rene in 1949.

Johnny Board said: *"Hawkins never wrote out a complete musical score for the band. He would bring in an*

Hawkins and his children, left to right Mimi, Rene and Collette.

alto part one night, a piano part the next and so on, until everyone had a part. I never figured out how the Hawk could remember the part he had written the day before or the day before that. Ordinarily an arranger will write a score and then he can see at a glance exactly who is playing what note at any given time, but to write it in segments as Hawkins did was mind-boggling."

In the mid-forties, Coleman Hawkins toured with Norman Granz's Jazz at the Philharmonic. Granz said: *"Hawkins is the first major performer on his instrument. He created the full bodied tenor style, his is the most emulated sound other than Louis Armstrong."*

On another occasion Bud Freeman, a tenor man who had worked for both the Benny Goodman and Tommy Dorsey Orchestras said to the writer: *I got my first in-depth lesson on the tenor saxophone while listening to Coleman Hawkins play at the Graystone Ballroom in Detroit, Michigan. On that occasion Hawkins told me I needed to develop a tenor style of my own. I noted that in addition to Hawkins being a great musician he probably was one of the* *most schooled musicians around, black or white. He had a degree in music, he played the piano, violin and cello, but he didn't really get his jazz wings until he listened to the great Louis Armstrong, who was to the trumpet what Coleman became to the tenor saxophone. Hawkins was a great melody man. He could take a song like **"Body and Soul"**, which was written by John Green, and put his talent around that construction, and develop a masterpiece. In fact, if you listen to Hawk, you'll find him doing his greatest work when he sticks very, very, very close to the melody. Lester Young also loved melody. He just had a different sound and a different way of expressing how he felt about it. Lester was a quiet, soft, gentle man, while Hawkins was very robust, outspoken, and in many instances, a very angry man. Ben Webster was also a very soft man, although when he got drunk, he could be vicious, a brute and cruel. But he was a lovely fellow if you knew him, and I knew him as a sober guy. Webster and I became very, very close friends.*

*Ben Webster was very strongly influenced by Coleman Hawkins. He was a melody man and would not go too far out harmonically speaking. If you listen to his records, you'll see that his best songs were those with strong melody lines, and near the end of his life, say the last five years, most, if not all, of the things that he recorded were lovely melodies with strong lines. He wasn't strong on improvisation. It's almost a contradiction when you think about it. The song that really made him famous was **"Cotton Tail"** which he recorded when he was with Duke Ellington, and **"Cotton Tail"** is not melodic, but a take-off on the chord structure of an upbeat standard called **"I've Got Rhythm."*** The words were by Ira Gershwin and music by his brother George Gershwin.

Genetics and lifestyle weigh heavily in determining one's longevity. Whisky and women had contaminated Coleman Hawkins' maternal genes. His mother lived to enjoy her 95th birthday and his grandmother lived to the ripe old age of 104. Both women were lucid until the day that they finally closed their eyes.

On the other hand Hawkins died at the age of 64. His last day on this planet ended as follows: He was scheduled to play a gig in the New York area on May 18, 1969. He was found by a friend crawling on the floor inside his apartment toward the door with his hat and jacket on and dragging his horn case alongside of him because he could not walk. He was both deathly ill and drunk.

Coleman Hawkins died in the early morning hours on May 19, 1969 in the hospital. The doctor said that bronchial pneumonia was the immediate cause of his death. Many of the great names of jazz attended the funeral. "He had a presence, even lying there in the casket," saxophonist Russell Procope, the Ellington alto sax man for thirty years, later told critic Stanley Dance. "I looked at his hands the way they were folded together, and I thought of how much they had achieved."

Shortly before he died, he had bought a new saxophone. It went back to Charlie Ponte's instrument shop on New York's 46th Street because he had not finished paying for it. Ten years later, it still hung in the window there. But it was not for sale.

Even after death, he will always be remembered by some of us old cats as "The Bean" which is a nickname that implies the best and only.

Ben "Cotton Tail" Webster

Cut X
Ben Webster: The Swinging Brute

Benjamin Francis Webster was conceived in Chicago on or about June 10, 1908. He saw the first light of day on March 27, 1909 in Kansas City, Missouri, the midwest cradle for both the down-home blues and the world of jazz. Baby Ben was delivered at 12:02 p.m. by a midwife in the home of his mother's aunt, Agnes Johnson at 2441 Highland Avenue.

Walter Webster, the boy's father first met Mayme Barker his future wife and a public schoolteacher from Kansas City, Missouri in 1907 at a social gathering held at Bob Mott's Pekin Temple of Music located at 2700 South State Street in Chicago, a metropolis that was also known by the brothers and sisters as Abraham Lincoln's City By the Lake. Miss Barker was in the "Windy City" studying

The Pekin Temple of Music at 2700 South State Street in Chicago. Where Shelton Brooks in 1917 composed *"The Darktown Strutters Ball"* and *"Some Of These Days"* in 1910 and 1917.

for an advance degree at the University of Chicago.

Ben's father was a tall 6.2 inch handsome dude who wore a tilted straw-hat and walked with a jazzy strut. He was an articulate, smooth talking streetwise guy who chose to share some of *Carl Sandburg's City Of The Big Shoulders* best smelling perfumes for the nostrils of his Kansas City country girl.

Following a short courtship, Walter begged Mayme on bended knees to marry him and melt away into Shangri-La. She accepted his proposal of marriage with a grin spread across her beautiful oval shaped copper colored face like grape jelly on white bread. Mayme had one contingency other than faithfulness and that was the marriage to her Black Knight had to take place in her own West Point Baptist Church in Kansas City, Missouri on Sunday September 17, 1907.

Following the wedding ceremony Walter Webster promptly whisked his cinderella off to Chicago via a railroad train in a dust filled Jim Crow car next to the coal car which was located directly behind the steam driven loco-motive engine. Their Shangri-La turned out to be a one room kitchenette apartment on the southeast side of the city's Black Belt. They shared a community bathroom and kitchen with three other families. In less than six months into the marriage Mayme discovered that marrying the Black Knight was a horrible mistake in that she had not married a fun loving and kind family man but a stone cold abusive, alcoholic skirt chaser.

Aunt Agnes got wind of her niece's dilemma with this man that she had married through a childhood girlfriend who worked as a schoolteacher for the Chicago Board of Education. Agnes immediately came to the rescue of the deflowered bride and literally kidnapped the pregnant woman and carried her back to their family home in Kansas City, Missouri.

Although Mayme's divorce papers had been filed the legal process had not been finalized when Ben was born, thus, the family decided overwhelmingly against permitting Walter Webster's face to be seen even as a shadow on the wall when the first family portrait was taken with the baby. Seven months after Ben's birth Mayme returned to her job as a kindergarten schoolteacher in the Kansas City Public School system. She was so bitter about her marital experi-ence she vowed to remain a divorcee and devote the balance of her life to her son.

Ben Webster was not permitted to have the typical lifestyle of an ordinary child in his community in that he was chaperoned and guided by his mother and Aunt Agnes at the age of five into taking both violin and piano lessons. He quickly learned the basic fundamentals of both instru-ments. The two women drilled a notion into the boy's head of his need to learn to play the diatonic scales in all of the major and minor keys. They also made it mandatory that he practice his music lessons in the Matthews Piano Method book for a minimum of one and a half hours daily.

The Kansas City three corner gang in his neighborhood began calling Ben a sissy because when his feet hit the street he was always dressed to the nines and looking like his mother's little prince. His walking gait was always straight-laced and prissy as he carried his violin case to and fro to the home of Mrs. Mable Simpson, his music teacher. To counteract any misnomer about his masculinity Ben at a young age went through a metamorphosis in that he transformed his persona from a nice smiley, squeaky clean face kid to that of a sun-baked sourpuss brute. Young Ben was muscular and built like a bantamweight boxer. He had the physical strength and the will to take on the street urchins one by one with the drop of a cap. He had no qualms about getting into a bare knuckle fistfight with any tormentors who did not believe that grits were white and fat meat was greasy.

In spite of his Dr. Jekyll and Mr. Hyde personality, in the classroom Ben's behavior was that of a model student in that he received three double promotions. The boy graduated from Crispus Attucks Elementary School at the age of eleven in 1921. Three years later he graduated from the Sumner High School in Kansas City with a B plus average and from there he went on to earn a bachelor's degree in American Literature from Western University in Kansas on June 2, 1927. At Western University he was also awarded athletic letters for the positions that he played on the varsity football squad.

Despite his undergraduate college training his mother and aunt felt that he was still too naïve in his knowledge on racial matters, therefore they sent him off to Wilberforce University in Ohio. It was an institution school that recruited middle class Negro students nationwide. During the two years he was enrolled at Wiberforce he was taught about his own culture as a person of the Colored persuasion in addition to the history of Black people in America generally. It was paramount in his mother's opinion that he also meet people of Color that were his educational and cultural peers.

Following his college years in lieu of going into teaching as a profession he opted to play jazz music for a living with territory bands in the Midwestern and the Western states. Luck was on his side in Albuquerque, New Mexico because it was there that he met and joined Willis Young, the leader of a family orchestra. He was hired as a piano player, Lester Young was playing sax in his father's band at that time. "Professor" Young who was educated at the Booker T. Washington Tuskegee Institute became over-whelmed with Webster's general demeanor and talents, thus

Andy Kirk, leader of the Clouds of Joy.

he took him under his wings and gave him some private music studies on both the trombone and tenor sax-ophone. In the nineteen thirties Webster moved on and played with a succession of excellent bands includ-ing Jap Allen in 1930, Blanche Calloway (Cab's sister) in 1931, Bennie Moten the composer of the *Moten Swing* in 1931-32; Andy Kirk in 1933; Duke Ellington briefly in 1935; Cab Calloway in 1936-37; and in 1940 he rejoined the Duke Ellington Orchestra during a period that became known as the Ellington orchestra's vintage years. He stayed with the Duke from 1940 to 1943.

It was in the Duke Ellington Orchestra that Ben Webster gained his national reputation as a tenor saxophone player via Ellington's composition and the band's record-ings. That period revealed some of Ben's very best work on such compositions as *"Cotton Tail;"* where Webster pushed the right notes and set the tempo that made *"Cotton Tail"* a masterpiece built around the chord changes of George Gershwin's *"I Got Rhythm."* He gave his recreation of the Gershwin song a permanent identity that stood on its own.

Billy Strayhorn, pianist, arranger and composer of "Take The a Train", "Just A Sitting And A Rocking", "Lush Life", "Passion Flower"' and other popular hits.

Webster was also featured with the Ellington Orchestra on such compositions as *"Chelsea Bridge"*, by Duke Ellington; *"All Too Soon"*, by Duke Ellington and Carl Sigman; *"Congo Bravo"*, by Duke Ellington and Juan Tizol; *"C Jam Blues"*, by Duke Ellington; *"Just A-Sitting and A-Rocking"*, by Billy Strayhorn , Lee Gaines and Duke Ellington; and *"What Am I Here For?"*, by Ellington and vocalist Frankie Laine.

Webster became the fifth member of what had been historically a four-man reed section. Ben was anointed as the Ellington Orchestra's first major tenor saxophone star. Ellington frequently said that: "No man in the band had ever played more beautiful - or caused him more trouble than Ben "The Brute" Webster."

Ben "The Brute" Webster

The following observations were made by two of Webster's band mates who chose not to go public for fear of being beaten up by the "Brute," they said: *Ben's drinking and short temper often got him in trouble. Once while in a wild drunken rage he pushed a beautiful young woman out of a window at the Dunbar Hotel in Los Angeles, California. The woman survived the fall but was hospitalized for several weeks with serious injuries. Duke Ellington intervened on Ben's behalf and managed to keep him from having to serve hard time in jail.*

In retrospect, when Ben Webster joined the Ellington Orchestra for the second time in 1940 the Duke said: *Ben Webster was really making some mighty important statements with the tenor saxophone. Therefore I thought it was most fitting for me to add him to our reed section. He immediately made the sax section more mature, he put a grip on its togetherness like no other section that I had ever had before or since."*

233

Duke Ellington's reed section. Left to right: Barney Bigard, Johnny Hodges, Otto Hardwick, Ben Webster and Harry Carney.

Webster had the benefit of more academic training than any of the other members of the Ellington band including the Duke who was a dropout from the Armstrong Manual Training School in Washington, D.C. Ellington did not make the cut that permitted him to matriculate at the Dunbar Academic High School for Colored students in the District of Columbia. The school was named after Paul Lawrence Dunbar, the great Negro poet. Dunbar was and still is the alma mater for many of the District of Columbia's elite movers and shakers.

Ellington further said: *Billy Strayhorn and Ben Webster almost strong-armed me into bringing Jimmy Blanton, into the orchestra, Blanton was a young man who at the age of twenty revolutionized bass playing.*

Dempsey J. Travis, a professional musician before and during World War II and shortly thereafter became a Roosevelt University graduate, businessman and writer. He said: *I heard and saw the Duke many times during his vin-*

tage years. However, there is no night for me that parallels Friday, December 6, 1940 at the Parkway Ballroom in Chicago at 4457 South Parkway (Dr. Martin Luther King Drive). It was approximately nine years after my mother Mittie Travis first took me downtown to see Duke at age ten on Friday January 13, 1931 at the Oriental Theater in Chicago.

On the Friday night of December 6, 1940 several musician friends and I stood just a few inches from the center of the bandstand where Ellington and his orchestra, were rocking in rhythm and giving the dancers and gawkers three and a half solid hours of melodic joy. We did not move even to go to the men's restroom when the band took several 15-minute intermissions, for fear of losing our precious space.

Ivie Anderson, vocalist and Jimmy Blanton.

To hold a position within arm's reach of the great Duke Ellington Orchestra was space worth fighting for. Duke had expanded the band and added Jimmy Blanton as the second chair in the bass section and Ben Webster was holding down his chair in the reed section. Johnny Hodges, Cootie Williams, Rex Stewart and Ivie Anderson also made some real musical contributions that night.

Jimmy Blanton had a tone and beat that created a propelling pulsation that synchronized the rhythm section

235

and rhythmically pushed the entire orchestra to another level of swing. His instrumental technique was unlike any other jazz bass player on the planet. Billy Taylor the other bass player in the first chair had quit earlier that week in the middle of a dance set at the Southland Café in Boston. As he walked off the bandstand Taylor said, "I am not going to let no young bass player embarrass me in public."

Webster's presence, like Blanton's gave the orchestra another dimension.. Along with other members of the sax section such as Barney Bigard, Johnny Hodges, Otto "Toby" Hardwick and Harry Carney. Ben Webster brought a cohesiveness and a Kansas City swing style to the sax section that was long overdue in light of what was happening in the reed sections of the Count Basie, Tommy Dorsey, Jimmie Lunceford, Benny Goodman, Woody Herman, Glenn Miller and the Andy Kirk Orchestras.

Ben Webster plays "C Jam Blues."

*Ben Webster had a style that was both harsh and tender, depending on the tune. For example, he figuratively kissed you when he played **"All Too Soon."** On the other hand, he made your backbone twitch and your toes itch when he blew **"Cotton Tail."***

*Everybody in the Parkway ballroom that cold December windy city night stopped dancing and stood still for several spellbound minutes while the copper-colored, handsome and slender, 22 year-old Jimmy Blanton soloed. The strong pulsations from the strings of his bass fiddle sent tremors through your soul as he plucked melodic solos on **"Jack The Bear"** and **"Sepia Panorama."** The young musician radically*

236

increased the scope of the four-string bass for all living bass players and those yet unborn. No electronic devices were needed in a ballroom or theater to hear Blanton because he played from scratch with his God-given talent, his imagination, his bow and his well-worn naked finger-tips.

Holmes "Daddy-O" Daylie, a Chicago jazz impresario and barkeeper at the DuSable Lounge said: *Although there was always something going on at the Lounge, which was located in the basement of the DuSable Hotel at 764 East Oakwood Boulevard 125 feet west of Cottage Grove Avenue. Daddy-O said the most memorable event that he could recall was the morning that Ben Webster, and Roy "Little Jazz" Eldridge got fired up on their horns. He said he will never forget Ben "The Brute" Webster playing "**All Too Soon**" and "**Cotton Tail**," and sending everybody in the joint into a musical high.*

*Ben Webster was called "The Brute" because he was always looking for a rumble, and he walked around talking about it. But privately, he was a very softhearted, sensitive man. How else could he have played "**All Too Soon**," in such a hypnotic, tender fashion. Gene "Jug" Ammons, Claude McLinn, and Tom Archer, were the young musical tenor sax "Turks" in Chicago at that time, they would sit at Webster's feet and soak up his solos like gin on the rocks.*

Webster disciples, left Claude McLinn and Gene "Jug" Ammons.

Johnny Griffin, the tenor sax man was recruited by Lionel Hampton shortly after he graduated from DuSable / Phillips High School in Chicago in 1945. Following his work with Hampton he played gigs with Art Blakey's Jazz Messengers, and Thelonious Monk, the piano player and composing genius. Griffin made the following observation while in high school: *I was playing alto sax in a tenor style, because musicians during the early 1940's were trying to imitate Ben Webster, and on slower tempos, I would play like Johnny Hodges, not realizing at that time that both Webster and Hodges played the same way, only one played alto and the other played tenor. But their styles were more or less the same.*

Johnny Griffin

Milton Hinton a popular jazz bass player, was a Chicagoan and Wendell Phillips High School graduate, who studied music under Major N. Clark Smith the high school's bandmaster. Hinton was a longtime friend of this writer, and was also a Phillips / DuSable graduate who studied piano under Captain Walter Dyett, Major Clark's successor. Hinton worked with the internationally famous Cab Calloway Orchestra from 1936 to 1951.

Hinton describes a classic jam session between Coleman Hawkins and Ben Webster as follows: *"After Ben Webster left the Ellington Orchestra in 1943 he got a gig playing at the Three Deuces Club located in New York City on 52nd Street which was commonly known as Jazz Row because of the numerous number of jazz joints on that strip. Ben was red hot as a result of his popular Ellington record-*

ings of "Cotton Tail" and "A-Sitting and A-Rocking." He told Milton that he wanted Coleman Hawkins' head on a silver platter.

Hinton promised that he would make it happen and he did by managing to get the club owner to advance Coleman Hawkins $20.00 which was double the union scale to perform on a one night gig. On the Sunday night of the special event Webster walked into the club and stepped up to the mike like Joe Louis, the world's heavyweight champion would step into a boxing ring. There he stood, big, bad and bold while growling out a red hot chorus of ***"Cotton Tail."*** Coleman Hawkins who was in the audience kept egging him on by shouting from the ringside for Ben to play some more choruses. Ben looked across the stage at Hawkins with a twinkle of suspicion in his eyes and continued spitting fire through his horn. The Hawk slowly took his horn out of its case and assembled it and checked his reed as Webster was finishing his first set. The Hawk then stepped up to the mike on the bandstand and figuratively blew Webster away in thirty-two bars of ***"Body and Soul."*** When Milton looked around for Ben Webster to come back on the bandstand and duke it out in the second set with the "Hawk" he discovered that Ben had split the scene and blew the gig.

The following week Ben Webster showed up at a jam session shortly before day- break at Minton's Playhouse which was located uptown in Harlem at 118th and 7th Avenue. The "Brute" was half crocked and feeling no pain as he waved his clarinet in mid-air with his right hand and shouted at the top of his lungs "Get me Barney Bigard, Ellington's clarinet player and I will blow the S.O.B. out of this damn room."

Norman Granz arranged to have an expanded version of the Harlem jam session in Los Angeles, California on Sunday June 28, 1944. Ben Webster shared the stage in a set with Lester Young and Joe Thomas the star tenor sax players with Jimmy Lunceford's great orchestra. The Downbeat reported that the three cats literally carved each other up like chopped liver.

Webster's future assignments in JATP jam sessions were cool in that he played several long solos over simple, harmonic chord changes such as those found in songs like *"I Got Rhythm," "Dinah"* and *"Honeysuckle Rose"*. He would close out his set with a medley of ballads such as *"In A Sentimental Mood", "Stardust," "Mood Indigo"* and *"Moonglow."* During the dreamy ballads he was able to play at his own speed, whereas on up tempo numbers he did not fair well in that he seemed to be screaming and hollering for help through the bell of his horn.

Lester Young earned $750.00 per week touring with Granz's JATP jam sessions whereas the famous Birdland Club on Broadway in New York City only paid him $125.00 for the same period. Ben Webster earned the same kind of money as Lester in addition to receiving recording royalties from Granz's record company.

In July 1952 Webster was in a jam session with Flip Phillips, Illinois Jacquet, Charlie Parker, Willie Smith, Howard McGhee, Johnny Hodges and Benny Carter. All of these musicians were boss cats. Granz's stable of cats in all of the musical disciplines were expansive. On hides he had the best in Gene Krupa, Buddy Rich, J.C. Heard, Louie Bellson, Jo Jones, Sid Catlett, and Dave Tough. On trumpet there was Roy Eldridge, Buck Clayton, Dizzy Gillespie, Charlie Shavers and Clark Terry.

On a cold Sunday afternoon in December 1957 the CBS Television Studio presented nationally a jam session entitled *"The Sound of Jazz"* it was a real Christmas gift for me and hundreds of thousand other jazz lovers. This session was miles ahead of what Federal Communication Commissioner Newton Minow once described television as being a "Vast Wasteland." In the writer's opinion and I am sure the commissioner would agree that *"The Sound of*

Jazz" was classic television.

On the *"Sound of Jazz"* program Billie Holiday sang a blues number entitled ***"Fine and Mellow"*** which she composed. *"Lady Day"* was accompanied by a group of all star musicians including Lester "Prez" Young, Coleman Hawkins, Gerry Mulligan and Ben Webster and Roy Eldridge. "Lady Day" lyrically told the story of the blues in the first four bars when she wailed: ***"My Man Don't Love Me He Treats Me All So Mean..."*** Ben Webster followed with a 12 bar solo which he played in a breathless, heart-breaking manner. Without missing a beat an ill Lester Young stood up and took two steps forward and blew one of the most moanful poetic blues sounds that one's ears will not likely ever hear again except on records. He and Billie were looking at each other softly eyeball to eyeball and their eyes were interlocked as he played while she nodded her head and smiled approvingly of his work. For those moments they both seemed to be mentally recalling some happier times - except for the two of them nobody will ever know if there had ever been anything more than a very warm friendship between them. Both Lester and Billie died several months apart in their forties within two years after that classic televised session. Billie made her transition in July 1959 at the age of 44 and Lester made his transition in March 1959 at the age of 49.

Gigs for Webster were slim to none in the "Big Apple" during the 1950s. In April 1958 he got a two week gig working at the Village Vanguard where he played with Jimmy Jones, a Chicago piano player and teenage friend and neighbor of this writer. In addition to Hawkins and Jones there was Joe Benjamin, on bass; and Dave Bailey, on drum.

Jimmy Jones was a class act who frequently substi-tuted for Duke Ellington on the piano and also directed the band during rehearsals in Duke's absence. Earlier he had been the accompanist for Sarah Vaughan from 1947-1952, and later with Nancy Wilson and Ella Fitzgerald and others. The music business did not improve for Ben Webster in the early sixties despite his reputation as a great musi-cian. As a young man he learned a great deal about music but he appeared to have skipped his university eco-nomic class on supply and demand. He continued to price his talents above their market value. At the time, he was living in the basement of the Hinton home gratis as a friend and guest by invitation

Milt Hinton and his wife Mona.

from Milton and Mona because he could not afford to pay his hotel room bills. In spite of his poverty his ego would not permit him to accept gigs that paid less than triple the union scale.

Late one morning, Mona Hinton asked Ben how he could sit around the house and eat and drink and yet at the same time refuse to take the many jobs that were being offered to him. She pointed out that her husband Milton was just a plain bass player and that he was a star. She told him that Milton worked nine hours many a day at his craft while Ben was just A-Sitting-And-A-Rocking. That truth coming from his friend Mona's mouth broke Ben's heart. After Mona's sermon, Ben was offered a job in Europe and he took it. The engagement was to last for a month and was to begin in London in mid-December 1964. Ben took a boat to England because he was afraid to fly. The Brute was welcomed with open arms in Europe. There he was still thought of and treated as a star. Webster never returned to the United States.

Webster died at age 64 in Amsterdam, Netherlands

on September 20, 1973. His ashes were brought to the Assistens Kirkagoard in Copenhagen, a very old renowned cemetery near the center of the city where Hans Christian Anderson the great writer had been buried. In the 1980s a street in Holland was named Ben Websterstraat after him. The cross streets in the same general area were named Fats Wallerstraat and Art Tatumstraat and just a short distance away was the Duke Ellingtonstraat.

Ben's gravesite, is in Assistens Kirkagoard, Copenhagen.

Charlie Parker

Cut XI
Charlie "Yardbird" Parker:
Co-Creator of Be-Bop
With John "Dizzy" Gillespie

Charlie Parker Jr. was born on August 29, 1920 in
Kansas City, Kansas. His mother, Adelaide "Addie" Bailey
was the offspring of an African-American and Choctaw
Native American Indian. Luckily, the Parker family moved
from Tulsa, Oklahoma to Kansas City, Kansas a year before
the devastating race riot in Tulsa. The racial pandemonium
created by the riot was a living hell on earth for a period of
forty-eight hours commencing just before daybreak on
Memorial Day, Tuesday May 31st 1921. The initial evidence of disorder was the crackling sounds of gunfire followed by bullets whizzing over and around their heads.
Black and white World War I vets and some civilians
exchanged firepower until almost midnight on Wednesday
June 1st, 1921.

Greenwood Street, Tulsa, Oklahoma, 1921-about a year before the great race riot of May 31-June 1, 1921. The main thoroughfare of Tulsa's relatively prosperous African American community,Greenwood was sometimes called the "Black Wall Street."

The warlike upheaval totally wiped out what was known as the "Black Wall Street" of Tulsa in the Greenwood area. This district had been heavily populated by Blacks and Native Indians. At the end of the craziness the Greenwood district was literally a ghost town blanketed with hunks of charcoal that had become tombstones for houses that will never stand or be filled with laughter again..

Partial view of the destruction in Tulsa following the 1921 race riot.

"Captured Negroes" being taken into detention by vigilante whites on June 1, 1921 during the Tulsa race riots.

The spark that ignited the race riot was caused by an innocent incident involving a Negro delivery boy accidentally stepping backward onto the toe of a white female elevator operator. The news accounts and rumors of the event were blown totally out of the realm of clear thinking individuals during the Memorial Day weekend. The heel and toe incident figuratively became a carnal relationship between a white woman and a Black man.

According to the white establishment it was considered un-American for a Black man to have any kind of touching relationship with an ofay woman. The mixing of races brought out the very worst kind of reaction from whiskey drinking, bloodshot eyed, white vigilantes that were diehard racists to the marrow of their bones. In retrospect the Tulsa riot was really a mini version of the Chicago 1919 Blood Red Summer.

Following five decades of many mini and major race riots a fourteen year old boy by the name of Emmett Louis Till from Chicago was one of several thousand Blacks who was kidnapped, lynched and left hanging from the blood drenched limbs of trees like pieces of Strange Fruit left to

Emmett Louis Till

rot and stink in the heat of the blazing sun.

Till's body unlike most lynched victims was thrown into theTallahatchie River near Greenwood, Mississippi on August 28, 1955 where his body was left to bloat and become ghastly disfigured. Master Till's only crime was having the audacity to whistle at the hip switching daughter of a white storekeeper. She was walking approximately forty feet away from him on the opposite side of the street.

When Till's grotesque and distorted body was discovered it was shipped to Chicago at the request of his mother Mamie Till and put on display in an open casket at a Chicago church in the Forty Hundred block on South State Street where thousands of people of all races viewed it for a period of several days.

Rosa Parks being fingerprinted by a police officer.

The Emmet Till case was still fresh in the minds of the world community when Dr. Martin Luther King under the umbrella of the Southern Christian Leadership Conference led a 12 month bus boycott that commenced on December 5, 1955 following Mrs. Rosa Parks' refusal to move to the back of the bus in Montgomery, Alabama.

During the Tulsa race riot a minimum of a thousand armed white men physically attacked unarmed African American women and old men on the public streets and in their homes. The mob burned down every Negro owned home and business and barbequed several of the black occupants who refused to run in terror from the thirty-five block area surrounding Greenwood Street which had historically been the center of the Black business and social activities.

Buck Colbert Franklin, a lawyer and the father of historian John Hope Franklin in tandem with Attorneys I. H. Spears and Amos T. Hall represented Black property owners who managed to escape with their lives as their homes were being burned to the ground.

Within five days following the Tulsa conflagration there were efforts made to exploit the surviving Colored landowners by white real estate developers and speculators operating with the blessing of a brand new Tulsa city council ordinance that was specifically designed to prevent the Black riot victims from rebuilding homes on the valuable sites that had been owned by some Black and Indian families when the state of Oklahoma was a territory.

Information on Charlie Parker Senior who became a Tulsonian via Mississippi, is very sketchy to say the least in that he has been described by some old-timers as a wandering alcoholic who had always traveled light. The old man legally separated from Charlie Junior's mother in 1928 shortly before the boy celebrated his eighth birthday. It has been said by several old time Kansans that Charlie Senior died violently in a drunken tavern brawl over a woman's affections in February 1940 in Kansas City, Kansas.

In 1930 Charlie Parker Jr. moved with his mother from Kansas City, Kansas across the river to Kansas City, Missouri where he was enrolled in the Crispus Attucks Elementary School. After graduating from the sixth grade

Jimmy Rushing, the Blues singer with the Count Basie Orchestra.

he enrolled in the seventh grade in the Abraham Lincoln Junior High School in 1932, it was there that he was introduced to music and a silver alto horn that was loaned to him by the music department. In the middle of the semester his position in the band was upgraded to a large baritone horn. Both horns were valved instruments much like a trumpet or trombone. Neither of the horns used reeds nor were they keyed like an alto or tenor saxophone. Parker's performance in the school band was graded as excellent.

The school bandmaster was Professor Alonza Lewis. Mr. Lewis once said: *"If Charlie Parker concentrated on his regular schoolbooks like he did on his horn he might qualify as an honor student."* Unfortunately,

The Count Basie Rhythm section. Left to Right: Walter Page (bass), Freddie Green (guitar), Joe Jones (drums) and Count Basie on the piano.

Parker was a perpetual truant in his academic classes, but a fly stuck on sticky paper in the band room.

During Parker's early teenage years he took advantage of the Kansas City Jazz scene. You could find him listening to the blues wailings of "Big" Joe Turner and Jimmy "Mr. 5x5" Rushing, both were band vocalist singers at some point in their careers, and they had worked with the swinging-blues playing orchestras of Count Basie, Benny Moten, Andy Kirk and his Clouds of Joy and also the Blue Devils.

Young Parker frequently watched the jazz musicians play as he pressed his nose or ears against the plate glass windows of the various juice joints that lined Vine Street. On other occasions he could be found eavesdropping through the keyholes and peepholes of the outdoor beer garden fences where he was usually denied admission because of his age.

Fats Waller taught Basie how to play the organ.

Parker's only formal music training was gained during his multiple years as a freshman in the Lincoln High School band. He was indeed a perpetual member of the freshman class. On the other hand, in the music class he displayed tremendous large ears and retention skills. These talents enabled him to instantly play back riffs and other musical ideas that he had harvested from seasoned cats in the juice joints and theaters in addition to listening to their recordings over and over. In contrast to his innate music retention he remained blind to the history, mathematics and social science studies. On the other hand, in the orchestra the boy had an ear that would amplify the sound of a fly pissing on cotton.

One night Charlie got hopped up on some of Louis Armstrong's golden leaf reefers and decided he was really ready to sit on his own tub, and blow some out of this world solos, side by side with some professional musicians. To his surprise and disappointment he was laughed off of the bandstand before he could complete the first eight bars of Fats Waller's standard *"Honeysuckle Rose,"* In the language of musicians he was really a sad cat.

At age fifteen Charlie Parker got hot pants and started playing footsie under the breakfast table with Rebecca Ruffin the teenage daughter of a boarder in his mother's rooming house at 1516 Olive Street in Kansas City, Missouri. Their footsie game became a very hot and heavy skin to skin game after school while the older women were at work.

Rebecca was not in a family way when the lovers decided to play footsie full time and therefore they got married on July 25, 1936. The young lady had graduated from Lincoln High School on June 7, 1935, shortly before she turned eighteen. Charlie played in the school band at her graduation and he just simply dropped out of school to be with his lady love fulltime after she got her diploma. Since Charlie was only fifteen years old he had to get his mother's written permission to marry Rebecca.

In 1937 when Rebecca discovered that she was three months pregnant, she also learned that Charlie was using hard-drugs. The couple became the parents of a son on January 10, 1938. They named the boy Frances Leon Parker. The middle name was selected by Charlie because of his admiration for Leon "Chu Berry" Brown, the dynamite tenor sax player with the Fletcher Henderson Orchestra in 1935-36 at the height of Henderson's popular theme song entitled *"Christopher Columbus."* The song was ideal for dancers who wanted to do the *Shuffle* or some

At extreme right is Charlie Parker; second from the left is Lester Young.

Trucking but too fast to do the Jelly. After leaving Henderson "Chu Berry" joined Cab "The Hi-De-Ho Man" Calloway and his international famous band in 1937. He starred with Cab until he was killed in 1941 at the age of 33 in an automobile accident.

The Parker family's burden got heavier when Rebecca got pregnant for the second time in 1940 it was then that she learned from her pediatrician that her husband's use of heroin would put a ceiling on his life span of not more than an additional eighteen to twenty years. Charlie Parker died on March 15, 1955 in the deluxe appointed apartment of Baroness Pannonica de Koenigsmarter in Manhattan on upper 5th Avenue in the Stanhope Hotel. Parker died three years earlier than the doctor's most favorable prognosis in 1940. On the brighter side of his death, it can be said that Charlie Parker packed

Lester Young plays with the grace of an eagle.

more jazz and bebop music into fifteen years than any other cat who had walked on this planet before and since his time.

Looking back to the summer of 1937 we find that Charlie Parker went to the top of the Ozark Mountains to play on a three months gig at a white summer resort, like all real jazz saints he fasted on a stack of Count Basie records and Lester Young solos. He carried a bushel basket of their recordings to the mountaintop gig with him. When he returned to Kansas City in the early fall of 1937 his soul had been cleansed of all of his musical inhibitions of the past. He could out Lester, note by note on Young's own material. Following the Count Basie and Lester Young diet his playing caused eyebrows to rise and mouths to gap among the Vine Street hip cats in Kansas City. His transformation was almost unbelievable. He was now considered a real contender and was never thought of again as a sad cat. He was indeed a super-cat in that everybody wanted a piece of the "Yardbird" and that meant more than wings or chicken feet.

Despite Parker's many talents he carried two wild animals on his back, a monkey (reefers) and a gorilla (heroin). He got a job with the Jay McShann Orchestra which he could not hold because of his drug habits and his erratic behavior.

Holmes "Daddy-O" Daylie a Chicagoan and a good friend of Charlie Parker said: *"Charlie Parker, the man was on a fast track to self-destruction. I have watched the narcotics and dope pushers work him over like vultures over a dead horse. Bird would come on a gig and play one set, and then leave with the dope dealer. Many times he would not come back."*

Eddie Johnson, a former tenor sax player with Louis Jordan, Cootie Williams, Horace Henderson, Coleman Hawkins and Moral Young, who subsequently years later became the musical director for the *I Love Lucy Show*, a very popular 1950-60s television sit-com. It was in Moral Young's band that Johnson and Parker worked together at the Swingland Café located in Chicago in the 1940s at 343 East Garfield Boulevard. Johnson said: *"Parker's tenure with the band lasted only three and a half weeks. He just did not seem to want to play the musical scores, for the show or even play the band's arrangements for dancing. Keep in mind that the "Bird" could read, however the only thing he wanted to do was solo. He would lay out and just wait until some measures were left open on the score for a solo. The empty measures may be marked for trombone, piano, drum and clarinet etc. Charlie just did not give a damn about the markings in those blank measures he would just simply jump up from his chair and start wailing on his alto sax. He and Moral Young had several conversations about his disregard for the music arrangements and this ultimately led to Charlie's termination.*

Parker was a top-flight musician but he was a pain in the ass. Dizzy Gillespie is a star witness to that fact. The proof of the statement is born out when Gillespie signed an eight week contract to bring a quintet into Billy Berg's Jazz Club in Los Angeles, California. Dizzy took six cats instead of five because Charlie Parker was not dependable.

A prime example of Parker's instability exhibited its

ugly head when Parker's L.A. heroin dealer Emery "Moose The Mooche" Byrd got busted. Parker's health deteriorated rapidly when he could not find another dealer to feed his habit. Thus, he turned to booze in an attempt to modify and ease the withdrawal pains from time to time. He obviously was a no-show many times at Billy Berg's gig. Howard McGee, the trumpet player found him sleeping on the concrete floor of an unheated garage. There was nothing between his body and the cement floor but his overcoat. On this trip Dizzy returned to New York without Parker.

Norman Granz, the wise one was aware of Parker's heroin problem and felt that he had found a solution to the Parker problem while on a very successful Jazz At the Philharmonic tour. Granz said: *"Well, Charlie was fine on the whole tour, which means, he had made connections in certain cities, and this enabled him to make time on the gigs. The old problem resurfaced again when we arrived in Los Angeles, on the JATP tour where the pushers were all over Parker like flies on a hot freshly broken watermelon.*

Granz changed his tactics and decided to stash Charlie where no one could find and tempt him before the tour ended. The last performance was an enormous advance sell-out at the biggest auditorium in Los Angeles. Parker was part of a big package which included the Hawk - and many other jazz stars. I called a friend of mine who was a captain in the L.A. detective division, he was a colored cat who was appropriately called Rocky - and he was just the kind of man I wanted. I went to Rocky, and I said, "Look, I have to keep this guy, away from everyone until after the show. Do you have some off-duty detective you can give me, and of course he had to be colored, too, that would pick up Charlie Parker and pretend he was gonna be his chauffeur?" And he said, "Sure, you can hire the guy, no problem." I found a motel on the outskirts of LA, and convinced Charlie, that he was going to have his own car and chauffeur. This idea appealed to Parker's ego. Charlie and his wife Doris came in on the flight, and I introduced him to this young man, and I said, "He's your driver, and we've got you a nice motel, and he'll pick you up for the gig," et cetera. Charlie thought that was great. So [the chauffeur] drove Charlie and his wife to this motel, where he was suppose to stay with them in an adjoining room. Charlie convinced the driver into thinking he was going to take a nap. The young police officer, decided that he would sack out, too. When the cop awakened he found that Charlie had taken the keys to the car and was gone.

I arrived at the concert hall early, around six o'clock - the hit was at eight, and it was a big concert, there were a lot of musicians, so I had to get the routine together and everything - [the detective] came, to me and said, "The Shit Has Hit The Fan, Mr. Granz I don't know what else to say. Charlie has disappeared." So I said, "Well, if we don't get him before the show starts, I will have to go out and make an announcement to the people and tell them that they can have their money back if they want it. But once the show starts, then they can see the whole show for nothing and still get their money back." Because Charlie was advertised and wasn't at the concert hall I said, "You better be sure that he's... going to be here at some time. Anytime before eleven o'clock, before the concert closes, I can effectively put him on anytime, if that is impossible, I have gotta make my announcement at eight o'clock." He didn't know what to say, and he didn't know what to do. And finally, Teddy Edwards, the tenor saxophonist -was backstage (he lives in LA), and he said, 'Well, let me see if I can find him.' And he went to some of the places that the detective never knew about. He found Charlie, and Charlie was virtually uncon- scious, he was really out of it, and he brought him back to the auditorium. And, I mean, there was no way for Charlie to go on effectively - but I didn't know what to do with him. Coleman Hawkins was playing, and I kept signaling when Coleman would finish a number, which finished his set, I'd say, "One more, one more". Poor Hawk was out there interminably, it seemed, and then I got Charlie, and I said, "Put his head under the cold water faucet." At the same time during this process I said, "Charlie, I'm gonna kill you if you don't get yourself together and he did. I did not have to make an announcement."

Milt Hinton and Duke Ellington reminiscing about old times

Milton "The Judge" Hinton the great bass player and a friend of the author later made an east coast observation about Charlie Parker in his book entitled *Bass Line.* He said: *"I remember an afternoon when one of the bartenders in a Midtown New York joint asked if I would help him pull out a guy who had slid down onto the floor in one of the front booths. He told me he could not understand what had happened because the guy had been in the bar a couple of hours and only had one or two Cokes. I crossed the aisle to the booth and when I looked down I saw it was Charlie Parker. He was conscious, but slobbering all over himself and nodding the way junkies do. I told the bartender the guy was a friend of mine and was feeling sick. We walked him to a booth in the back and laid him across one of the benches so he could sleep it off.*

Charlie Parker's final big sleep was a composite of all of his negative habits such as alcohol, drugs and an unsatisfied thirst for women, too many women can be as poisonous as a rattlesnake bite. According to the old testament Samson was not the first or the last victim of a Delilah. His first marriage to Rebecca, ended in divorce, he knotted a tie with his second wife Geraldine, which also ended in divorce. He went through a third marriage ceremony with a woman named Doris, his last known widow was a common-law white female dancer who answered to the name of Chan Richardson Parker. She died in a hospi-

tal on September 9, 1999 at the age of 74 in Etampes, France, which is located southwest of Paris.

Although Parker died in New York he was buried in Kansas City. Trumpeter Dizzy Gillespie, plus four of his sidemen played a jazz concert at the gravesite of the immortal Charlie Parker on October 4, 1961.

Gene Krupa

Cut XII
Gene Krupa: The Drummer Man

The very first time that I was within arm's reach of Gene Krupa and Benny Goodman was on the evening of June 22, 1937. A battle of the bands session was scheduled to be held at the Eighth Regiment Armory which is currently a remodeled military academy at 3515-33 South Giles Avenue that night. The location of the hop was in the heart of Bronzeville on the near southeast side of Chicago, Illinois. Today that community is turning from Black to white by the minute. The program was billed to feature the Roy "Little Jazz" Eldridge Orchestra and the nationally famous Benny Goodman Band.

Earlier on, the evening of June 22nd Joe Louis defeated James Braddock for the title of the world's heavyweight championship of the world at Comiskey Park which

Joe Louis
Ring Announcer Hal Totten on left and co-manager Julian Black on right.

is located less than eight short blocks west of the Armory. After I left the fight I had to claw my way east to the regiment because the Black community had gone berserk celebrating the Joe Louis victory. Streetcars, cabs and jitneys could not move an inch because the streets were jampacked from curb to curb with celebrants. Although my car was blocked in at the ballpark parking lot I was determined to get to that Battle of the Bands at the Armory if I had to crawl on my knees.

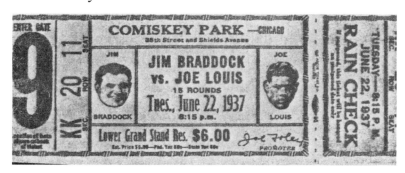

Eighth Regiment Armory at 35th and Giles in Chicago.

When I finally reached the doors of the Eighth Regiment Armory I could hear Roy Eldridge blowing one of his super fast skyscraping trumpet solos on one of my favorite songs **After You've Gone** by Henry Creamer and Turner Layton (1918). There must have been 2,000 people in the hall when I arrived. My first inclination was to get close enough to the bandstand to greet some of my old buddies who were working with the Eldridge Orchestra. The cats in the band were George "Scoops" Carey, an excellent alto sax man who always referred to me as the chief, my buddy Dave Young, was the tenor sax man, he must have known a thousand jokes and he always carried X rated card size pictures to match. In the rhythm section there was Truck Parham, on the string bass, Zutty Singleton on the drums, Teddy Cole, at the piano and Johnny Collins on guitar. All of the players including me were fellow members of the Colored Musicians Union Local 208. "Little Jazz" the leader of the group always purchased at least one shoebox full of reefers on pay night at the Three Deuces night-

Roy Eldridge and his band at the Three Deuces in Chicago.

club which was located at 222 North State Street in Chicago. Art Tatum and Gladys Palmer entertained at the piano bar upstairs on the street level.

Early on I frequently listened to the Goodman Orchestra on their nightly radio broadcast from the Urban Room in the Congress Hotel on South Michigan Boulevard in Chicago, Illinois, that is, when I was not overloaded with school assignments. The following year, I was a regular listener to their weekly broadcasts on a popular radio music commercial show called the Camel Caravan sponsored by a major tobacco company.

The first time I actually saw Goodman and Krupa play was in a bit part in a motion picture musical-comedy entitled *The Big Broadcast of 1937* starring Jack Benny, the comedian and radio star; Martha Raye, the jazz singer; and Leopold Antoni Stokowski, British born American conductor of the Philadelphia Symphony Orchestra.

By the time the Goodman Group arrived at the

Benny Goodman and his orchestra.

Armory on the night of June 22, 1937 there were 5,000 people waiting in a non air conditioned, mammoth size, sweaty hall. The crowd was so overwhelming it became necessary to call out the riot squad police to keep order. We teenagers figuratively went through the roof when the Goodman Orchestra opened their first set with "Jelly Roll" Morton's **King Porter's Stomp** and that was followed with **Big John Special,** arranged by Fletcher Henderson and then there was

Gene Krupa with Harry James at the right.

Sing, Sing, Sing which was a take off of on the Christopher Columbus song featuring Krupa on the tom toms and Harry James with a quartet of wailing trumpets. Each number was sending the crowd of 5,000 higher and higher into a musical frenzy. Krupa egged the band on with his tom-tom-ming, grunting, grinning and shaking his tangled jet-black hair like Cab Calloway as he sweated like John Henry the steel driving man. Krupa's beat was in sync with Vido Musso's bellowing and bawling on his tenor sax and then overriding everything except Harry James' quartet of trumpets spewing out a fanfare of screams reminiscent of a Spanish bullfight. The trumpets punctuated through and around Krupa's drumbeating and tom tomming and Musso's bellowing. The spirit of the evening was best captured in a nineteen twenties blues song entitled: *"It Was Tight Like That."*

At the end of the first hour Gene Krupa had to change all of his clothing from his socks in addition to his under and outer garments because everything he had on was soaking wet from the sweat he had generated in driving, lifting and propelling the orchestra. Without question, Krupa was the hardest working jazz drummer in the business.

The drive of Gene Krupa's drums and the screams of Harry James' trumpet rocked the foundation of the Eighth Regiment Armory. Those white boys were playing Black music like it had never been played before. The Goodman formula for making your feet happy was to swing. Equally important was the fact that he hired some of the best trained white musicians in the country and they in turn played the arrangements of three of the best Black arrangers in the nation, namely, Fletcher Henderson, Jimmy Mundy and Mary Lou Williams. Hence, the Goodman sound was Black America speaking through a white Ambassador of Swing.

A little less than a month earlier on May 4, 1937

266

Chick Webb

Goodman's Orchestra was in a battle of the bands with Chick Webb's Orchestra at Harlem's uptown Savoy Ballroom which was also known as "The Home of Happy Feet" in New York City. Many drummers copied Gene Krupa but few could top him. The exception was Chick Webb who wiped him to a fair do well the night of May 4th after a four-hour intensive battle of the bands. Gene gracefully conceded to his mentor when he said: "I have never been cut by a better man." Gene had learned his art from Black drummers like Chick Webb, Baby Dodds, and Zutty Singleton, who worked with Louis Armstrong and Roy Eldridge.

Krupa was born in Chicago's Polish neighborhood on January 15, 1909 and died in Yonkers, New York on October 16, 1973. He was the youngest of nine children of Bartley and Ann Krupa. Both of his parents were of Polish descent. Both his father and his mother's parents were natives of Poland. His father died early, thus, Gene went to work at age 11 to help his mother who was a milliner. He helped her, like his siblings, keep the family's skin and bones together.

Baby Dodds

At age 12 he played his first professional musical gig with Frivolian. He could not read a

267

note as tall as Chicago's Water Tower but he could beat the hell out those skins with his strong wrist and bubbling personality.

Glenn Miller

Fast forwarding nine years we find that Krupa got a job playing in a pit band at the Times Square Theater in New York City. The year was 1930 the gig was playing Gershwin music for a show called *Strike Up The Band.* Both Benny Goodman and Glenn Miller were also members of the pit band. Krupa had not learned the difference between a quarter note and an eighth note. However, luck was on Gene's side in that Glenn Miller sat directly in front of him and from time to time he would tap the rhythm of the song with his fingers on the seat of his chair until Gene got the beat in his head.

Even though Krupa could not read, Gerswhin was impressed with him because he introduced the "Freeze Beat" to the score in lieu of the four bar solo on temple blocks that had been written by the arrangers. It was something that he had picked up while watching Duke Ellington and Sonny Greer play drums in a Cotton Club stage show.

In 1931 Krupa joined an orchestra that had been organized by Benny Goodman for the very popular radio crooner Russ Columbo. Following the breakup of the Russ Columbo Orchestra in 1932 he freelanced until he joined the Benny Goodman organization in 1934 where he stayed put until 1938 at which time he decided to organize his own band.

The Krupa Orchestra was at the height of its popu-

Benny Goodman and Gene Krupa.

Roy Eldridge, the trumpet wizard.

larity during the early years of World War II when he brought Anita O' Day and Roy Eldridge on board. Eldridge's contribution over and above the Krupa Band was his soul stirring solo on **Rockin Chair** which is still a classic. Roy's vocal duet with Anita O' Day entitled **"Let Me Off Uptown"** was good music and also the first time that a Black male worked publicly with a white female on a world stage.

The whole Krupa outfit became a big family until 1949 when he got some bad press that he did not need. Three members of his band were caught and booked for using marijuana. Krupa threatened to fire anybody in his organization caught using drugs. (See the FBI report on the following pages).

In 1951 Gene was released from the hospital following an appendicitis attack. Norman Granz nagged and jostled him into joining the JATP tour along with other big time stars like Ella Fitzgerald, Oscar Peterson, Flip Phillip, Illinois Jacquet and Lester Young, et al. Krupa stayed with the Granz group intermittently from 1951 to 1959 touring throughout the States and Europe.

In 1960 Krupa was hospitalized suffering with heart problems. He stated that he was not concerned about dying as much as he was about being able to playing a little with his favorite mistress, the drum.

Standing left to right: Norman Granz, Gene Krupa, Ella Fitzgerald, Ray Brown, unidentified man, Barney Kessell,Oscar Peterson and Lester Young. Kneeling: Flip Phillips, Charlie Shavers and Willie Smith.

Lionel Hampton

Cut XIII
Hamp: The Champ
of The Vibraphone

Lionel Hampton was born in Birmingham, Alabama on April 20, 1908. The family of Charles Edward and Gertrude Morgan Hampton lived in "Bombingham" a Confederate Metropolis following the Civil War, and they stayed there until after World War I.

The Hampton family had not been made aware of the fact that Charles Edward Hampton had been killed on a battlefield in Belgium until after the Armistice with Germany had been signed on November 11, 1918. However, following a respectful mourning period Gertrude Hampton married Samuel Davis a gentleman who lived directly across the street from her parent's home at 1513 Seventh Avenue in Birmingham.

Pvt. Charles E. Hampton and Gertrude Hampton, Hampton's parents.

Lionel was raised by his maternal grandparents Richard and Louvenia Morgan after his mother Gertrude decided to move into her new husband's home across the Avenue at 1514 Seventh Avenue which is adjacent to the corner of Fifteenth Street. Hampton's grandfather Richard Morgan made his final transition in less than a year after his daughter married the very gentle pint-size Mr. Samuel Davis.

Grandmother Louvenia received a modest lump sum pension from the railroad company as a result of Grandpa Richard's death. It was at this crossroad in her life that she decided to use the pension money as a stake for starting a new beginning in Chicago, Illinois, a metropolis that Blacks affectionately referred to as Abraham Lincoln's City by the Lake. The pension money was in tack when they reached Illinois Central Railroad Station at 12th and South Michigan Boulevard in Chicago. The train ride was gratuitous in that her late husband had worked a lifetime for the Southern Railroad Company.

When they settled down in Chicago during the prohibition period which lasted from January 1920 to February 1933 Mamma Louvenia discovered that her brother Richard had become a big shot working with the Al Capone gang in the bootleg whiskey business. Oversize greenbacks flowed freely through Uncle Richard's fingers like flour in a sifter. Some of the money must have stuck because in a very short period of time he had accumulated enough capital to buy a spanking brand new Nash automobile and a brownstone two story house at 2837 South Wabash Avenue.

Louvenia Morgan, Grandmother

Although Mama Louvenia enjoyed all the luxury that was showered upon her by her brother she repeatedly reminded him, "that crime don't pay", his rubuttal was always "but whiskey does".

Lionel's grandmother was very concerned about her grandson growing up in an environment of prostitutes, bootleggers and mobsters. Therefore, she decided after praying all night for an answer, that she had no choice but to get her grandson out of Chicago's Douglas Elementary School at 32nd and Calumet Avenue and into a Christian school. The Sunday following her all night prayer, Uncle Richard drove her and Lionel north over pothole riddled, bumpy roads for approximately ninety miles North to the Holy Rosary Academy in Kenosha, Wisconsin, it was a school for Black and Indian children.

The Holy Rosary Academy was an offspring of St. Benedict The Moor, a Catholic boarding school in Milwaukee, Wisconsin where Harold Washington, Chicago's first Black mayor, and Redd Foxx, the NBC television comedian, were students in residence approximately a decade following Lionel's brief tenure at the Academy.

At the Academy he learned the basics of playing the

snare drum, xylophone, orchestra bells and the timpani under the watchful eyes of Sister Petra. It was unfortunate for him that the school closed fourteen months after he had enrolled. Therefore, when the kid returned to Chicago, his grandmother was still not comfortable with the idea of enrolling him in either the Doolittle or Douglas Public Elementary Schools.

The only place for a Black child to get a good education in the Windy City in her opinion was in a Catholic school like the St. Monica School, at Thirty-sev-

enth and Wabash Avenue. That institution was run by the Sisters of the Blessed Sacrament, they were also dedicated to teaching Black and Indian children. The school was just a half block south from where Lionel lived with his Grandma. On the other hand, Saint Monica did not have a band, therefore Lionel did not get a chance to develop his early music training until he got hooked up with Mr. Robert S. Abbott, the publisher of the Chicago Defender

Mr. Robert S. Abbott, publisher of the Chicago Defender

Newspaper. Mr. Abbott had started a band for the Black boys who sold his weekly red headline newspapers on the street corners of Chicago every Friday and Saturday.

276

The icing on the cake came when Mr. Abbott, a patron of the Insull Opera House succeeded in convincing Madame Schumann-Heink a star singer with the Opera company to give one of the mansions she owned at 37th and Michigan Boulevard to the Defender boys' cause. The house was used as a conservatory where the young boys could study and practice their various musical crafts.

David Young, a preteen aspiring tenor sax player recalls: *"My first major step up the musical ladder was with the Chicago Defender Newsboys Band under the direction of Major N. Clark Smith. Lionel Hampton had become a member of that organization shortly before I joined, he like others who trained under Major Clark Smith became a top-notch musician. Others such as Bill Oldham, the tuba player who doubled on string bass with Louis Armstrong; Scoops Carry, the great alto sax man in Earl Hines' Orchestra; Ray Nance, a violinist and trumpet star with the Duke Ellington band; and Milt Hinton, Cab Calloway's top string bass man for fifteen years; there were hundreds of other kids who later did very well in the music business because of Major Smith. We all got a real solid musical foundation in the Chicago Defender Band under the direction of the Major.*

Samuel Insull

In 1923, Mr. Samuel Insull, the Chicago financial tycoon who controlled utilities and holding companies, providing electricity, gas and transportation in Chicago purchased an old mansion at 3947 South Michigan Boulevard (presently the site of the Donnelly Youth Center) and had it completely renovated. Insull and his lawyer, Daniel J. Schuyler, organized the South Side Boys Club for

*Negroes. The big mansion became our youth center. It was
a large-scale, well-financed facility that included vocation-
al training, recreation and a music department. Mr. Insull
hired Major N. Clark Smith, who was a full time band
instructor at the Wendell Phillips Public High School, to
direct the band after his regular school hours. Mr. Insull
took Major Smith downtown to the Lyon & Healy music
store on the northeast corner of Jackson Boulevard and
Wabash Avenue to purchase instruments for a seventy-five
piece symphony orchestra.*

*Apparently Major N. Clark Smith a dark complex-
ion man was either one of Sam Greenlee's characters in
"The Spook Who Sat Behind The Door" or a non-person
in the eyes of the white clerk who said to Mr. Samuel Insull
in Smith's presence, "Mr. Insull, these aren't the kind of
instruments you should buy for Negroes."*

*Mr. Insull thanked the clerk for his advice and asked
him in a very acid tone, "What time can I expect delivery?"
The clerk momentarily came to his senses and replied,
'Within forty-eight hours, sir!"*

*When the Lyon and Healy instrument delivering
truck arrived at the South Side Boys Club loaded with
oboes, flutes, English horns, French horns, bassoons and
the traditional trumpets, trombones, saxophones, clarinets,
and drums; man the kids' eyes lit up like Christmas tree
lights because they had never seen that many brand new
instruments in their lives. Once the excitement of seeing the
instruments wore off, we became cry babies because there
were not enough trumpets and saxophones to go around.*

At the age of thirteen, Lionel Hampton a Chicago
Defender Band member and paperboy started hanging out
at the Vendome Theater stagedoor entrance which was in
the alley under the "L" tracks at the rear of 3145 South State
Street where Erskine Tate and his great Symphonic Jazz
Orchestra was featuring the great Louis Armstrong on trumpet and Jimmy Bertrand on drums. Bertrand became

Lionel's mentor in that through him he learned what it meant to be a first class professional drummer.

In addition to the excitement Lionel got from playing the drums, he also got a thrill riding the elevated "L" train with its windows down. The ride was a substitute for a giant size electric fan on a hot Sunday afternoon. Every time the train looped around downtown and made that sharp left turn on Lake Street heading, west he always got the feeling that the leaning "L" train was going to fall into the side of a building.

Uncle Richard gave Lionel a set of drums exactly like Mr. Bertrand's set for Christmas. Lionel the sophomore student was hot to trot with his new toy. Lionel dropped out of high school before he completed his fourth semester and joined Les Hite's teenage band. Les was an excellent alto saxophone player who lived directly across the street from his Uncle Richard at 2837 South Wabash Avenue. The youthful Les Hite's band was very popular with the Roaring Twenties Teenage Rugcutters.

Lionel was very disappointed when Hites decided to break-up his band and move to sunny Los Angeles, California. To soften the blow Les promised the guys in the band that he would send for them once he got his west coast act together. Lionel was the only member of the old Chicago band that Les ever offered a job in his new orchestra at Frank Sebastian's Cotton Club in Culver City, California.

Following his engagement at Sabastian's Cotton Club with Les Hite, Hampton took a gig at a small club in Los Angeles known as the Paradise Café. It was there that he was discovered by Benny Goodman's future brother-in-law, John Hammond, the wealthy New York critic and promoter in 1935. Hammond told Goodman who was playing a two week engagement at the Palomar Ballroom in Los Angeles about the Colored kid at the Paradise Café with a new sound. He suggested to Goodman that he check the kid out. However, before Goodman got around to digging Hampton at the Paradise Café, Hymie Schertzer and Pee Wee Irwin two of Goodman's sidemen heard the vibraphonist at the café and reported back to Goodman that Lionel was a "bad motor scooter." Benny was still too busy to follow-up on the reports about Hampton, however he sent his brother Harry over to the Paradise Café to validate the rumors about Hampton's skills.

During a 'Take Five' intermission break Hampton learned that Benny Goodman was also in the house. Following the rest period, Benny joined Hampton on the bandstand. They jammed the rest of the night. At the end of the jam session Goodman simply said to Hampton "I am very pleased to have met you."

The next night while Hampton was on the bandstand playing he heard someone playing a mighty mean clarinet behind him. Lo and behold it was Benny Goodman but this time he had brought Gene Krupa and Teddy Wilson along. The four musicians jammed together for a solid four hours without a break. Benny fell in love with the mix that the four of them brought to the sound of the music. Therefore, before he departed he asked Lionel to join him at the RCA Victor recording studio in Hollywood the next day. Needless to say, Lionel showed up bright and early and they recorded two standards: **Moonglow and Dinah.** Within a month after the recordings were released, they became instant jukebox hits. All the cats across the country were bending their ears over the Nickelodeon and listening to the Goodman Quartet's brand new sounds. (Hampton had recorded his first vibraphone solo with Louis Armstrong in 1930, the song was **Memories of You** by Eubie Blake and Andy Razaf).

Benny and his orchestra finished their engagement at the Palomar in late August 1936 and went back to the 'Big Apple", and Hampton went back to his local gig at The Paradise Café. One night a month later, Tyree Glenn,

Hampton's trombone player, shouted from a telephone booth across the room to tell Hampton that Benny Goodman was on the phone. Tyree was a known prankster and Hampton thought that the call was another one of his tricks.

Several nights later Benny Goodman called again. This time Lionel's common-law wife Gladys answered the telephone, she and Goodman got down to basic business and talked about Hampton joining the Goodman group. She was grinning like a kid on Christmas morning when she told Lionel that Benny had offered him a one year contract at a salary of $550.00 per week. Benny also told her that she could travel on the road with the band. Lionel couldn't believe the good news because that money could buy a giant size slice of bread in the heart of the country's worst economic depression in history. His monthly salary would exceed a postal clerk's annual salary.

Gladys never asked Lionel what he thought about the deal. She talked in detail about the transition with her brother Dr. Riddle, who came up from Texas to Los Angeles to discuss the matter. Once she had resolved any doubts in her mind, she simply turned to Hampton and said, "Lionel! We are going to New York." There was no query like: "Do you want to go?"

The couple packed their belongings and hit Route 66 and drove from Los Angeles to New York City although Benny Goodman had offered to pay for their train tickets. Milt Hinton thought that Gladys and Lionel were married when he came out to the west coast in 1933. Contrary to his thoughts, Gladys and Lionel were simply doing what we use to call some very heavy rooming. However, enroute to New York in November 1936 they stopped off in Yuma, Arizona and got married as they had promised her mother that they would do. They mailed the marriage certificate back to the old lady in Texas as bonafide proof that they had "jumped the broom."

Gladys Hampton, his wife

Hampton made his debut with the Benny Goodman Quartet in the Manhattan Room of the Pennsylvania Hotel which was located directly across the street from the Pennsylvania Railroad Station. The telephone number of the hotel was Pennsylvania 6500. (Glenn Miller later composed a glee club type song called Pennsylvania 6500). The evening of Hampton's debut on November 21, 1936 was a bit disappointing because Lionel thought that he was going to be playing with the big orchestra, instead he played with the Goodman Quartet which was an extra attraction for the show.

Gene Krupa did not like the new arrangement because he was working while the rest of the band was taking a half hour break. Goodman satisfied Krupa by doubling his salary. Teddy Wilson was a part timer in that he didn't sit on the bandstand with the white musicians, he simply came onstage to play intermission piano in addition to playing with the original Goodman Trio. Back in those days an integrated band was not even a good pork chop night's dream.

Benny Goodman Quartet, left to right: Hampton, Teddy Wilson, Benny Goodman and Gene Krupa

It was with the Benny Goodman Quartet that Lionel Hampton gained international fame as a vibraphonist. Those coast to coast nightly broadcasts from the Pennsylvania Hotel made him a household name.

After four years with the Goodman organization Gladys decided it was time for Lionel to start thinking about organizing his own band again. She went to Goodman and Joe Glaser of the Associated Booking Corporation to get them to put up some seed money to lift them off the ground, and they did. She also signed an exclusive recording contract with Norman Granz. Gladys decided that they would make their home base in Los Angeles.

When they got back to L.A. they immediately started calling around in an effort to recruit guys who they hoped would be the nucleus of their new orchestra.

Hampton and "Sugar Child" Robinson

They arranged to rehearse daily at the Club Alabam on Central Avenue the main drag in the Los Angeles Colored community. Guys like Marshall Royal, Lee Young, Lester's brother, Illinois Jacquet, Sir Charles Thompson, on piano, Karl George and Jack Trainer on trumpet and others started dribbling into rehearsals until they had grown like topsy into a full-fledged orchestra ready to hit the road.

When the band came to Chicago, Illinois Jacquet was red hot playing **Flying Home** Hampton's composition and theme song. The band

Samuel Davis, Jr. Hampton's half brother.

was at the Regal Theater with Sugar Child Robinson during the Christmas holidays of 1942. It was during that period that the author was formally introduced to Lionel Hampton by his half brother Private Samuel Davis, Jr. The meeting took place backstage in Hampton's dressing room at the Regal Theater . Both Davis and the author came to town together on a weekend furlough from Fort Custer, in Battle Creek, Michigan. While in Chicago Hampton recruited Dinah Washington, a washroom attendant at the Garrick Stage Bar on Randolph Street off of Clark and Joe Williams the blues singing backstage doorman at the Regal Theater and part-time singer with Tiny Parham for the roller skaters next door to the Regal at the Savoy Ballroom.

Lionel Hampton and Johnny Board at the Apollo in New York City.

A month later, Hampton was appearing at the Apollo Theater in New York City. The Hampton Orchestra was closing out a set as Illinois Jacquet was rocking and wailing with Hampton's theme song **Flying Home.** A reefer smoking cat in the second balcony started shouting, "I am **Flying Home,** I am **Flying Home"** then he quickly climbed over the balcony railing and jumped down two stories to the main floor. Fortunately, no one was hurt but the leaper. As a result of this incident Earl Hines later wrote a composition entitled **"Second Balcony Jump."**

Hamp was the boss in the spotlight but Gladys was the boss in the wings offstage in that she hired, fired and always got first count on the money. Without Gladys Hamp would have been just another booty bug.

When Gladys died of a sudden heart condition in 1971 Lionel figuratively broke into small pieces like a very thin and expensive crystal glass. It took a lot of glue to partially put him back together. I am not sure that all the pieces were ever put in place again.

Hampton died like his wife Gladys of a heart failure thirty-one years later on August 31, 2002. Many of the twentieth century musical giants participated in the funeral ceremony. The cats involved included Wynton Marsalis, Clark Terry, Hank Jones, Illinois Jacquet, Roy Hargrove, and Jon Faddis among many others. Twenty-five hundred people attended the service. The cats of yesteryears like Louis Armstrong, Duke Ellington and Cab Calloway would say Hamp died standing pat.

Hamp was laid to rest at the Woodlawn Cemetery in the Bronx where Louis Armstrong, Duke Ellington and Miles Davis were also buried.

The Last Goodbye, left to right at the Chicago Historical Society: Art Hodes, Dempsey J. Travis and Benny Goodman.

Left to right: Harold Washington who became Mayor of Chicago 30 years after this picture was taken on December 26, 1953, Marcella Davis, Duke Ellington, Moselynne E. Travis and Dempsey Travis, the Author.

Cut XIV
An Epilogue From The "Duke" To The "White Moses"

"In 1966 my orchestra went to Europe for Norman Granz for the first time. Norman did very well, he represented us beautifully as an impresario, and thus left me feeling very much indebted to him. He took us back several times after that, and later that year he sent us back to the old country with Ella Fitzgerald, which was a bang.

Norman Granz is one of those people I have often spoken of as encountering at various intersections of my road through life, he was one of those persons who was always there to point me in the right direction. He got some very good deals for me, too, like the Francis Sinatra picture, *Assault On A Queen*. The movie people were not talking as much money as he was thinking but he got it, and fairly quickly, too. It was one of those situations where someone says, "That's it, or nothing." He kept his cool, called an hour later, and the price was upped from $5,000 to $15,000...

The representation he gave me was great. It makes a lot of difference when the man who is doing the talking is a millionaire. He had no qualms. Everything had to be cleared through him and he took full responsibility. Although he was acting in effect as my manager, he never took a percentage or a fee...

One of the highest honors paid me was when Norman Granz presented us at the St. Tropez Art Festival in 1966 along with Ella Fitzgerald and a host of top masters in their own different fields. At that time I had the enormous pleasure of appearing in a film made with Joan Miro, the great Spanish painter. The movie was made at one of the worlds finest museums, La Fondation Maeght, in St Paul de Vence.

Music Is My Mistress
by Edward Kennedy Ellington(1973).

Edited by Dempsey J. Travis
October 2002.

Bibliography

Interviews

(Interviews were conducted and taped by the author between 1940 and 1999).

Ernie Anderson, was interviewed via telephone on March 9, 1995 and a half dozen subsequent days.
Occupation: Concert promoter
He was a friend and traveling companion of Louis Armstrong. Letters and other materials from Anderson relating to Louis Armstrong were mailed to the author on the following dates: April 8, 1995, April 9, 1995, April 12, 1995 and June 3, 1995. Ernie died in Palm Beach Shore, Florida, on June 12, 1995 according to a regret announcement from Allie, his daughter, in London, England.

Lil Armstrong, June 16, 1970.
Occupation: Bandleader, Pianist, Arranger and Composer
She studied music at Fisk University in Nashville, Tennessee. She was a trained classical pianist. After graduating from Fisk she moved to Chicago where she played jazz and blues with King Oliver, Freddie Keppard in addition to her husband, Louis Armstrong and a sundry of other bands. She was interviewed by the author at least a dozen times between 1940 and 1952.

Louis Armstrong, was interviewed by the author on May 18, 1937, June 19, 1940 and September 2, 1940 plus sound bites at various venues where they met across the country up until the mid sixties. He played with Kid Ory, Fate Marable, King Oliver, Fletcher Henderson, Erskine Tate, Carroll Dickerson, Clarence Jones, Lil Armstrong, Luis Russell and Les Hite.

Louie Bellson, the drummer was interviewed on June 31, 1983 in Chicago.
He played with Tommy Dorsey, Benny Goodman, Harry James, Duke Ellington, Charlie Shavers, Pearl Bailey, and Terry Gibbs. Recorded several LPs with Louis Armstrong.

Ken Blewett, manager of the Regal and Tivioli Theaters in Chicago, Illinois. Their initial in-depth interviews took place in his home commencing on April 7, 1982, followed by numerous visits and tapings when the author reviewed his catalogues of pictures taken onstage and backstage at the Regal and Tivoli Theaters in Chicago.

Johnny Board, A tenor and alto saxophone player was interviewed several times in July 1982.
He worked with Lionel Hampton, Count Basie, Coleman Hawkins, Woody Herman, Red Saunders, Johnny Long, B.B. King, Jesse Miller, Bobby Blue Bland and Ruth Brown.

Roy Butler, interviewed on March 16, 1982.
He played alto saxophone and clarinet with Sammy Stewart, Leon Abbey, Jimmy Wade, Harry Fleming in Europe, and South America, and also Teddy Weatherford in the U.S.A.

Cab Calloway, was initially interviewed on January 14, 1983 and several times thereafter between real estate transactions. He gained fame as an international bandleader at the New York Cotton Club in Harlem. In addition to directing an orchestra he was vocalist and the "Hi-De-Ho" King. Early in his career he worked with Louis Armstrong, Blanche Calloway (his sister), as a master of ceremonies at the Sunset Café in Chicago and later with the Alabamians and the Missourians in New York City.

Floyd Campbell, the drummer was interviewed several times in April, 1982.
He worked with Jabbo Smith, Louis Armstrong, Charlie Creath, Fate Marable, Al Trent and for years directed his own band at social events on the south side of Chicago and on the road.

Carol Chilton, interviewed June 14, 1982 was a dancer, singer, pianist and composer.
She worked with Al Jolson, Kate Smith, Eddie Cantor, Jimmy Durante, Duke Ellington, Don Redman, Noble Sissle, The Whitman Sisters, Mills Brothers, Bill Robinson, Milton Berle, Mae West, George Burns, Gracie Allen, Eubie Blake and Louis Armstrong. She and her husband were the first two Negro stars to do a command performance before the King and Queen of England at the Palladium in London, England on May 22, 1930.

Oliver Coleman, the drummer was interviewed on February 2, 1981.
He worked with Ray Nance, Earl Hines, Erskine Tate and Horace Henderson. He played in several jam sessions with Louis Armstrong.

Holmes "Daddy-O" Daylie, interviewed September 18, 1982 and many times thereafter.
Occupation: Radio/Television Personality and Bartender. He served Louis Armstrong, Billie Holiday, Ben Webster, Fats Waller and numerous other Negro stars as a bartender in the late 1930s and early 1940s at the DuSable Hotel Lounge located at 764 East Oakwood Boulevard in Chicago, Illinois.

Barrett Deems, called himself the world's fastest drummer. He interviewed on October 17, 1982 in Chicago. He worked with: Paul Ash, Joe Venuti, Jimmy Dorsey, Tommy Dorsey, Charlie Barnet, Woody Herman, Red Norvo, Muggsy Spanier, Louis Armstrong, Jack Teagarden and The Dukes of Dixieland.

George Dixon, played violin, trumpet and saxophone. He was interviewed on April 21, 1982 and at least a dozen more times over a period of a year.
He played with Sammy Stewart, Earl Hines, Floyd Campbell and Eddie King. George will always be remembered for his uncontrollable shout "Play it to 1951" during the bridge of "Boogie on the St. Louis Blues". Earl Hines was really wiping the piano ivories on that 1938 recording. As a teenager in the late 1930s, the year 1951 sounded to me like a year in the great beyond.

Dorothy Donegan, the pianist was interviewed June 1982 and countless other times before and after that date. She was a high school and elementary school classmate of the author in 1935 and 1939. Donegan was a prodigy who played in concert with the Chicago Symphony Orchestra at age fourteen at Orchestra Hall in Chicago. She was also featured in several movies during World War II, in addition to performing in Nightclubs, Broadway Plays and Concert Halls throughout America. The lady also played on several gigs with Louis Armstrong and Cab Calloway. The writer heard Dorothy beat out ten of the best piano jazz players in the world in a cutting contest at Carnegie Hall in New York City in the late 1950s.

Billy Eckstine, was interviewed on July 7, 1982 in Chicago. He was a vocalist, songwriter, and bandleader and a jive time trumpet player.
He worked with Tommy Myles and Earl Hines. Billy formed his own band in the 1940s with sidemen Dizzy Gillespie, Miles Davis, Fats Navarro, Budd Johnson, Kenny Dorham, Gene Ammons, Dexter Gordon, Budd Johnson, Lucky

Bibliography

Thompson, Frank Wess, Charlie Parker and Sarah Vaughan.

Duke Ellington, was interviewed on December 23 and 26, 1953 at the Blue Note in Chicago and in later years at the Palmer House on Monroe and Wabash in Chicago, and several times backstage at the Regal Theater on the south side of Chicago.

Mercer Ellington, was interviewed for a week commencing on October 29, 1994 during a Caribbean cruise. He was a composer, bandleader and trumpet player.
He played trumpet with his father Duke Ellington and also for Cootie Williams a former Ellington star trumpet player however at the beginning of his career formed his own band shortly after coming out of the Juilliard Music School in 1939.

Henry Fort, a bass fiddle player was interviewed on February 16, 1983 in addition to being lifelong friends.
His first memorable gig was with Nat "King" Cole and his Original Twelve Royal Dukes in 1934. He later went on the road with Nat in the Shuffle Along Vaudeville Production

Bud Freeman, was interviewed on October 12, 1982. He was a tenor saxophone player of note. He played with the original Austin High School Gang, Husk O'Hare Wolverines, Ben Pollack, Red Nichols, Meyer Davis, Tommy Dorsey, Benny Goodman and Eddie Condon.

Dizzy Gillespie, the unforgettable trumpet player was interviewed on June 2, 1982 and on several other occasions. He played with Cab Calloway, Lucky Millinder, Charlie Barnet, Fletcher Henderson, Benny Carter, Earl Hines, Duke Ellington, John Kirby and Billy Eckstine and participated in many after-hour jam sessions with Louis Armstrong and Roy Eldridge. He was co-founder of the Be Bop school with Charlie Parker.

Harry Gray, [President of Local 208, affiliate of the American Federation of Musicians], October, 1982. Armstrong, Ellington and other road bands had to get Mr. Gray's approval to perform in Chicago.

Sonny Greer, interviewed on July 14, 1969, but missed other opportunities because of my heavy schedule. He played drums with Duke Ellington for 31 years.

Johnny Griffin, tenor saxophone and clarinet man was interviewed on June 4, 1982 and on sundry of other dates. He started playing with Lionel Hampton almost as soon as he could remove his DuSable High School graduation robe in June 1945. He worked with Hampton from 1945 to 1947. He also worked with The Jazz Messengers, Thelonious Monk, Gene Ammons, Lester Young, T-Bone Walker, Dallas Bartley and he studied under Captain Walter L. Dyett at DuSable High School.

Fred Guy, was interviewed on September 11, 1952, but talked to him daily about things that in retrospect were not important because I was on another page .
He played guitar with Duke Ellington for 25 years.

Lionel Hampton, the drummer and vibraphonist was interviewed in 1942, 1944, and 1985 in Chicago, Illinois. The author met Hampton through his half brother Samuel Davis Jr. (no relation to the song and dance Candyman) It was during a furlough to Chicago during the Christmas holidays in 1942 that Davis introduced the author to Hampton backstage at the Regal Theater. In 1985 the author and Hampton were the sole guests on Kup's Television Show in Chicago.

Al Hibbler, the vocalist was interviewed on October 6, 1993 and December 10, 1995.
Hibbler sang with Dave Jenkins, Clifford Douglass, Jay McShann and with Duke Ellington for 8 ½ years.

Earl "Fatha" Hines, a trumpet style piano player was interviewed on July 21, 1982 in Chicago for one of several sessions.
In addition to playing with his own band for twenty years he worked with the Louis Armstrong All Stars, the Duke Ellington Orchestra, Carroll Dickerson, Jimmie Noone and the Erskine Tate Vendome Theater Orchestra.

Milton Hinton, the bass violin player was interviewed on February 22, 1983 and on several other occasions. Hinton played the bass violin on gigs with Earl Hines, Jabbo Smith, Eddie South, Fate Marable, Count Basie, Louis Armstrong, Bing Crosby, Pearl Bailey, Zutty Singleton and worked with Cab Calloway for fifteen straight years.

Art Hodes, the piano man was interviewed on March 17, 1982.
In addition to gigging with Louis Armstrong , Eddie Condon, Sidney Bechet, Bix Beiderbecke, Bud Freeman, Pops Foster Pee Wee Russell, Wingy Manone, Gene Krupa, Chippie Hill and Bunk Johnson. He also played piano for Dempsey J. Travis at two jazz SRO lectures, the subject was the author's best selling book entitled An Autobiography of Black Jazz at the Chicago Historical Society in the spring of 1984.

Franz Jackson, tenor sax man was interviewed on January 5, 1982 and on several other sets. He worked with Earl Hines, Jabbo Smith, Eddie South, Cab Calloway, Count Basie and Louis Armstrong. Jackson also played with Roy Eldridge, Fats Waller, Cootie Williams, Fletcher Henderson, Earl Hines and Jimmie Noone.

Viola Jefferson, the vocalist and a friend of many years
She worked with: Ray Nance, Horace Henderson, Jimmy Johnson and in Larry Steele's "Smart Affairs." Because of her dark complexion she was forced to work as a single in Europe's nightclubs from 1949 to 1954. She was a European success.

Herb Jeffries, was interviewed on October 28, 1994.
A vocalist with Duke Ellington, Earl Hines and later worked as a single.

Eddie Johnson, was interviewed on August 1982. He was a teenage friend of the author.
He played the tenor and alto saxophone. He worked with: Johnny Long, Horace Henderson, Moral Young, Cootie Williams, Louis Jordan and Coleman Hawkins.

Nat Jones, a Chicago boy was interviewed on March 20, 1983.
He played alto saxophone in Johnny Hodges' old chair with Duke Ellington in the Spring and Summer of 1943 at the Hurricane, on Broadway and earlier in Chicago with Tony Fambro, Johnny Long and Red Saunders at the Club Delisa, Savoy Ballroom, and The Warwick Hall.

George Kirby, was interviewed on June 11, 1982.
Occupation: Mimic Extraordinaire, Singer, Dancer and Comedian
Featured On: All of the major television shows, including Johnny Carson and Ed Sullivan. Starred in nightclubs and theaters in the Continental United States. He was Louis Armstrong's downstairs neighbor in 1929 and 1930.

Bibliography

Ray Nance, was interviewed on May 20, 1972.
Occupation: Instrumentalist, Arranger, Vocalist, Composer and Bandleader
Instruments Played Trumpet and Violin. He played with: Horace Henderson, Earl Hines and Duke Ellington. His trumpet and singing style were greatly influenced by Louis Armstrong.

Sy Oliver, was interviewed on April 30, 1982.
Occupation: Instrumentalist, Arranger, Vocalist, Composer and Bandleader
His instrument was the trumpet.
He played with Zack Whyte, Alphonso Trent, Jimmie Lunceford and Tommy Dorsey. And he was an Honorary pall-bearer for Louis Armstrong.

Kilner T. Randolph, was interviewed on September 14, 1982.
Occupation: Composer, Arranger and Director
Instruments Played: Trumpet and Piano
Arranged For: Earl Hines, Duke Ellington, Fletcher Henderson, Blanche Calloway, Woody Herman, Carroll Dickerson and Dave Peyton. He also arranged and directed the orchestra for Louis Armstrong with whom he wrote "Old Man Mose Is Dead" in 1938. It was Armstrong's best selling recording until "Hello Dolly."

William Samuels, was interviewed on June 1983.
Occupation: Secretary of Local 208 of the American Federation of Musicians.

Arvell Shaw, was interviewed on September 8, 1996.
Occupation: Musician
Instrument Played: Bass
Played With: Louis Armstrong, Fate Marable, Teddy Wilson, Benny Goodman and Sidney Bechet.

Lonnie Simmons, was interviewed on July 4 and 14, 1983.
Occupation: Bandleader
Instruments Played: Tenor Saxophone, Clarinet and Organ
Played With: Fats Waller, Chick Webb, Hot Lips Page, Savoy Sultans and Ella Fitzgerald. Jammed with Louis Armstrong several times at Club DeLisa in Chicago.

Maxine Sullivan, was interviewed March 1982.
Occupation: Vocalist
She sang with her husband John Kirby, Louis Armstrong, Benny Goodman, Glenn Gray, Henry Busse, Bobby Hackett and Fats Waller.

Mark Terry, was interviewed on April 4, 1983, December 27 and 29, 1995, November 22 and 29, 1996.
Occupation: Instrumentalist, Composer, Vocalist, Bandleader and MasterTeacher Instruments played: Trumpet and Flugelhorn
Played With: Fate Marable, George Hudson, Charlie Ventura, Charlie Barnet, Eddie "Cleanhead" Vinson, Count Basie, Duke Ellington and the NBC Staff Band for the Johnny Carson Tonight Show. He was a Corona, New York neighbor of Louis Armstrong.

Joe Williams, was interviewed on August 26, 1982.
Occupation: Vocalist
Sang With: Jimmie Noone, Coleman Hawkins, Lionel Hampton, Count Basie, Red Saunders, Tiny Parham and Johnny Long.

Nancy Wilson, was interviewed on June 1983.
Occupation: Vocalist and Actress

Sang With: Cannonball Adderley and Larry Steele's "Smart Affairs" and others.

Dave Young, was interviewed on June 12, 1982.
Instruments Played: Tenor Saxophone and Clarinet
Played With: Roy Eldridge, Carroll Dickerson, Fletcher Henderson, Horace Henderson, Lucky Millinder, Walter Fuller and King Kolax.

John Young, was interviewed on May 12, 1982. A fellow pianist and a high school classmate of the author.
Occupation: Arranger and Bandleader
Instrument Played: Piano
Played With: Andy Kirk's Orchestra, Joe Williams, Nancy Wilson, Dick Gregory, Lurlene Hunter and Redd Foxx.

Books

Dahl, Linda. Morning Glory, A Biography Of Mary Lou Williams. Berkeley, CA: University of Chicago Press, 1999.

Daniels, Douglas Henry. Lester Leaps In: The Life and Times of Lester "Pres" Young. Boston: Beacon Press, 2002.

De Valk, J. Ben Webster, His Life And Music. Berkeley, CA: Berkeley Hills Books, 2001.

De Veaux, Alexis. Don't Explain A Song Of Billie Holiday. New York: Harper Row, 1980.

Epstein, Daniel Mark. Nat King Cole. New York: Ferrar, Straus Giroux, 1999.

Feather, Leonard and Gitler, Ira. The Biographical Encyclopedia of Jazz. New York: Oxford University, 1999.

Fidelman, Mark. First Lady Of Song: Ella Fitzgerald For The Record. New York: Birch Lane Press, 1994.

Gillespie, Dizzy. To Be Or Not To Bop. New York: Doubleday & Company, 1979.

Hampton, Lionel With James Haskins. Hamp, An Autobiography. New York: Amistad Press, 1989.

Haskins, James With Kathleen Benson. Nat King Cole: The Man And His Music. London, England: Robson Books, 1986.

Holiday, Billie With William Duffy. Lady Sings The Blues. Garden City, New York: Doubleday & Company, 1956.

Jones, Quincy. Q The Autobiography Of Quincy Jones. New York: Doubleday, 2001.

Lees, Gene. Oscar Peterson, The Will To Swing. New York: Cooper Square Press, 1988.

Murray, Albert. The Blue Devils Of Nada. New York: Patheon, 1996.

Nicholson, Stuart. Ella Fitzgerald A Biography. New York: Charles Scribner & Sons, 1993.

Nicholson, Stuart. Billie Holiday. Boston: Northeastern University Press, 1995.

Pearson, Jr., Nathan W. Going to Kansas City. Chicago/Urbana: University of Illinois Press, 1987.

Travis, Dempsey J. The Autobiography of Black Jazz .

Bibliography

Chicago, IL: Urban Research Press, 1983.

Travis, Dempsey J. The Duke Ellington Primer. Chicago, IL: Urban Research Press, 1996.

Travis, Dempsey J. The Louis Armstrong Odyssey: From Jane Alley To America's Jazz Ambassador. Chicago, IL: Urban Research Press, 1997.

Travis, Dempsey J. J. Edgar Hoover's F.B.I. Wired The Nation. Chicago, IL: Urban Research Press, 2000.

Travis, Dempsey J. The F.B.I. Files: On The Tainted And The Damned. Chicago, IL: Urban Research Press, 2002.

Ward, Geoffrey C. and Ken Burns. Jazz: A History of America's Music. New York: Alfred A. Knoff, 2000.

Wordeck, Carl. Charlie Parker: His Music and Life. Ann Arbor, MI: The University Of Michigan Press, 1996.

Newspapers

At Home With Farina of "Our Gang" Fame. March 1, 1930, The Afro-American, Baltimore.

Jabbo Smith, 82, Trumpeter, Dies; Called Rival to Louis Armstrong. Died in New York City, January 18, 1981, New York Times.

'Soul on Soul' Jazz Composer Pianist Mary Lou Williams. Died in Durham, North Carolina on May 30, 1981, Chicago Tribune.

'Bud" Freeman, 84, Jazz Sax Legend Dies in Chicago, Illinois. March 16, 1991, Chicago Sun-Times.

A Tribute and a Triumph: Natalie Cole Conquers Her Past, With a Little Help From Her Dad. October 20, 1991, Chicago Tribune.

Rites Set For William "King Kolax" Little. December 21, 1991, Chicago Tribune.

Thelonious Monk, Master Of the Deceptively Simple. Died in New York on October 4, 1992, New York Times.

Franz Jackson, Turning 80, Does the Honors. November 1, 1992, Chicago Tribune.

Services To Be Held For Retired Defender Worker and Former Jazz Tenor Sax Man David Young. December 28, 1992, Chicago Defender.

Dizzy Gillespie Age 76 Gave Us a Lot To Enjoy, But Even More To Think About." Died on January 6, 1993, New York Times.

Jazz Virtuoso Dizzy Gillespie Dies of Cancer at 75. January 7, 1993, Chicago Defender.

Sammy Cahn, Weaver of Words for Hit Songs, Is Dead at 79 In Englewood, New Jersey. January 16, 1993, New York Times.

Billy Eckstine Dies At 78; Helped To Launch Bebop. March 1993, Crisis.

Art Hodes, a Pianist Known for the Blues In the Old Style, 88. Died in Chicago on March 4, 1993, New York Times.

Billy ('Mr. B') Eckstine, A Stroke Victim, Dies Of Cardiac Arrest At Age 78. Died March 8, 1993, Jet Magazine.

Billy Eckstine, 78, Band Leader And Velvet-Voiced Singer. Died in Pittsburgh, PA on March 8, 1993, New York Times.

Jazzman's Return: Saxman Johnny Griffin Will Turn 65 Here At Home. April 18, 1993, Chicago Tribune.

Dorothy Donegan In Dreamland: As She Proved at the White House, You Can't Keep Dorothy Donegan Down. Died in Los Angeles on September 19, 1993, Chicago Tribune.

Tales of a Texas Tenor: All The Big Bands Heard a Blast From Illinois Jacquet's Sax. October 3, 1993, Chicago Tribune.

Zilner Randolph, Music Teacher, Songwriter. Died in Chicago on February 3, 1994, Chicago Sun-Times.

George Dixon, 85, Jazz Pioneer, Saxophonist With Hines Orchestra Dies in Chicago on September 4, 1994, Chicago Sun-Times.

Lonnie Simmons, 80, Jazz Musician, Sideman to Stars. Died in Chicago on February 9, 1995, Chicago Sun-Times.

A Voice That Always Brings a Happy Ending: Ella Fitzgerald Dies on June 16, 1996 in Beverly Hills, California. She Will Always Remain An Immutable Force In A Musical World Where Everything Else Is Crumbling. New York Times.

Henry Fort, Real Estate Exec, Bass Player For Nat 'King' Cole Dies in Chicago on January 22, 1997, Chicago Sun-Times.

Betty Carter, Innovative Jazz Vocalist, Is Dead in Brooklyn New York at 69 on September 26, 1998, New York Times.

Joe Williams Remembered For 'Down Home Elegance'. March 29, 1999, New York Times.

Joe Williams, Jazz Singer of Soulful Tone and Timing, Died at 80 in Las Vegas, Nevada. March 31, 1999, New York Times.

Singer Mel Torme A Chicago Native Died in Los Angeles at 73. June 5, 1999, Chicago Sun-Times.

Trumpeter Harry 'Sweets' Edison Dies. July 28, 1999. Chicago Sun-Times.

Bebop Jazz Vibraphonist Milt Jackson Dies. October 12, 1999. Chicago Sun-Times.

Donald Mills; Brother Act Broke Barriers. Died November 15, 1999, Chicago Sun-Times.

Saxophonist Grover Washington Jr. Dies At Age 56. December 18, 1999, Chicago Sun-Times.

Chicago South Side's Wilbur Campbell, 72, Jazz Drummer. Died January 2, 2000, Chicago Sun-Times.

Nat Adderley, Jazz Cornetist, Composer. Died January 4, 2000, Chicago Tribune.

Bibliography

Nat Adderley, Jazz Cornetist, Composer. Died January 4, 2000, New York Times.

Jonah Jones, 91, a Master Jazz Trumpeter. Died on May 3, 2000, New York Times.

Barry Ulanov, 82, a Scholar Of Jazz, Art and Catholicism. May 7, 2000, New York Times.

Tex' Beneke, 86, Hit with Glenn Miller Band. Died May 31, 2000, Chicago Tribune.

Stanley Turrentine, 66, Dies; Known for Earthy Blues Style. September 14, 2000, New York Times.

Les Brown, Swing Bandleader, Dies at 88. January 6, 2001, New York Times.

Jack McDuff, 74, Longtime Jazz Organist, Bandleader. January 26, 2001, Chicago Tribune.

Frankie Carle, 97, Band Leader Who Wrote 'Sunrise Serenade'. Died March 10, 2001, New York Times.

Modern Jazz Quartet Founder John Lewis Dies: Writer, Arranger, Jazz Pianist Was 80 When He Died on March 31, 2001, Chicago Sun-Times.

John Lewis, 80, Pianist, Composer and Creator of the Modern Jazz Quartet Dies. March 31, 2001, New York Times.

The Matchmaker of Bach-Gillespie: John Lewis' Legacy Hard to Overstate. April 8, 2001, Chicago Tribune.

Jazz Singer Al Hibbler Dies at 85 in Chicago, Illinois on April 6, 2001, Chicago Sun-Times.

Al Hibbler, A Singer With Ellington's Band, Dies at 85. April 6, 2001, New York Times.

Grammy-Winning Saxophonist Joe Henderson. July 2, 2001, Chicago Tribune.

Larry Adler, Political Exile Who Brought the Harmonica to Concert Stage, Dies at 87. August 8, 2001, New York Times.

Panama Francis, 82, Jazz Drummer of Swing Era Died in New York City on November 17, 2001, New York Times.

Tommy Flanagan, Elegant Jazz Pianist, Died in New York City at 71. November 19, 2001, New York Times.

Truck Parham, 91, Jazz Bassist for 7 Decades Died in Chicago on June 23, 2002, New York Times.

Nellie Monk, 80, Wife, The Wings And Mainstay of a Jazz Legend. Died June 27, 2002, New York Times.

Magazine Articles

Afro-American, Fetchit Balks When Salary Is Withheld: Screen Star Abruptly Closes Philly Engagement After Squabble with Manager, June 7, 1930.

Arts Midwest Jazz Letter, The 1992 Arts Midwest Jazz Masters: John Young, Summer 1992.

Jazz Unites Inc., 9th Annual Historical and Musical Perspective to Marian Anderson, February 14, 1993.

Jazz Unites Inc., 16th Annual Tribute To Duke Ellington & Dizzy Gillespie, May 16, 1993.

The Mary Herrick Scholarship Fund, Dorothy Donegan Internationally Acclaimed Jazz Pianist, October 13, 1993.

Hot Man, The Life of Art Hodes, October 24.

Art Hodes Autograph Party, October 24.

Stop-Time, Center for Black Music Research Launches Project Stop-Time, Fall 1998.

Photo Credits

Photo Credits

Index

Index

Index

Index

Index

Index